The Canadian Conveyancer and Hand-Book of Legal Forms

C. B. ROBINSON,
PRINTER,
JORDAN STREET, TORONTO.

PREFACE.

The two former editions of the present work having met with considerable acceptance from the public, and the last having been for some time out of print, the Author has been induced to undertake the task of compiling a new edition, adapted to the present state of Canadian practice, and the recent statutes and decisions upon the subject, and for which his long experience may in some measure qualify him.

The design has not been to interfere with or supersede any established work on Conveyancing, but to compress within the limits of a single volume a large number of Conveyancing Precedents, which have come before the Compiler in his business of a Law Stationer during the last twenty-five years, and which he conceives by a careful revision to be adapted to more extensive usefulness, as an introduction to a more elaborate and scientific system of Conveyancing.

The Compiler would acknowledge the advantage the present edition has derived from the careful revision of the original matter by J. E. Rose, Esq., Barrister-at-Law, whose name will be a sufficient guarantee for the accuracy of that portion of the work.

The alphabetical and other arrangement has been adhered to as the most convenient of reference.

The volume is offered to the Legal Practitioner, Justice of the Peace, Conveyancer, &c., in the hope that it will be found a useful and convenient, as well as correct and reliable, compendium of all ordinary Legal Instruments.

J. RORDANS.

88 King Street East, Toronto,
     July, 1879.

TABLE OF CONTENTS.

1.—INDEX TO TREATISE.

2.—INDEX TO PRECEDENTS.

INTRODUCTION

ON THE

LAWS RELATING TO REAL PROPERTY

IN ONTARIO.

IN submitting our new book of Forms, we have revised and corrected our synopsis of the real property law which appeared in our last issue, bringing the same down to the year 1879.

The criminal law of England was first introduced by the treaty signed at Paris on the 10th February, 1763. Afterwards certain other laws were introduced from time to time, by proclamations and other official instruments, and especially on the 7th October, 1763, in the reign of George the 3rd.

When the Canadas were separated as to civil rights in 1791, the laws of Canada, that is to say, the French laws, were conceded to Lower Canada, while the civil laws of England were, by express enactment of our own Legislature, declared to be in force in Upper Canada. By 32 Geo. III. cap. 1, and by the Revised Statutes of Ontario, cap. 93, sec. 1, it was enacted that, " In all matters of controversy relative to property and civil rights, resort shall be had to the laws of England, as they stood on the 15th day of October, 1792, as the rule for the decision of the same * * * —except so far as the said laws and rules have been since repealed, altered, varied, modified or affected by any Act of the Imperial Parliament still having the force of law in Ontario, or by any Act of the late Province of Upper Canada, or the Province of Canada,

B

or of the Province of Ontario, still having the force of law in Ontario, or by the Revised Statutes of Ontario."

On that day the unwritten or common law and the written or statute law of England, as it then stood, became law in Upper Canada, and generally speaking no Imperial Statute passed since 1792 has any effect in this province, unless Canada is expressly mentioned or unless re-enacted in our own Parliament.   But by the 2nd section of cap. 92, of the Revised Statutes of Ontario, "The Statutes of Jeoffails of Limitations, and for the amendment of the law, excepting those of mere local expediency, which previous to the 17th January, 1822, had been enacted respecting the law of England, and then continued in force shall be valid and effectual for the same purposes in Ontario, excepting so far as the same have since the day last aforesaid been repealed, altered, varied, modified or affected in the manner mentioned in the first section of this Act."

The laws of this Province as to real estate are much more simple than those of the mother country, as this is comparatively a new country. All our titles to real estate are of recent date, and where evidence has been preserved can be traced to the Crown. There are several species of property in England which are not to be met with among us, owing to the difference in the customs and usages existing here from those which exist in the mother country, such as copyholds, advowsons, tithes, rights of common, and rights of common of Turbary, of Piscary, and Pasture, and Seigniories or Lordships ; neither have we tenure by customs of Gavelkind, or Borough English, nor are our conveyances subject to the Stamp Duty.   Tithes were abolished in this Province by 2 Geo. IV. c. 32.

The periodical revision and consolidation of the Public General Statutes afford greater facility of reference, although to secure accuracy, careful attention must be paid to the repealed as well as to the repealing Statutes.

. *Real* property comprehends all such things as are permanent, fixed, indestructible, immovable, and which cannot be carried out of their place, and is usually denoted by the terms, "*lands, tenements and hereditaments*," although under the authority of our statutes relating to real property the general denomination "*land*" is often used. It legally includes all houses and other buildings thereon, so that by a conveyance of the land or ground the structures pass therewith, as well as everything else both above and below the surface. *Hereditaments* is the most comprehensive term of the three in signification, and literally embraces whatever may be inherited. The term "*premises*" strictly denotes that which has been before mentioned, and *property* is seldom spoken of as premises unless a description of it is contained in some prior part of the instrument. The terms *messuage or house* comprise all outbuildings, the orchard, yard and garden attached and adjoining thereto ; and *appurtenances* embrace all easements attached to or used with the property.

We are bound therefore by the law of England prior to 1792, and it has been the policy to adopt from time to time such improvements as have been made in the English law, so far as they have been applicable to the circumstances of this country.

It follows that the law of real property in this Province in a great measure resembles that of England. It is unnecessary in a synopsis like the present to notice at much length the objects, effects, and operation of the several important Statutes of Uses, DeDonis, Quia Emptores, Wills and Frauds, however interesting to the antiquary and legal student. It is sufficient to remark, that after a lapse of nine or ten centuries, we have come almost back to the same system of unfettered alienation of real property as existed in England before the Norman Conquest and the feudal system. It may appear strange that a common deed of a piece of freehold land in this Province cannot be explained without going back to the reign of Henry the Eighth, when the Statute of Uses was passed (27 Henry VIII. c. 10), that no man is in law the absolute owner of land, and that he can only hold an *estate* in it. One of the objects of the Statute of Uses was, that all uses or equitable estates should become *legal* estates, and subject to the common law rules. Under its provisions an estate of freehold could commence *in futuro* or upon a contingency, whereas at the common law no such thing was permitted. The modern system of alienation is more simple, and tends more to the happiness of the possessor and the increase of the nation's wealth. In this Province we have abolished the law of Primogeniture, though retained in England. The establishment of registry offices in each county secures a public record for titles, certain and convenient of access.

OF TITLE.

On every purchase of real estate or mortgage thereon the purchaser or mortgagee should submit the investigation of the title to some experienced conveyancer, and great care should be taken with regard to wills, many of which being drawn up by the parties themselves, or by persons ignorant of the law, are frequently unskillfully or incorrectly worded. Even in purchasing from the original grantee from the Crown this precaution should be observed.

In all cases a search should be made in the County Treasurer's Office for arrears of taxes or sales for taxes, in the Sheriff's Office for executions against lands, and in the office of the Clerk of the Queen's Bench in Toronto for Crown debts. Before paying over the purchase money or advancing a loan, the deed should be registered and a final search made to ascertain that no conveyance has been recorded or *fi. fa.* lands placed in the Sheriff's hands, since the preliminary investigation. Registration is notice to the world.

All these precautions are requisite, although the purchaser may have from the vendor covenants for title. There are five usual convenants for title in most modern conveyances, namely: That the vendor is seized in fee, that he has good right to convey, for quiet enjoyment,

free from incumbrances, as a for further assurance. Those
as a rule are limited or qualified covenants, that is, covenants limiting the liability to the acts of the vendor. On
the other hand, a mortgagor is generally required to give
absolute covenants. The vendor should furnish the purchaser with an abstract of all the deeds, wills and other
instruments affecting the land, and produce the original
title deeds, or account for their non-production.

The furnishing of the abstract is generally waived in
simple titles, reliance being had upon the title deeds produced, and on the search in the registry office.

Revised Statutes, cap. 107, sec. 7, provide that "the
bona fide payment, of any money to, and the receipt
thereof by any person to whom the same is payable upon
any express, or implied trust, or for any limited purpose,
and such payment to and receipt by the survivors or survivor of two or more mortgagees or holders, or the executors or administrators of such survivors, or their or his
assigns, shall effectually discharge the person paying the
same from seeing to the application or being answerable
for the misapplication thereof, unless the contrary is expressly declared by the instrument creating the trust or
security."

When a sale is made by trustees who have no beneficial
interest in the property, they merely covenant that they
have done no act to incumber the premises. In some
cases it might be advisable to have covenants for title
from the person beneficially interested. A person who
has bought a piece of land and has taken a deed and given
a mortgage thereon for the balance of the purchase
money, should be very careful how he disposes of such
land before the mortgage has been satisfied. He should
have it stated in the deed to the purchaser from him that
the land is sold subject to such mortgage. He should
consider the solvency of the purchaser, and have inserted
in the deed a covenant of indemnity against the mortgage
and costs incurred on account thereof. On any sale or
mortgage of lands all the title deeds in the hands of the

vendor or mortgagor which relate exclusively to the property in question should be handed over to the purchaser or mortgagee. Where the title deeds relate also to other property of greater value than that conveyed, the purchaser is only entitled to a covenant from the vendor for their production, and also to copies thereof at his own expense. The custody of title deeds is, however, of less importance than formerly, since the passing of the late Registry Act (Revised Statutes, cap. 111) hereinafter mentioned, under which duplicate originals of all deeds relating to land are registered at the time of execution. Where the vendor is married the purchaser should see that his wife joins in the deed in order to bar her dower, and care should be taken that both vendor and wife have attained the age of twenty-one years. Purchasers at sheriff's sales should be as careful as in other cases, as the sheriff's deed conveys no better title to the land than the judgment debtor himself had. In a contract for the sale of real estate time is not of the essence of the contract unless so stipulated, but either party has in equity the power to make it so by giving the other reasonable notice to perform his part of the agreement.

On taking an assignment of a mortgage also, much of what has been said will have to be observed.

QUIETING TITLES.

A defective system of conveyancing, as also carelessness in the preservation, and irregularity in the registration, of title deeds, together with incorrect surveys, have rendered many titles unmarketable, and litigious purchasers, especially where purchases have turned out unfavourably, have put the vendor to much expense and then been able to refuse to carry out the purchase because the proofs of title required by law were not forthcoming.

To remedy this defect, the very important and useful statute for quieting titles to real estate in Upper Canada, 29 Vic. cap. 25, was passed, by the provisions of which any person may have any title, legal or equitable, which he claims in any land in Upper Canada, investigated at any time in the Court of Chancery, which Court has framed a set of orders for regulating the proceedings under that Act.

The application is made by petition, a certificate of the filing whereof is required to be registered in the county where the lands are situated, and the petition must be supported by the production of all muniments of title and the certificates and proofs required by the Act, and before a certificate of title is granted by the Court, a notice must be inserted in the *Gazette*, and if the Court so directs, in a local newspaper also.

Where an adverse claimant is known to the Court, notice must be given as prescribed, and finally the Court grants such certificate of title as the circumstances warrant ; that is a certificate showing the title as it really exists with all defects which have not been removed during the investigation. Any one purchasing after such certificate is signed, sealed and registered must accept the same as conclusive at law and in equity.

By this Act also, any resident of Upper Canada claiming real estate therein, upon a similar application supported by proper proofs, is enabled to establish his legitimacy or the marriage of himself or of his progenitors, or that he is the heir or one of the co-heirs of any one deceased or that he is a natural born subject of Her Majesty.

It is worthy of note that *for the purposes of this Act*, a married woman is deemed a *feme sole*.

ESTATE FOR LIFE.

This estate arises when a conveyance is made of lands to a man to hold for the term of his natural life or for that of any other person or for more lives than one. When one holds an estate by the life of another he is usually styled a tenant *pur autre vie,* and the other person is called the *cestui que vie.* A grant by deed to a person simply without adding the words "and his heirs," confers an estate for life only. He may part with it if he pleases, but it will terminate at his death into whosesoever hands it may come. Any person remaining in possession of lands after the determination of a life estate, without the consent of the persons next entitled in remainder, is considered a trespasser. A tenant for life has an estate of freehold and he that hath a less estate cannot have an estate of freehold. Some estates which may not last a lifetime, are considered in law as life estates and estates of freehold. Thus an estate granted to a woman during her widowhood, an husband's tenancy by the courtesy, a widow's tenancy in dower, and a wife's jointure, are all in law life estates. A tenant for life has merely a limited interest and cannot of course make any disposition to take effect after his death and cannot make leases to endure beyond his life, unless empowered so to do by the deed or will under which he holds.

ESTATES TAIL.

This is an estate given to a man, and the "*heirs of his body.*" It will descend on the decease of the first owner to all his lawful issue, children, grand-children and remote descendants, so long as his posterity endures in a regular course of descent, but not to collateral relations, and on the other hand, if the first owner should die without issue, his estate will then determine. It' may be either in possession or expectancy. A tenant in tail has the power to acquire an estate in fee simple, either in possession or remainder, by *barring* the entail, as it is termed. Revised Statutes, cap. 100, regulate the law as to barring estates tail. Previously to this statute, estates tail were barred by the cumbrous and antiquated machinery of a fine or common recovery. This Act has established the office of *protector*, who is generally the owner of the first existing estate for life, under the settlement prior to the estate tail. When the estate tail is not an estate in possession, but is preceded by a life estate in some other person, the consent of the protector is requisite to enable the tenant in tail to bar the entail and dispose of the lands as a tenant in fee simple, and such consent may be given either by the same assurance by which the disposition is effected or by a distinct deed, and is to be executed on or at any time before the day on which the assurance effecting such disposition shall be made. Every disposition of lands by a tenant in tail, is to be effected by some one of the common assurances to pass an estate in fee simple absolute, but must be by deed and not by will or by contract incomplete. The assurance by deed must also be registered in the Registry Office of the county or city in which the lands are situated, within six calendar months from the execution thereof and the consent of the protector, if given by distinct deed, must also in like manner be registered either at or before the time of registering of such assurance. The protector is under no restraint in giving or withholding his consent, but is left entirely to his own discretion. When the estate tail is in possession, that is when there is no previous estate for life, there can very seldom be any protector, and the tenant in tail may at any time by deed duly registered, bar the entail remainder and reversions at his own pleasure. A tenant in tail is empowered however to make leases without the necessity of registration, for any term not exceeding twenty-one years from the date, or from any time not exceeding twelve calendar months from date, where a rack rent or five-sixth parts of a rack rent shall be thereby reserved.

The above sketch gives a brief and therefore very imperfect view of the provisions of the statute. To secure anything like a correct idea of the law most careful attention must be given to the whole statute.

ESTATE IN FEE SIMPLE.

This is the greatest estate or interest which the Law of England allows any person to possess in land. A tenant in fee simple is one that holds land to him and his heirs, so that the estate descends not merely to the heirs of his body but to collateral relations according to the canons of descent. The unfettered right of alienation, which is now inseparably incident to this estate, is by far its most valuable quality. A tenant in fee simple holds his land free from any qualification or condition, save such as are contained in the Patent from the Crown, and he may alien his estate subject to any conditions not repugnant to law.

Aliens in this Province may hold and transmit real estate as natural born subjects.

Infants or all persons under the age of twenty-one years, and also idiots and lunatics, though they may hold lands, are incapacitated from making a binding disposition of any estate in them. Revised Statutes, cap. 40, contain provisions for the sale of estates of lunatics and infants.

Married women are under a limited incapacity to alienate as will hereafter appear.

And a conveyance can be made only to such *corporations* as are authorised by their Acts of Incorporation to purchase, hold, and convey lands for the uses of the corporation.

Prior to the 15th of August, 1866, Crown debts formed a lien on the lands of the debtor, but by cap. 43 of 29 & 30 Vic. Crown debts were placed on the same footing as obligations entered into between subject and subject. By 36 V. cap. 6, sec. 5 (O), lands theretofore bound were released in so far as the authority of the Government of Ontario extended, except where proceedings had been taken on such obligations. No similar provision as to release exists as to the bonds or obligations given to the Dominion Government.

LIABILITY OF ESTATES IN FEE SIMPLE TO THE PAYMENT OF DEBTS.

This liability is not so extensive in this Province as in England, as we have no statute corresponding with the Imperial Act 3 & 4 Wm. IV. c. 104.

This liability to what may be called an involuntary alienation has been established by slow degrees. It is laid down by Britton, who wrote in the reign of Edward I., that the heir was not bound to pay the debt of his ancestor to any other person than the King, unless the heir were by the deed of his ancestor specially bound to do so. On this footing the law of England long continued. The heir was liable only to the value of the assets which had descended from his ancestor. When the power of testamentary alienation was granted, a debtor who had thus bound his heirs became enabled to defeat his creditors by devising his estate by his will to some other person than his heir, and in this case neither heir nor devisee was under any liability to the creditors. At length by 3 & 4 Wm. & Mary, c. 14, all devises by will are made void as against creditors by specialty, in which the heirs were bound, but not further or otherwise. This statute was made perpetual by 6 & 7 Wm. III. c. 14. A testator may, however, of his own accord by will charge his lands with the payments of his debts, in which case the Court of Chancery allows all creditors to be equally entitled to the benefit, and the lands are then called equitable assets.

The courts in Upper Canada had held, that under the Imperial Act of 5 Geo. II. c. 7, the title of a testator or intestate in real estate in Upper Canada might be seized and sold under a judgment and execution by a creditor of the testator or intestate, recovered against an executor or administrator of the deceased, in the same manner and under the same process that the same could be seized and sold if the judgment and execution had been against the testator or intestate if living, and many sales had taken place and titles been acquired under such proceedings, and it being desirable to quiet the same, it was enacted by 27 Vic. c. 15, entitled, An Act respecting sales of land under execution against executors and administrators, that under the said Imperial Statute the title and interest of a testator or intestate in real estate in Upper Canada

might be seized and sold under a judgment and execution
recovered by a creditor of the testator or intestate against
his executor or administrator, in the same manner and
under the same process that the same could be sold under
a judgment and execution against the deceased if living.
And all such sales theretofore made and titles given thereunder are thereby declared to have passed and conveyed
the title or interest of the testator or intestate in his real
estate so sold and conveyed as against any objection that
might be made, on the ground that real estate could not
be seized and sold in manner aforesaid under the said act;
Provided always, that that act should not affect any case
pending at the time of the passing of the same in or
theretofore finally adjudged by the courts of law or
equity in Upper Canada.

The lands of a defendant as also a contingent, an executory, and a future interest and a possibility coupled with
an interest in any land, whether the object of the gift or
limitation of such interest or possibility be or be not ascertained, also a right of entry whether immediate or future,
and whether vested or contingent into or upon any land ;
and also a mortgagor's legal and equitable interest in the
lands mortgaged may be sold by the sheriff of the county
where the lands lie under an execution against lands; and
the moment such execution is placed in the sheriff's hands
any land or interest therein as aforesaid of the defendant
in that sheriff's county becomes bound for the payment of
the judgment upon which such execution has been issued.

Lease-hold interest in lands may be sold under execution against goods.   The law is consolidated by cap. 66 of
the Revised Statutes.

DESCENT OF AN ESTATE IN FEE SIMPLE.

A person is said to die intestate when he departs this
life without having made a will.   If he make a will sufficient according to the statute to pass real estate, the latter
will be distributed in accordance with the wishes of the
testator, but if he does not exercise the right of making a

will, then the statute law declares how his real estate shall decend.

There are two acts on the subject in this Province, viz., 4 Wm. IV., cap. 1, and 14 & 15 Vic. cap. 6. As it is very seldom that any case at the present day can be affected by the statute of 1834, the former of such statutes, we content ourselves with giving the course of descent according to the latter statute, stating the order for the sake of clearness as briefly as possible, referring the reader, as particular cases calling for adjudication may arise, to the statute itself. Vide. Rev. Stat. Cap. 105.

The real estate in Upper Canada of all persons dying intestate, after 1st January, 1852, descends as follows :

1. To lineal descendants and those claiming by or under them equally *per stirpes.*

2. To the father.

3. To the mother.

4. To collateral relatives.

5. To the brothers and sisters of the father of intestate, equally if all be living.

6. To their descendants.

7. To the brothers and sisters of the mother of intestate, equally, and their descendants.

8. To the next of kin according to the English Statute of Distribution of Personal Estate, 22 & 23 Car. II. cap. 10.

This Important Act brought in the doctrines of the Civil Law, abolished the right of primogeniture in Upper Canada and enables the half blood to inherit equally with the whole blood, unless the inheritance came by descent devise, or gift of some one of intestate's ancestors, in which case those not of blood of the ancestor shall be excluded. All the children take equally, males and females, as under the Roman Law. Posthumous children inherit equally with those born in the intestate's lifetime. Illegitimate children cannot inherit. Where an inheritance descends to several persons, they take as *tenants in common.* Advancements to children by settlement or portion, are taken into consideration, and affect the shares of the

children so advanced, but the maintaining or educating or
the giving of money to a child without a view to a portion or
settlement in life, shall not be deemed an advancement within the Act.   The interpretation clauses should be carefully
read in order to see the extent of the meaning of the words
used in the Act.   It is only in cases of high treason, and
of abetting, procuring or counselling the same, that an
attainder for felony extends to the disinheriting of any
heir or to the prejudice of the right or title of any person
other than that of the offender, during his natural life.
See 3 Wm. IV, cap. 4. (C.S. U.C. Cap. 116.)

TENURE.

This term is used to denote the manner of holding lands
and tenements.   The most familiar instance of a tenure
is   given   by   a   common   lease   of   a   house   or   land
for a term of years.   This is not however a freehold tenure,
as the lessee has only a chattel interest.   A tenant in
fee simple has a fredhold tenure.   The seller or giver of
an estate in fee simple, is only a tenant to the Crown, with
the liberty of putting another in his place.   By 12 Car.
II, cap. 24, all the tenures by Knight Service were abolished, and all tenures turned into free and common
socage, except copyholds and frankalmoign, and the
honorary services of grand sergeantry.   But by the Con-
stitutional Act of 31 Geo. III., it is expressly enacted
that "all lands which shall be hereafter granted within
the Province of Upper Canada, shall be granted in free
and common socage in like manner as lands are now holden
in free and common socage in that part of Great Britain
called England."

Free and common socage in this Province is therefore
synonymous with the term "freehold" or "fee simple."

JOINT TENANTS AND TENANTS IN COMMON

A joint tenancy arises where any persons hold property
between them in equal shares by purchase, as where two or

more persons purchase lands and take a conveyance to them and their heirs. This is a joint tenancy, and the legal estate will go to the survivor. During the time they hold jointly neither of them has an estate in any particular part. Each has the whole with benefit of survivorship unless the tenancy be severed, and has been held to be incapable of devising his respective share by will. On the severance of a joint tenancy, a tenancy in common is created.

By Rev. Stat. Cap. 106, S. 11, wherever, by any letters patent, assurance or will executed after 1st July 1834, land has been or is granted, conveyed, or devised, to two or more persons (other than executors or trustees) in fee simple, or for any less estate it shall be considered that such persons took or take as tenants in common and not as joint tenants unless an intention sufficiently appears on the face of the letters patent assurance or will that they are to take as joint tenants. The proper mode of conveyance from one joint tenant to another of his interest is a deed of release.

Tenants in common take also by purchase but hold by distinct titles and have separate freeholds, being not seized *per mie et per tout* as joint tenants are. Tenancies in common descend to the heirs of each of the tenants because they have several freeholds and not an entirety of interest as joint tenants, and therefore there is no survivorship between them, but each may alienate or devise his moiety to any person. This tenancy is more preferable to a joint tenancy as it is not subject to the right of survivorship.

All joint tenants, tenants in common, coparceners, doweresses and parties entitled to dower, tenants by the courtesy, or other creditors having liens on and all parties whosoever, interested in, to, or out of any lands in Ontario, may be compelled to make or suffer partition or sale of the said lands or any part or parts thereof under the provisions of cap. 101, of the Revised Statutes. A partition may also be voluntarily made by the parties by deed (2 Wm. IV. C. 35.) The proceedings for a compulsory partition are

carried on in the Court of Queen's Bench, or Common
Pleas, or the Court of Chancery, when the lands are situated in two or more counties; but in the County Court,
or in any of the Superior Courts of Law or Equity when
the lands are situated in one county only. The proceedings are commenced by filing a petition in any of the said
courts, praying that a partition or sale of the lands may be
made, and the practice is principally regulated by said
cap. 101.

TRANSFER OF REAL PROPERTY.

A feoffment with *livery of seisin* is the most ancient
means of conveyance. Seisin signifies the feudal possession, and is to be distinguished from actual or simple possession. Thus a tenant for a term of years has not the
feudal possession or freehold, but his possession, like that
of a bailiff or servant, is that of his landlord. Livery of
seisin is the delivery of the feudal possession. In every
conveyance (except by will) of an estate of inheritance
the word "*heirs*" is necessary. A deed is a writing sealed
and delivered, and the sealing and delivery constitute its
execution. By sec. 3, cap. 98, Revised Statutes, a feoffment must be by deed. An *escrow* is a deed delivered
conditionally and not with a view to its immediately taking effect. If the condition be performed the delivery thus
becomes complete and the deed ceases to be an escrow.

The usual mode of conveyance in this Province is by
what is known as the Statutory Conveyance—the opera-
tive word in which is "grant." See cap. 102 Revised
Statutes. Considerations in a deed are either good or
valuable. A good consideration is founded upon natural
love and affection between near relations by blood. A
valuable consideration is founded on something deemed
valuable, as money, goods, services or marriage.

Every deed or contract is void when made for fraudulent purposes, or in violation of law, and by 13 Eliz. c. 5,
conveyances of landed estates and also of goods made for
the purpose of delaying, hindering or defrauding credi-

tors, are void as against them unless made upon valuable consideration and *bona fide* to any person, without notice of such fraud. And by a subsequent statute 27 Eliz. c. 4, *voluntary* conveyances of any estate in lands are also void as against subsequent purchasers for valuable consideration.

The Insolvent Act of 1875 declares all conveyances made in contemplation of insolvency an unjust preference and void. See Davidson v. Ross, 24 Gr. p. 22. Revised Statutes, cap. 95, enact that all corporeal tenements and hereditaments shall, as regards the conveyance of the immediate freehold thereof, be deemed "*to lie in grant as well as in livery,*" that is to say, shall require a deed in writing and under seal for their effectual conveyance. It further enacts, that a feoffment otherwise than by deed shall be void at law, and that no feoffment shall have a "*tortious operation,*" that is to say, the feoffee shall not take an estate larger than that possessed by the feoffor. A reference is here made to the previous law under which if a tenant for his own life should have made a feoffment for an estate in fee simple the feoffee would not thereby have acquired an estate for the life of the feoffor, but would have become seized of an estate in fee simple *by wrong*. By the same statute it is also enacted, that a *partition* and *exchange* of any land and lease required by the law to be in writing of any land, and an *assignment* of a *chattel interest* in any land, and a *surrender* in writing of any land not being an interest which might by law have been created without writing shall be void unless made by deed. That a contingent, an executory, and a future interest, and a possibility, coupled with an interest in any land, whether the object of the gift or limitation of such interest or possibility be or be not ascertained, and also a right of entry, whether immediate or future, and whether vested or contingent into and upon any land, may be disposed of by deed, and that neither the words "*grant*" or "*exchange*" in any deed shall create any warranty or

C

right of re-entry or covenant by implication, except in cases where by any act in force in Ontario it is declared that the word "grant" shall have such effect. The same statute declares that any corporation aggregate in this Province capable of taking and conveying land shall be deemed to be capable of doing so by deed of bargain and sale, in like manner as any person in his natural capacity, subject nevertheless to any general limitations or restrictions as to holding or conveying real estate which may be applicable to such corporations. Formerly a corporation could not convey by bargain and sale, because they could not be seized of a use or trust for another person. A deed of bargain and sale does not require registration as indispensable to render it a valid conveyance, but the necessity of registration is to prevent a subsequent purchaser from gaining priority.

Until the passing of 9 Vic. c. 6, (Revised Statutes, cap. 102), commonly called, "*The Act to facilitate the conveyance of Real Property,*" forms of deeds in use in this Province were comparatively long and cumbrous. Deeds under this statute are called "*Statutory Deeds*," are much shorter than the old form although in effect the same, and since the passing of the late Registry Act have come into general use in the Province on account of the saving of expense in their registration. There are two schedules to the act, the one containing the covenants in the short the other the long form. The act then enacts, that any deed made in pursuance of that statute or referring thereto, and containing the short covenants, shall be taken to have the same effect and be construed as if containing the covenants in the long form. It also enacts that a deed or part of a deed failing to take effect by virtue of the act shall still be as valid as if the act had not been passed.

The Act 14 & 15 Vic. c. 8, (Revised Statutes 105), is the corresponding act with respect to leases, and the provisions are of the same nature, but it may be useful to notice the effect of some of the usual covenants in a statutory lease, so that a lessee may know what constitutes a oreach of them. The short form of covenant to pay taxes includes all taxes, whether parliamentary, municipal or otherwise, whether charged upon the premises or the lessor in respect thereof. The covenant not to cut down timber does not prevent the lessee from cutting timber for necessary repairs, firewood, or for the purpose of clearance. The notice to repair must be in writing and left at the premises, and the lessee has after such notice three calendar months to make such repairs. The consent to assign or sub-let must be in writing. The covenant that the lessee will leave the premises in good repair is subject to the exceptions of reasonable wear and tear and damage by fire, while the preceding covenants to repair and repair according to notice are unqualified. Every conveyancer should see that the same qualification is made of these covenants as is made of the covenant to leave in good repair else the lessee may be compelled to rebuild in case the premises be consumed by fire. Every lessee should have a proviso inserted in his lease, that the rent shall in case of destruction by fire cease from and after the happening thereof, otherwise he may be compelled to pay rent during the remainder of the* term, although the premises may prove a total loss. The proviso for re-entry by the lessor on non-payment of rent, comes into operation at the end of fifteen days after any of the days on which the rent ought to have been paid, and no demand of such rent is necessary ; and for non-performance of covenants, it comes into operation at any time after such breach or non-performance. Although the landlord under this covenant has the right of re-entry, it is, however, necessary for him to bring an action of ejectment to recover possession of the premises, or proceed under the Over-holding Tenancy Act.

If a tenant holds the premises demised beyond his term, he is called an *over-holding tenant*, and may be proceeded against under the 27 & 28 Vic. cap. 30, (Revised Statute, cap. 107), under the provisions of which Act, the Judge of the County Court where the lands lie has power to

deal summarily between the landlord and an over-holding
tenant, and where no "colour of right" is shown the
Judge will issue process to the sheriff of his county to turn
out the over-holding tenant forthwith.

The statutes regulating conveyances by married women
seized of or entitled to real estate in their own right in
Upper Canada, are 59 Geo. III. cap. 3 ; 1 Wm. IV. cap.
2 ; 14 & 15 Vic. cap. 115, and 29 Vic. cap. 28, (Revised
Statutes, caps. 125, 126 and 127.)   According to these
statutes, the married woman must be twenty-one years of
age and must convey the land by deed executed by her
in her proper person or by her attorney duly appointed
by power or attorney, jointly with her husband, unless
she obtain an order from the Judge permitting her to execute the deed alone.   Revised Statutes, cap. 127.

An important enactment of the session of 1865 is the
Act to amend the Law of Property and Trusts in Upper
Canada, 29 Vic. cap. 28 (Rev. Stat., cap. 107, s. 35), and
among its most useful provisions it provides that trustees,
executors, &c., may apply by petition to the Court of
Chancery, for opinion, advice, &c., as to the management
of Trust Property, adopting the provisions of the Imperial
Acts 22 & 23 Vic. cap. 35.

A WILL OF LANDS.

The right of testamentary alienation of lands is a matter
depending upon Acts of Parliament, viz. 32 Henry VIII.
cap. 1 (the Statute of Wills) explained by 34 & 35 Henry
VIII. cap. 5, 12 Car. II. cap. 24, and by "The Wills
Act of Ontario."   By sect. 10, every person may devise
all real and personal estate to which he may be entitled
at the time of his death and which otherwise would
devolve upon his heir-at-law, or upon his executor or
administrator.   After-acquired property also will pass.
By sect. 11, wills made by persons under 21, are declared
invalid.   By sect. 9, s. s. 4, "Person" and "Testator"
are declared to include a married woman, so that as to
will since 1st January, 1874, married women are placed

on the same footing as any other person, an evidence of
that increasing civilization which tardily recognizes the
fact that a married woman is a person. By sect. 5,
wills executed after 6th March, 1834, and prior to
1st January, 1874, are valid, if executed in presence
of two or more witnesses, who have signed in the presence of each other, although not in the presence of the
testator.

By sect. 12, since 1st January, 1874, a will to be valid,
whether of personalty or realty, must be in writing, signed at the foot or end thereof by the testator, or some
one in his presence and by his direction, and such signature must be made or acknowledged by the testator, in
presence of two or more witnesses, present at the same
time, who shall subscribe the will in the presence of the
testator—but no form of attestation shall be necessary.
By sect. 14, it is declared that soldiers being in actual
military service, and mariners, or seaman being at sea,
may dispose of their personal property as before the
passing of this Act.

By section 17, gifts to a witness or husband or wife of
a witness, are declared invalid, and the will valid.

By sect. 20, wills are declared revoked by marriage
with certain exceptions in favour of wills made in the
exercise of a power of appointment. And that whenever land shall be devised in a will, it shall be
considered that the devisor intended to devise all
such estates as he was seized of in the same land, whether
fee simple or otherwise, unless it appears upon the face
of such will that he intended to devise only an estate for
life, or other estate less than he was seized of at the time
of making the will. The Statute of Frauds, it may be
observed, requires that the witnesses should be credible.
Under the Provincial Act, however, the incompetency of
the witnesses at the time of the execution of the will or
at any time afterward, is not sufficient to make the will
invalid. Creditors also are good witnesses, although the
will contains a charge for the payment of debts, and the

mere circumstance of being appointed an executor, is no objection to a witness. It may be mentioned, however, that the statute authorizing the devise of lands by married women does not require the witnesses to sign in the presence of the testratrix or of each other. As a will does not take effect until the decease of the testator, it may in the meantime be revoked, and this may be done in various ways, as by marriage, or by burning, tearing or otherwise destroying the same, by the testator or some one in his presence and by his direction, with the intention of revoking the same, and also by any writing executed in the same manner as a will and declaring an intention to revoke, or by a subsequent will or codicil executed as before. By sect. 23, it is declared that no alteration, interlineation, or other alteration, made in any will after execution, shall have any effect except so far as the words or the effect of the will are not apparent unless the alteration be executed in like manner, as required for the execution of the will. The signatures of the witnesses and testator are well placed if made in the margin or some other part of the will, opposite or near to such alteration, or at the foot or end of, or opposite to a memorandum referring to such alteration, and written at the end or in some other part of the will. Where a codicil is added, it is considered part of the will, and the disposition made by the will is not disturbed further than is necessary to give effect to the codicil. The testator may, if he choose, part with any of the property comprised in his will before his death, and this is called *ademption.* The failure of a devise by the decease of the devisee in the testator's lifetime, is called a *lapse* of the devise, and this is not prevented by the lands being given to the devisee and his heirs.

In the construction of wills, the courts have always borne in mind that a testator may not have had the same opportunity of legal advice in drawing his will as he would have had in executing a deed, and the first maxim of construction accordingly, is that the "*intention of the tes-*

tator ought to be observed." In a deed, on the other hand, technical words are always used. If a testator devise land to the person who is heir-at-law, it is provided by 4 Wm. IV. cap. 1, that such heir takes as devisee and not by descent

As soon as possible after the testator's death, the will should be proved in the proper Surrogate Court, and wills or devises affecting lands should be registered in the Registry Office where such lands are situated. A will, however, or probate, if recorded within twelve months after the death of the testator, will be as valid against subsequent purchasers as if the same had been recorded immediately after such death. Further time may be allowed for registration in certain cases of inability to record the will by reason of its being contested, or by any other inevitable difficulty without the devisee's wilful neglect or default, in which case it will be sufficient to register within 12 months after removal of the impediment. Rev. Stat. cap. 111, s. 75.

MUTUAL RIGHTS OF HUSBAND AND WIFE.

1. *Rights of the husband in respect of the lands of his wife.*

By the act of marriage at the Common Law the husband and wife become in law one person, and so continue during the marriage. The wife is, as it were, merged in the husband, and before the statutes hereafter mentioned the husband was entitled to the whole of the rents and profits arising from his wife's lands, and acquired a freehold estate therein during the continuance of the marriage. But property might then, and may still be vested in trustees for the separate use of an intended wife making provision for her independent of the debts and liabilities of the husband.

Another consequence of the unity of husband and wife was the inability of either of them to convey to the other. But a man might, and still may leave lands to his wife by his will. And by means of the Statute of Uses a man might, and may still convey lands to a third person in trust for the use of his wife.

By the Statutes 22 Vic. cap. 34, and 35 V. (O) cap. 16, Rev. Stat. (O), cap. 125, very important alterations were made in the law relating to married women's rights in property.

By the provisions of these statutes, any woman, who married on or before the 4th of May, 1859, whose husband had not previous to that day, by himself or his tenants, taken possession of her real property, and any woman who married since that time, and prior to 2nd March, 1872, may hold all her real estate acquired in any way before or after marriage, except property received by a married woman from her husband during coverture, and except also property included in or affected by her marriage contract or settlement, free from her husband's debts contracted since the passing of the Act, and from his control or disposition, in as full a manner as if she were unmarried, except only that it shall be liable under execution against her husband for her *torts*. The real estate of any woman married after 4th March, 1872, may also be held by her free from any estate therein of her husband during her lifetime, and from his debts and obligations, and from any claim or estate by him as tenant by the curtesy; but this shall not prejudice any claim of the husband as tenant by the *curtesy* in any real estate of the wife which she has not disposed of *inter vivos* or by will. But this or any other estate which the husband may by virtue of his marriage be entitled to in the property of his wife, shall not during her life be subject to his debts. A married woman's property not settled by ante-nuptial contract is liable for her debts contracted before marriage in all cases where the marriage was since the 4th May, 1859, and in case of marriage settlement on the husband the husband is liable for such debts to the extent of the property taken under such settlement.

A tenancy by the curtesy occurs where the husband survives his wife, in case he has had issue by her born alive who might by possibility have inherited the estate as her heir. He thus becomes entitled to an estate for the residue of his life in such lands of his wife as she was solely seized of in fee simple, or fee tail in possession. If the wife's estate should be *equitable* only, her husband will be entitled to this estate in the same way. The wife's estate must be a several one or else held under a tenancy in common, and must be an estate in possession.

2. *Rights of the wife in the lands of her husband. Dower.* Rev. Stat. (O), cap. 126.

By the act of marriage the wife becomes entitled to an estate for life upon surviving her husband in a third part of all estates of inheritance of which he was solely and legally seized at any time during the marriage, and which her issue by this marriage might by possibility have inherited. This interest of the wife is termed her dower. Where there is an exchange of lands the widow may elect from which of the lands she will have her dower. In regard to the husband's seisin the law has been altered by our statute, 4 Wm. IV. cap. 1, sec. 14, of which gives the wife dower without seisin, if the husband shall have been entitled to a right of entry or action, provided such dower be sued for or 'obtained within the period during which such right of entry or action might be enforced. Under the same statute widows are entitled *in equity* to dower, also in *"equitable estates in possession,"* except an estate in joint tenancy. Dower is not recoverable out of land which, when aliened or at the time of the death of the husband, was in a state of nature and unimproved by clearing, fencing or otherwise, for the purposes of cultivation or occupation. A woman may bar her dower by joining in her own proper person or by her attorney, with her husband in a deed of conveyance thereof in which a release of dower is contained. A married woman may also bar her dower by executing, in her own proper

person or by her attorney, either alone or jointly with
other persons, a deed to which her husband is not a party,
containing a release of such dower.   Where the husband
is not a party the order of the Judge must be obtained
to give effect to the deed or power of attorney.   See
"The Married Women's Real Estate Act," cap. 127,
Rev. Stat. (O).

No arears of Dower, nor any damages on account thereof, can be recovered for a longer period than six years.

INCORPOREAL HEREDITAMENTS.

An incorporeal hereditament is a right issuing out of a
thing corporate, whether real or personal, or concerning
or annexed to, or exercisable with the same, as a rent
issuing out of lands or houses or the like.   Reversions,
remainders, executory interests, rights of way, and annuities are all examples of incorporeal hereditaments. They
must be conveyed by deed or will.   This kind of property
is not of a visible and tangible nature, and does not in
itself admit of actual delivery.

A TERM OF YEARS.

The two principal interests of a personal nature derived
from landed property, are, a term of years and a mortgage
debt.

And first, a *term of years* may be created by an ordinary lease, by settlement, will or mortgage deed.   All terms
of years, of whatever length, possess the same attributes
in the eye of the law, whether for one or a thousand
years.

A *tenancy at will* may be created by parol or by deed.
It arises when a man lets land to another to hold at the
will of the lessor.   The tenant may be evicted whenever
his landlord pleases, and the tenant himself may leave at
any time.   This kind of tenancy is very inconvenient and
seldom adopted.

A *tenancy by sufferance*, is where a person who has
originally come into possession by a lawful title holds over

after his title has determined. A special remedy against *over-holding tenants*, is provided by the Canadian Statutes, 4 Wm. IV. cap. 1, and 27 & 28, Vic. cap. 30. Rev. Stat. (O), cap. 137.

A lease from year to year is a mode of letting very commonly adopted. Its advantage is that both landlord and tenant are entitled to notice before the tenancy can be determined by either of them. This notice must be given at least six months before the expiration of the current year of the tenancy. A yearly tenancy can be created by parol or word of mouth, if the rent reserved amount to two-thirds at least of the full improved annual value of the lands; for if the rent do not amount to so much, the Statute of Frauds declares that such a parol lease shall have the effect of a *lease at will* only. A lease from *year to year* reserving a less rent, must be by deed. A lease at an annual rent made generally, without expressing it to be at will, and without limiting any certain period, is a lease from year to year.

A lease for a fixed number of years may, by the Statute of Frauds, be made by parol, if the term do not exceed three years from the making thereof, and if the rent reserved amount to two-thirds at least of the full improved value of the land. Leases for a longer term or at a lower rent, are required to be in writing and to be made by deed. See Rev. Stat., (O), cap. 98.

There is, as before mentioned, no limit to the number of years for which a lease may be granted, so long as there is a fixed time at which the term must end and from which it is to begin, and this latter may be at a future period. The leasee is liable on his express covenants during the continuance of the term, notwithstanding any assignment which he may make; but the assignee is only liable for such covenants as run with the land, which may be broken during the time the term may be vested in him, and not after he has assigned it over to another. On assigning leasehold premises, therefore, the assignee should enter into a covenant with the assignor to indemnify him against the payment of rent and performance of covenants contained in the lease. Covenants which are binding on the assignee are said to *run with the land.*

Assignments of a chattel interest in any lands are also required to be by deed by Rev. Stat. (O), cap. 98. Leasehold estates may be bequeathed by will. They are considered as personal property and devolve in the first place on the executor or administrator. A tenant for a term of years may, unless restrained by express covenants, make an underlease for any part of his term. Any assignment for any less period than the whole term, is in effect an underlease. But an underlease which comprises the whole term of the underlessor and more properly called an assignment of the lease, gives him no right to destrain for rent reserved since it leaves in him no reversion to which the rent can be incident. Between the original lessor and an underlessee, no *privity* is said to exist, and consequently the original lessor's remedy for any breach of the covenants contained in the original lease, is only against the original lessee or any assignee of the whole term.

A surrender of a term is also required by Rev. Stat. (O), cap. 98, to be by deed. If an estate of freehold should be vested in any person who at the same time is possessed of a term of years in the same land, and no other estate should intervene, the estate of freehold will swallow up the term which will, as it is expressed, become *merged* in the freehold.

Leases for a term not exceeding seven years, when the actual possession goes along with the lease, need not be registered.

Attornment is the consent of a tenant to become the tenant of another landlord, and was formerly necessary to the validity of the grant of the reversion. Its necessity, however, in nearly every case, was abolished by 4 Anne, cap. 16. Notice should be given to the tenant, as prior to such notice he may pay to the prior owner.

MORTGAGES.

A mortgage debt is an interest in land of a *personal* nature. It is the conveyance by the mortgagor of his estate to the mortgagee in fee simple, or by demise for a term of years as a security for the payment of a sum of money with a condition that the instrument shall be void or that the mortgagee shall re-convey the premises upon payment of the mortgage money and interest within a limited time. Upon the failure of this condition, called the proviso for redemption, the mortgagee's estate becomes absolute at law, and he may recover possession of the premises by ejectment without any demand of possession. If, when the day of payment comes, the mortgagor should repay the mortgage money and interest, the mortgagee or, in case the mortgage has been assigned, then the person entitled to the mortgage money must discharge the mortgage at the mortgagor's expense. This is done by a certificate of discharge of mortgage under the late Registry Act.

From the date of the mortgage the legal estate in fee simple belongs to the mortgagee, and the mortgagor is thenceforward unable to create any legal estate or interest in the premises. Although the day fixed for payment of the money has passed, the mortgagor has still a right to redeem the premises on payment of principal, interest and costs up to the time of payment. This right to redeem is called the mortgagor's *equity of redemption*, and no agreement with the mortgagee expressed in any terms however stringent can deprive the mortgagor of this equitable right on payment within a reasonable time. But the mortgagor's right will be barred by the Statute of Limitations after 10 years from the time the mortgagee takes possession of the mortgaged premises. When the mortgagee is in possession, the Court of Chancery will compel him to keep a strict account of the rents and profits. If the mortgagor does not repay the amount on the day fixed for payment, the mortgagee can file a bill of foreclosure in the Court of

Chancery against the mortgagor at any time within 10 years next after the last payment of any part of the principal or interest secured by the mortgage, in order that the mortgagee's estate in fee simple in the premises conveyed to him when the mortgage was first executed may be made absolute. The Court of Chancery, however, can direct a sale of the property at the request of either party. The action at law on the covenant is not barred until after the lapse of 20 years.

In addition to the remedy by foreclosure, involving as it does, the necessity of a suit in Chancery, a more speedy and sometimes less expensive remedy is often provided by inserting a power of sale in the mortgage, giving the mortgagee power to sell the premises in case of default in payment. This course prevents the delay of applying to the Court of Chancery. The mortgagee is a trustee, and it is contrary to a well-known rule in equity for a trustee to purchase the estate ; and if a morgagee purchases the estate under a power of sale contained in his mortgage he still continues mortgagee, and is liable to be redeemed by the mortgagor. *Watkins* v. *McKellar*, 7 Grant, 584. A *mortgagee* may also, on default being made, serve a notice on the person in possession to pay all rents to the mortgagee ; and he may sue the tenant for use and occupation of the premises. A mortgagee after default, has three remedies in order to obtain his rights. 1st. To foreclose. 2nd. To sue at common law, on the covenant to pay contained in the mortgage, and 3rd, To bring ejectment against the mortgagor or those in possession. By foreclosure alone the mortgagee takes the land, and it becomes his own absolutely.

By Rev. Stat. (O), cap. 99, s. 5, executors are empowered to convey, assign, release or discharge the mortgage debt and the legal estate in the land.

By Rev. Stat. (O), cap. 104, similar provisions are made as in the case of the statutes authorizing short forms of conveyance, and short forms of lease. By the provisions of this Act that cumbrous verbiage which is for the most part only intelligible to a mind trained in the law, is dispensed with ; and a few simple and clearly understood words are declared to mean all that is stated in the long covenants. Reference should be made to the full covenants in the statute, as otherwise misconception of the force of the covenant is probable. This also, as before mentioned, now that duplicate originals of all deeds are registered in full, effects a considerable saving in the item of registration.

An *equitable mortgage* is defined to be a *deposit of title deeds* without any writing as security for a debt or loan of money.

The Registry Act, Rev. Stat. cap. 111, enacts that no equitable lien, charge or interest affecting land shall be declared valid in any Court in this Province as against a registered instrument, executed by the same party, his heirs or assigns, and "*tacking* shall not be allowed in any case to prevail against the provisions of this Act."

By 14 & 15 Vic. cap. 45, any mortgagee or any assignee of a mortgage, may receive from the mortgagor or his assignee, a release of the equity of redemption, or may purchase the same under any judgment, decree or execution, without merging the mortgage debt as against any subsequent incumbrancer, or person having a charge on the same property.

Leaseholds are also frequently the subjects of mortgage. The term of years of which the estate consists is assigned by the mortgagor to the mortgagee, subject to a proviso for redemption or re-assignment, on payment at a given time by the mortgagor to the mortgagee, of the sum advanced with interest. As the mortgagee is assignee of the term, he will be liable to the lessor during the continuance of the mortgage, for the payment of rent and performance of covenants in the lease ; and against this liability the covenant of the mortgagor is his security. To obviate this liability, where the rent and covenants are onerous, mortgages of leasehold are frequently made by ay of *demise or underlease* for the residue of the term, less a few days at a nominal rent. By this means the mortgagee becomes tenant only to the mortgagor, and no privity is created with regard to the lessor.

OF TITLES BARRED BY LAPSE OF TIME AND OF THE LIMITATION OF ACTIONS.

By Rev. Stat. (O), cap. 108, no person shall make any entry or distress, or bring any action for the recovery of land or rent, but within 10 years next after the time at which the right to make such entry or distress, or bring such action shall have first accrued to him or to some person through whom he claims. But a written acknowledgment of the title of the person claiming will extend the time to 10 years from such acknowledgment. If when the right first accrues, the person entitled should be under disability, by reason of infancy, coverture, lunacy or absence from the Province, 5 years are allowed from the time the person entitled shall have ceased to be under disability notwithstanding the period of 10 years may have expired, yet so that the whole period do not, including the time of disability, exceed 20 years.

Sec. 17 enacts that in case of lands granted by the Crown of which the grantee has not taken actual possession, and some other person not claiming under such grantee has been in possession, then unless such grantee had knowledge of the land being in the possession of such other person, the lapse of 20 years shall bar the right of such grantee to bring ejectment to recover the land.

Lands of the Crown not duly surveyed and laid out, are also excepted from the above provisions, in accordance with the maxim, " No time runs against the King." But by the 9 Geo. III. cap. 16, the Queen's prerogative is limited to 60 years. By Revised Statutes (Ontario), cap. 108, s. 19, it is also enacted that whenever a mortgagee has obtained possession of the land comprised in the mortgage, the mortgagor shall not bring a suit to redeem, but within 10 years next after the time when the mortgagee obtained possession or next after any acknow-ledgment of the title of the mortgagor or his'right to redeem. The mortgagee has also 10 years, from the last payment of mortgage money, within which to bring his suit to foreclose or recover such land.

Money secured by mortgage, judgment or lien or other-wise charged upon or payable out of land and also legacies, are to be deemed satisfied at the end of 10 years, if no interest should be paid or acknowledgment in writing given in the meantime.

The several lengths of uninterrupted enjoyment which will render indefeasible, rights of way or other easements, water-courses, the use of any water and the use of light for buildings, are regulated by the same statute. By the same statute no arrears of rent or of interest in respect of any sum of money charged upon or payable out of any land, or rent, or in respect of any legacy or any damages in respect of such arrears of rent or interest, shall be recovered by any distress, action or suit, but within six years after the same respectively became due, or next after an acknowledgment in writing.

The same statute enacts that no person claiming any land or rent in equity, shall bring any suit to recover the same, but within the period allowed at law.

In every case of a concealed fraud, sec. 32 enacts that the right in equity to bring a suit for the recovery of any land or rent of which one may have been deprived by such fraud, shall be deemed to have first accrued at and not before the time at which such fraud shall, or with reasonable diligence, might have been first known or discovered, unless in the case of a *bona fide* purchaser for valuable consideration and without notice.

REGISTRATION OF TITLES TO REAL ESTATE.

The registry of any instrument affecting lands will in equity constitute notice of such instrument to all persons claiming any interest in such lands, subsequent to such registry.

D

Priority of registration will in all cases prevail, unless before such prior registration there shall have been actual notice of the prior instrument to the party claiming under the prior registration.

The Revised Statutes, cap. 111, now comprises the whole Registry Law as it exists in this Province.

By its provisions there is to be a "separate Registry Office in every riding, county, union of counties and city in Upper Canada." A registrar is appointed for each whose duty it is to attend at and keep his office open each day from 10 to 4 o'clock, holidays excepted, and no instrument shall be registered by him on any holiday, nor received except within such mentioned hours.

Grants from the Crown are now registered in the County Registrar's Office, and any instrument whatever, in any manner affecting land in Upper Canada, either in law or equity, may now be registered, and all instruments are registered at full length.

The registration of Crown Grants is done by producing the original to the registrar and filing a true copy thereof, sworn to by some one who has compared the same with the original. All other instruments, except wills, are registered by depositing with the registrar the original or a duplicate, with the necessary affidavits. Wills should in every case be registered within one year after the death. of the testator, and are registered by producing the original and filing with the registrar a true copy, accompanied by an affidavit of one of the witnesses to the will, proving its execution, or by the production of probate or letters of administration with the will annexed, under the seal of any Court in this Province, or in Great Britain and Ireland, or any British Colony, Province or Possession, having jurisdiction therein, and by filing a copy of such probate or letters and an affidavit verifying such copy.

The proof required for the registration of other instruments than Crown Grants or wills, is as follows, viz. :— An affidavit by one of the witnesses to such instrument, written on the instrument, setting forth the witness' name, residence and occupation; that he was present at the execution of the original and duplicate (if any); where the instrument was executed; and that he knew the parties executing or some of them, as the case may be, and that he is a subscribing witness thereto.

The Superior and County Courts have power by order to compel a witness to any instrument, to make the necessary affidavit for registration, upon being tendered his necessary expenses therefor.

In case of the death of a witness, the execution of the instrument may be proved before the judge of any County Court, and the instrument may be registered upon such judge's certificate endorsed upon such instrument.

Notarial copies of instruments executed in Lower Canada, the originals whereof are filed in any Notarial Office, are treated as originals for the purposes of registration.

Sheriff's deeds for taxes must be registered within 18 months after the sale by the Sheriff, and deeds of lands sold under process of a court, must be registered within 6 months after the sale, to preserve priority against subsequent purchasers in good faith, who have registered their deeds.

Any person entitled to receive the money due upon a mortgage, may execute a certificate discharging such mortgage, and such certificate, when registered is valid and effectual in law as a release of such mortgage and a reconveyance of the estate to the mortgagor and those claiming under him.

After a grant from the Crown and patent issued, any one neglecting to register any instrument to him affecting such land, shall lose his priority as against a subsequent purchaser or mortgagee for value, who shall have registered, and this extends to equitable mortgages and all other liens. But a lease for a less term than seven years, accompanied by possession, need not be registered.

Plans of sub-divisions of lands are required to be lodged
with the registrar under a penalty of $20 a month for
refusing to register the same.

By this statute the appointment of an officer, called the
Inspector of Registry Offices is authorised, whose duty
it is to inspect all Registry Offices and the books, documents, and papers therein, and to preserve a general
uniformity of practice the want of which has been so
long felt by conveyancers. He is in fact to have a general supervision of the Registry Offices, and when necessary,
to enforce the provisions of the law in respect to the same.

Hitherto, inconvenience has often been felt by regis-
trars refusing personal inspection of the books of the
office. This statute expressly declares the right of every
one upon payment of the proper fees to inspect the books
for themselves and the facilities for searching titles are
very much increased by its provisions.

CLAIMS TO LANDS IN UPPER CANADA FOR WHICH NO PATENTS HAVE ISSUED.

The Heir and Devisee Commission under cap. 25 of the
Rev. Stat. of Ontario, is composed of the Judges of the
Superior Courts of Law and Equity, and such other
persons as may be appointed by commission under the
great seal. The duties of the commissioners are to ascertain, determine, and declare in all cases brought before
them, who is the party to whom the patent ought to issue .
for the lands to which such claims relate, whether made
by heirs, devisees, or assignees, of the original nominee
of the crown.

Every assignee of a crown land claim should give
notice thereof to the proper crown lands agent as soon as
possible after the assignment to him.

PROPERTY OF RELIGIOUS INSTITUTIONS.

By Revised Statutes (Ontario,) cap. 216, religious socie-
ties and congregations of Christians in Ontario can hold
lands for the site of a church, chapel, meeting-house,

burial ground, or residence of a minister, book store, printing or publishing office, or for any other religious or congregational purpose whatsoever. They must appoint trustees to hold and possess the lands and to maintain and defend actions.

A deed to such trustees must be registered within 12 months after its execution. The trustees may mortgage lands so held, to secure a debt contracted for the building, repairing, extending or improving the church, etc., or for the purchase of the land, or may borrow money on mortgage for such purposes.

Grantees in trust named in any patent, or trustees appointed in manner prescribed in the letters patent may lease lands for 21 years, and renew such lease at the expiration of any or every term of 21 years, and may bind their successors to pay for improvements on a valuation. The consent of the congregation to such leases must be signified by the votes of a majority of the members present at a meeting duly called for the purpose. Trustees may sue or distrain for rent in arrear as ordinary landlords. When lands held by trustees become unnecessary to be retained for the use of a congregation or religious body, and it is deemed advantageous to sell the land, the trustees after giving public notice of an intended sale for four successive weeks in a weekly paper may sell the land by public auction or private sale, and before the deed is executed the congregation must be duly notified thereof, and their assent, or the sanction of the Judge of the County Court of the County in which the lands lie must be obtained to the sale.

We have thus endeavoured to call attention to the more practical portions of the law relating to real property in Ontario. For more accurate knowledge reference must be had to the statutes named. He who relies on this introduction as an index directing him to fuller sources of knowledge will be benefitted, while he who is content to rely upon this short treatise as containing all that is necessary to know on the subject, will be most unwisely negligent.

THE CANADIAN CONVEYANCER.

AFFIDAVIT.

(General Form.)

County of
    to wit :
or United Counties
of   and
    To wit :

I   of   in the County of   yeoman *(or other proper designation)* make oath and say :

1. That, &c., *(Here state the matter to be sworn to, plainly and accurately. If the affidavit relates to more matters than one, then, having disposed of one matter in the first paragraph, go on to a second, as follows :)*

2. That, &c., *(and so on with as many paragraphs, as may be necessary, confining each paragraph to a distinct matter, and commencing each in a new line.)*

Sworn before me at
in the County of   this
    day of   A.D. 18
    J.P., or Commissioner, &c., for County of

AFFIDAVIT OF EXECUTION OF DEED.

County of
    To wit : of

I
    of   make oath and say :

1. That I was personally present and did see the with-

in Instrument and Duplicate   thereof duly signed, sealed, and executed by   the part   thereto.

2. That the said Instrument and Duplicate were executed at the

3. That I   know the said part

4. That I am a subscribing witness to the said Instrument and Duplicate.

Sworn before me at
in the said County of
this   day of
A.D. 18

A Commissioner, for taking Affidavits in B.R., &c.

AFFIDAVlT OF PERFORMANCE OF SETTLEMENT DUTIES.

Ontario,   of the
    Count· of   } of   in the County of
        To wit: and
of the same place *(insert here names in full, residence and occupation)* each for himself maketh oath and saith,

That he is well acquainted with   Lot Number in the   Concession of the Township of

And that it is occupied by   and has been continuously occupied by *(names of previous owners or occupiers if any)* for   years last past.

That there are   acres of it cleared and laid under crop, and a habitable house of the dimensions of   feet by   feet erected thereon.

That these improvements were made by and on behalf of the said *(names of owners and occupiers by whom improvements were made.)*

And that he this deponent is not aware of any adverse claim to or occupancy of the said lot.

Sworn before me, &c.,

A Commissioner, &c.

I have no reason to question the correctness of the above affidavit.

Crown Lands Agent.

OATH OF RESIDENCE.

(For Naturalization.)

I,   do swear, (*or being one of the persons allowed by law to affirm in judicial cases,* do affirm) that I have resided   years in this Province, with intent to settle therein, without having been during that time a stated resident in any foreign country. So help me God.

OATH OF ALLEGIANCE.

(Ditto.)

I,   do sincerely promise and swear (*or, being one of the persons allowed by law to affirm in judicial cases,* do affirm) that I will be faithful and bear true allegiance to Her Majesty Queen Victoria, as lawful Sovereign of the United Kingdom of Great Britain and Ireland, and of the Province of Canada, dependent on and belonging to the said United Kingdom, and that I will defend her to the utmost of my power against all traitors, conspiracies, and attempts whatever which shall be made against her Person, Crown, and Dignity ; and that I will do my utmost endeavour to disclose and make known to Her Majesty, Her Heirs and Successors, all treasons and traitorous conspiracies and attempts which I shall know to be against Her or any of them ; and all this I do swear. without any equivocation, mental evasion or secret reser vation, and renouncing all pardons and dispensatiqns from any person or persons whatever, to the contrary· So help me God.

AFFIRMATION.

(General Form.)

County of
To wit :
or United Counties
of and
To wit:

I, of in the County of yeoman, *(or other proper designation)*, do solemnly and sincerely affirm and declare as follows :

1. That, &c., *(As in an Affidavit.)*

Affirmed before me
at in the County
of this day
of A.D. 18

J.P., or Commissioner, &c., for the County of

STATUTORY DECLARATION.

County of
To wit :

I of the of
in the County of

Do solemnly declare, that, (*Here state subject matter declared to*)

And I make this solemn declaration, conscientiously believing the same to be true, and by virtue of the Act passed in the Thirty-seventh year of Her Majesty's Reign intituled "An Act for the Suppression of Voluntary and extra Judicial Oaths."

Declared before me
at   in the
County of   this
day of   A.D. 18

DECLARATION AS TO AGE AND MARRIAGE.

County of   }   I   of the
     To wit :   of   in the County of

Do solemnly declare that I well knew   of the   of   in the County of   prior to the   day of   A.D. 18   when he and that he was at that date of the full age of   years and   married.

And I make this solemn declaration conscientiously believing the same to be true, and by virtue of the Act passed in the Thirty-seventh year of her Majesty's reign intituled "An Act for the suppression of Voluntary and extra Judicial Oaths."

Declared before me
at the   of
   in the County
of   this
day of   A.D.
18

APPRENTICESHIP INDENTURE.

—

THIS INDENTURE, made the   day of   A.D.
18   WITNESSETH, that   of   in the
County of   in the Province of Ontario, in the
Dominion of Canada,   Hath put and placed out, and by
these presents doth put and place out   And the
said   ,   doth hereby put, place, and bind out
himself as an Apprentice to   of   ,
To Learn the Art, Trade, or Mystery of   And
with his Master after the manner of an Apprentice to
serve from the   day of   18   until the full
end and term of   years from thence next ensuing,
and fully to be complete and ended.   During all which
time the said Apprentice shall well and faithfully serve his
said master, his secrets keep, and his lawful commands
everywhere, and at all times, readily obey.   He shall do
no damage to his said master, nor suffer any to be done
by others ; and if any to his knowledge be intended, he
shall forthwith give his said Master seasonable notice
thereof.   He shall not waste the goods of his said Master, ,
nor lend them unlawfully to any.   He shall not play at
cards, dice, or other unlawful games.   He shall not contract matrimony during the said term.   He shall not
haunt or frequent taverns, drinking saloons, or places of
gaming, nor absent himself from the service of his said
master ; but in all things and at all times, during the said
term, he shall behave himself towards his said master and
all his, as a good and faithful Apprentice ought to do.

For the due and full observance and performance of all
which said articles by the said Apprentice the said

and   with the said   Do
hereby respectively Covenant, Promise and Agree ;

In consideration whereof, the said   Doth
hereby covenant with the said   that he will
at all times, during the said term, to the best of his
means and ability, teach and instruct, or cause to be
taught and instructed, his said Apprentice in the Art,
Mystery or Trade of a   which he useth ; and
also pay unto the said   for the use of the said
Apprentice the several sums following, that is to say :

And the said   agrees to find unto the said
Apprentice, during the said term,

In witness whereof the said parties have interchangeably to these indentures set their hands and seals.

Signed, Sealed and Delivered }
          in the presence of   }

INDENTURE OF APPRENTICESHIP TO LEARN HOUSEWORK.

THIS INDENTURE, made the   day of   18 ,
BETWEEN   of the Township of   in the County
. of   widow of the first part   her daughter now
of the age of   of the second part, and   of the
same township,   of the third part, WITNESSETH that
the said   by and with the consent of the
said   her mother, testified by her execution of
these presents, hath bound and put herself, and by these
presents doth bind and put herself apprentice to the said
                        with him to dwell and serve from the day of
date hereof until the full end of the term of   next

ensuing, fully to be completed and ended; during which term the said   her said master faithfully shall and will serve in all lawful business, according to her power and ability, and honestly and obediently in all things demean and behave herself towards her said master during the term aforesaid.

AND the said   . shall and will teach and instruct, or cause to be taught and instructed, the said apprentice in sewing, knitting, and house-wifery, the management of the dairy, and all matters connected with the calling of a farmer, properly to be taught to her the said apprentice; and shall and will during the said term find, provide, and allow her sufficient meat, drink, clothing, lodging, washing, and all other necessaries; and at the expiration of the term aforesaid shall and will give unto the said apprentice two suits of apparel.

In Witness, &c.

Signed and sealed, &c.

ARTICLES OF AGREEMENT.

—

MEMORANDUM OF AGREEMENT made and entered into this ` day of   A.D. 18 . BETWEEN

WITNESSETH that the said parties hereto do hereby mutually covenant, promise and agree to and with each other in manner and form following, that is to say :—

1. That, &c., *(here add the particular agreement entered into between the parties)*

As WITNESS the hands and seals of the said parties the day and year first above written.

Signed, Sealed and Delivered }
    in the presence of   }

AGREEMENT FOR SALE OF LAND.

—

ARTICLES OF AGREEMENT, made this   day
of   A.D. 18   ,   BETWEEN

WHEREAS, the said part   of the first part   ha
agreed to sell to the part   of the second part, and the
part   of the second part ha   agreed to purchase of and
from the said part   of the first part the lands, hereditaments and premises hereinafter mentioned, that is to say:
All and singular th   certain parcel or tract   of land,
being composed of   Together with all the privileges and appurtenances thereto belonging at or for the
price or sum of   of lawful money of Canada,
payable in manner and on the days and times hereinafter mentioned, that is to say :

Now IT IS HEREBY AGREED between the parties aforesaid in manner following, that is to say : The said part
of the second part, for   heirs, executors, and
administrators, do   Covenant, Promise and Agree to and
with the said part   of the first part,   heirs, executors,
administrators and assigns, that he or they shall well and
truly pay or cause to be paid to the said part   of the first
part,   heirs, executors, administrators and assigns
the said sum of money above mentioned, together with
the interest thereon, at the rate of   per cent. per
annum, on the days and times and in the manner above
mentioned ; And also shall and will pay and discharge
all taxes, rates and assessments, wherewith the said land
may be rated or charged from and after this date.

In consideration whereof, and on payment of the said
sum of money, with interest thereon as aforesaid, the

said part of the First Part, Do for   heirs executors, administrators and assigns Covenant, Promise,
and Agree, to and with the said part of the Second
Part,   heirs, executors, administrators or assigns, to
convey and assure, or cause to be conveyed and assured,
to the part of the Second Part,   heirs or assigns, by
a good and sufficient deed in fee simple, All that the said
piece or parcel of land above described, together with the
appurtenances thereto belonging or appertaining, freed
and discharged from all dower and other incumbrances,
But subject to the conditions and reservations expressed
in the original grant thereof from the Crown, and such
Deed shall be prepared at the expense of the said part
of the   part and shall contain the following covenants, namely

And also shall and will suffer and permit the said
part of the Second part,   heirs and assigns to occupy and enjoy the same until default be made in the
payment of the said sums of money, or the interest
thereof or any part thereof, on the days and times and in
the manner above mentioned ; Subject, nevertheless, to
impeachment for voluntary or permissive waste.

And it is expressly understood that time is to be
considered the essence of this agreement, and unless the
payments are punctually made at the times and in the
manner above mentioned, the said part of the First
Part   at liberty to re-sell the said land.

In witness whereof, &c.

Signed, Sealed, &c.

(Usual affidavit of execution)

AGREEMENT FOR SALE OF LAND.

—

(Shorter Form.)

THIS AGREEMENT made the   day of   A.D.
18   BETWEEN   hereinafter called the Vendor   , of the First Part ; and   hereinafter
called the Vendee   , of the Second Part :

WITNESSETH, that the Vendor   agrees to sell to the
Vendee   , and the Vendee   agrees to purchase from the
Vendor   , all that parcel of land situate, known and described as follows, viz :   for the price or sum
of   payable as follows : the sum of   on
execution of this agreement ; and the remainder thus :
that is to say :   Upon payment of the sum of   the
Vendee   is to receive a deed, and is then to execute a
mortgage, securing the balance of the purchase money in
manner above mentioned.

The Deed and Mortgage shall be prepared by the Vendor   or his Solicitor, and the expense of the Mortgage
(which shall contain the usual covenants and insurance
clause) shall be borne by the Vendee   .

The Vendee   shall examine the title at his own expense.   The Vendor   shall not be required to produce
any title deeds other than those in his possession ; nor
shall the Vendor   be required to pay for the production
of any deeds not in his possession ; or to pay for any
evidences of title or expenses connected with, or incidental to the examination of the same.

The Vendee   shall have one week to examine the title ;
and if not objected to prior to that time, he shall be
deemed to have accepted the same.

E

If the title be objected to, the Vendor shall have the privilege of putting an end to the above contract, if he desires to do so, by notice in writing to that effect, to the Vendee   or his solicitor ; and in that event the deposit shall be returned, but the Vendee shall not be entitled to any compensation or to any expenses incurred in the examination of the title.   The said notice shall be sufficiently served by mailing the same in a registered letter to the post office address of the Vendee   , or the solicitor employed by him to examine the title.

The Vendee agrees to pay the taxes upon the said land for the current year.

It is further understood and agreed that time, both in payment of the principal money and interest under this agreement, shall be considered the essence of this agreement, and unless payments are punctually made in manner above mentioned, these presents shall at the option of the Vendor   be null and void, and he shall be at liberty to resell the said land, and the payments made by the Vendee   shall be forfeited.

As WITNESS our hands the day and year first above written.

In presence of, &c.

(*Usual affidavit of execution.*)

AGREEMENT FOR SALE OF LAND.
—

(*Another form.*)

ARTICLES OF AGREEMENT, made this   day of   18   BETWEEN

WHEREAS the said part   of the First Part ha   agreed

to sell to the part   of the Second Part, and the part   of the Second Part ha   agreed to purchase from the said part   of the First Part the lands and premises hereinafter mentioned, that is to say :

All and singular th   certain parcel or tract of land, being composed of   Together with the appurtenances, for the price or sum of   of lawful money of Canada, payable in manner following, that is to say :

Now it is hereby agreed as follows, that is to say : The said part   of the Second Part, for   heirs, executors and administrators do   Covenant, Promise and Agree, to and with the said part   of the First Part, heirs, executors, administrators and assigns, that he or they shall well and truly pay, or cause to be paid to the said part   of the First Part,   heirs, executors, administrators and assigns, the said sum of money above mentioned, together with interest thereon, at the rate of   per cent. per annum, as above mentioned ; And also shall and will pay and discharge all taxes, rates and assessments wherewith the said land may be rated or charged from and after the   day of   And will cotemporaneously with the execution of the deed as hereinafter mentioned, execute a mortgage of said premises to secure payment of the balance of   which mortgage shall contain the usual statutory covenants, including a covenant to insure for not less than two-thirds of the insurable value of the buildings on said premises, and in which mortgage the dower of the mortgagor's wife shall be barred.

In consideration whereof, and on payment of the said

consideration sum of   dollars, the said part   of the First Part, do   for   heirs, executors, administrators, and assigns, Covenant, Promise and Agree, to and with the said part of the Second Part,   heirs, executors, administrators or assigns, to convey and assure, or cause to be conveyed and assured to the part   of the Second Part   heirs or assigns, by a good and sufficient deed in fee simple, All that the said piece or parcel of land above described, with the appurtenances, freed or discharged from all Dower or other incumbrances, but subject to the conditions and reservations expressed in the original grant thereof from the Crown, and such deed shall be prepared at the expense of the said part   of the   part, and shall contain the following covenants, namely: And said mortgage shall be prepared at the expense of the said part   of the part; and said deed to be delivered cotemporaneously with the payment of said sum of   and delivery of said mortgage.

And also, shall and will suffer and permit the said part   of the Second Part,   heirs and assigns, to occupy and enjoy said premises until default be made in the payment of the said sum of money, or the interest thereof, or any part thereof, on the day and time, and in manner above mentioned; Subject, nevertheless, to impeachment for voluntary or permissive waste.

And it is expressly understood that time is to be considered the essence of this agreement, and unless the payments are punctually made at the time and in the manner above mentioned, the said part of the First Part to be at liberty to re-sell the said land.

It is hereby expressly agreed, that said part of the First Part, is not to be bound to furnish any abstract of title or produce any title deeds not in possession or control, or give copies of any title deeds, but that the part of the Second Part to search the title at own expense, and if said part of the First Part, without any default on part unable to make a good title to the said land within days from the date hereof, then may withdraw from this contract on payment to the said part of the Second Part of all expenses reasonably incurred in investigating said title or otherwise by reason of the making of this contract.

In witness, &c.

Signed, sealed, &c.

(Usual affidavit of execution.)

AGREEMENT FOR SALE OF STANDING TIMBER.

This Indenture, made the day of A.D. 18 , Between of the of in the County of and Province of Ontario, of the first part; and of the of in the County of in the Province aforesaid of the second part, as follows:

The said party of the first part, for and in consideration of the payments hereinafter mentioned to be made to him, hereby grants, bargains, sells and assigns to the said party of the second part, his heirs, executors, administrators and assigns, all the standing trees and timber now standing, growing, lying or being in and upon that certain parcel of land and premises, situate, lying and being in the Township of   in the County of   and Province of Ontario, containing by ad-measurement   acres, be the same more or less, and being composed of

To have and to hold the said trees and timber to the said party of the second part, his heirs, executors, admin-istrators, and assigns, to and for his and their sole and only use. The said party of the second part, his agents, servants and workmen, with or without horses, carts, waggons or sleighs, shall at all times within   years from the date hereof, have full liberty to enter into and upon the said lands, and to fell the said trees and timber in such manner as he or they shall think fit, and cut and convert the same into such convenient logs, bundles or stacks as he or they shall think proper, with full liberty to bring horses, cattle, waggons, trucks, carts and sleighs in and upon the said land for the purpose of removing the said trees and timber at such times and in such man-ner, as he or they may think proper.

The said party of the second part hereby agrees to and with the party of the first part to pay him for the said trees and timber so being upon the said land the sum of   in manner following :

And the said party of the first part, for himself, his heirs, executors and administrators, covenants, promises and agrees to and with the party of the second part, his heirs, executors, administrators and assigns, that he has a good title in fee simple to the said lands, and good right, full power and absolute authority to sell and dispose of the said timber and trees, and that they are free from all incumbrances of any kind whatsoever.

In witness, &c.

Signed, sealed, &c.

(Usual affidavit of execution.)

AGREEMENT FOR SALE OF STANDING TIMBER.

(Another form.)

THIS INDENTURE, made in duplicate this   day of   A.D. 18   , in pursuance of the Act respecting short forms of conveyances, BETWEEN   of the   of   in the County of   and   his wife of the first part ; And   of the second part.

WITNESSETH that the said part   of the first part for and in consideration of the sum of   dollars of which   dollars are now paid to   by the said part of the second part (the receipt whereof is hereby by acknowledged) and the balance is to be paid as hereinafter set out, Do   hereby Grant, Bargain, Sell and Assign unto the said part   of the second part   heirs and assigns all the pine   timber now standing, growing or being in or upon all and singular that certain parcel or tract of land and premises situate lying and being in the Township of   in the County of   and more fully described as follows :

To have and to hold the same unto the said part of the second part   heirs and assigns for ever Together with full power, liberty, right and authority for

the said part   of the second part   servants, workmen and agents from time to time and at all reasonable
times hereafter during the term of   years to fell,
cut down, grub up, saw, dress, hew and work up the said
timber.   And together with full and free ingress, egress
and regress for the said part   of the second part
servants, workmen and agents with or without horses,
oxen, waggons, carts, sleighs, trucks and teams to enter
into and upon and over the said lands and premises for
the purposes aforesaid, and also for the purpose of taking
and carrying away the said timber, with liberty also to
make all such roads as may from time to time be necessary for getting out and removing the said timber, and for
that purpose to cut, fell, hew and remove such trees, logs
and brush as may be deemed necessary.

And the said part   of the first part hereby for
heirs, executors and administrators covenant   with the
said part   of the second part   executors, administrators and assigns that   ha   the right to convey the
said timber to the said part   of the second part.   And
that the said part   of the second part shall have quiet
possession of the said timber free from all incumbrances,
and that   will execute such further assurances of
the said timber as may be requisite, and that   ha
done no act to encumber the said timber.

And the said part   of the first part hereby release   to
the said part   of the second part all   claims upon
the said lands in so far as the same may affect the said
timber.

And the said part   of the second part for   heirs,
executors and administrators covenant   with the said

part of the first part executors, administrators and assigns that will pay the said part of the first part executors, administrators, or assigns the said sum of ' dollars as follows, that is to say :

In witness, &c.

Signed, sealed, &c.

RECEIVED from the said part of the first part the sum of dollars part of the consideration money within mentioned.

Witness,

* (*Usual affidavit of execution.*)

AGREEMENT TO SELL ON COMMISSION.

—

AN AGREEMENT made this day of A.D. 18 , between of manufacturer of and of traveller on commission.

1. The said for himself, his executors and administrators agrees that upon receiving a written order from the said the said his executors and administrators, will, from time to time, at his warehouse aforesaid, and according to such order, supply to the said the as now manufactured by the said

2. The said is to be invoiced to the said at the rate of per pound, and the said is to account for the same at that price every months, beginning from the date hereof.

3. The said his executors and administrators shall not be bound to supply more than lbs. on any one day, nor more than lbs. in any one week, withou

a week's notice in writing with a written order from the said   nor shall the said   his executors or administrators be bound to continue supplying
as aforesaid after   lbs shall have been delivered and shall remain unaccounted for, whether the said period of
     months shall have elapsed since such delivery or not.

4. This agreement shall continue in force for
years from the date hereof, but subject to determination at any time by   months' previous notice in writing from either of the said parties or the executors or administrators of the said   to the other of them and delivered at his usual or last known place of abode.

5. During the continuance of this agreement the said
     his executors and administrators shall not employ, nor shall knowingly suffer any other person than the said
     to sell on commission for them the said
beyond a radius of   miles from
and in case of a breach of this clause the said
     for himself his executors and administrators
undertakes to pay the said   the sum of   by way of agreed and liquidated damages.

In witness, &c.

Signed, &c.

AGREEMENT DEPOSITING GOODS AS A SECURITY.

An Agreement made the   day of   A.D. 18 , Between   of   , and   of   .

The said   having deposited this day at his risk, with the said   the following goods, namely, [*here give list of goods*], as a security for the payment of and interest, on the   day of   A.D. 18 it is agreed that, in default of payment, the said after   day's notice in writing, may sell the same goods, or any part thereof, by auction or otherwise, towards payment of the said principal sum and interest, and of the expenses of sale and insurance, but until such default no such sale is to take place, nor is any action or suit to be brought to enforce payment of the said sum and interest.

In witness, &c.

Signed, &c.

AGREEMENT GIVING A GENERAL LIEN, WITH POWER OF SALE.

AN AGREEMENT, made the   day of   A.D. 18 , BETWEEN   of   and   of   , WITNESSETH.

1. In consideration of the promise of forbearance, hereinafter contained, on the part of the said   the said agrees to give him a general lien on all property that may at any time be in his possession belonging to the said   or to any person on his account, and that such general lien shall at all times be a security to the said   his executors and administrators, for all moneys that may from time to time be due from the said   to the said   or to the said and any partner or partners of his in his business of   , and that, if at any time the sum of   shall be due as

aforesaid, the said   his executors and administrators may, after seven day's notice in writing, sell the same property or any part thereof, by auction or otherwise, towards payment of such sum and interest, and of the expenses of sale and insurance.

2. But unless the sum of   shall be due, as aforesaid, no such sale is to take place, and, after the said sum shall be due, no action or suit shall be brought for the recovery of the same or any part thereof until after the sale of any such property as aforesaid.

In witness, &c.

Signed, &c.

AGREEMENT FOR LETTING UNFURNISHED LODGINGS.

An Agreement made this   day of   A.D. 18 , Between A.B. and C. D.

The said A. B. lets, and the said C. D. takes, the two rooms on the first floor of the house No.   , in   street, for a week, at the rent of   , and so on, from week to week, until the tenancy is ended by a *week's* notice.

In witness, &c.

Signed, &c.

AGREEMENT FOR LETTING A FURNISED LODGING.

An Agreement made this   day of   A.D. 18 , Between A. B. and C. D.

1. A. B. lets to C. D. the rooms on the first floor of the house No.   in   street, ready furnished, from the   day of   18 , and agrees to supply customary attendance, together with the use of suitable linen, plate, china, and glass, for a *week* at the rent of   per week, and so on from week to week till the tenancy is ended by a *week's* notice on either side.

2. The said C. D. takes the said rooms with such attendance and use at the rent aforesaid, and agrees that if he shall damage the said rooms, or any articles used or being therein, he will restore them to their present condition, or replace them (damage by reasonable wear and tear excepted).

In witness, &c.

Signed, &c.

AGREEMENT FOR LETTING A FURNISHED HOUSE.

An Agreement made this   day of   A.D. 18 , Between A. B. and C. D.

1. The said A. B. lets, and the said C. D. takes, the house No.   in   steeet, with the appurtenances and the furniture and effects therein, for a month from the day of   18 , at the rent of   per month and so on, from month to month, till the tenancy is determined by a month's notice on either side.

2. If the said C. D., his family, or servants, shall damage the said house, or any of the said furniture and effects, he shall restore them to their present condition,

or replace them (damage by reasonablv wear and tear expected).

3. The said A. B. is to defray all outgoings in respect of the said premises.

4. The said A. B., or his agents may enter upon, and inspect the premises during the tenancy, on the first day of every month ; but if the same falls on a Sunday, or public holiday, then on the first day thereafter.

5. If the said C. D. continues the tenancy from the   day of   18 , he shall pay thenceforth   rent per month.

In witness, &c.

Signed, &c.

SCHEDULE.

AGREEMENT FOR A YEARLY TENANCY OF A HOUSE.

AN AGREEMENT made this   day of   A.D. 18 , BETWEEN A. B. and C. D.

1. The said A. B. lets, and the said C. D. takes, the house No.   in   street, with the appurtenances, from the   day of   18 , from year to year, at the yearly rent of   , payable quarterly on the usual quarter days.

2. The said C. D. will not assign or underlet, or part with the possession of the premises, nor let any portion thereof as lodgings, nor use the same save as a dwelling-house.

3. The said C. D., when the tenancy ends, shall deliver

up the premises in good order and repair, reasonable wear and unavoidable accidents excepted.

In witness, &c.

Signed, &c.

AGREEMENT FOR TENANCY OF HOUSE.

Another form.

MEMORANDUM OF AGREEMENT entered into this day of   A. D. 18 , BETWEEN   of the one part, and   of the other part.

WHEREBY the said   agrees to let and the said   agrees to take All that messuage or tenement and premises with the appurtenances.

To hold for the term of   years, to commence from the   day of   18   , at the clear yearly rent of   payable quarterly, free from any deduction in respect of taxes, rates or impositions, the first quarterly payment to be made on the   day of   next. And the said   agrees to pay the said rent on the   days of   in each year, free from deduction as aforesaid, and that he will not do, commit or permit on the said premises any waste or damage or anything which may be or become a nuisance or annoyance to any of the tenants or premises adjoining, and that on the expiration or determination of the tenancy hereby created, he, the said   will quietly deliver up the said messuage or tenement and premises to the said   in as good repair and condition as the same now are in (reasonable wear excepted), and also that in the event of any one quarter's rent or any part thereof being in arrear and unpaid for one week after it shall have become due and payable by virtue of this agreement and no sufficient distress càn be had or levied for the amount so due, or in the event of the said premises being untenanted in the usual and ordinary acceptation of such term, or if the said premises or any part thereof shall be let to disorderly or disreputable persons, then, and in any such case, it shall and may be lawful for the said   and any other person entitled to the said premises to enter into and take possession of the same and expel the said   therefrom without bringing any ejectment or other proceding at Law for the recovery of such possession, and that thenceforth this Agreement shall as to everything (except the recovery of any arrears of rent or damages then due or incurred) be utterly void, and the interest of the said   absolutely forfeited and the said   shall be barred and precluded from commencing or maintaining any action of trespass or otherwise by reason of such possession being taken as aforesaid, AND IT IS HEREBY FURTHER AGREED that at the expiration of the said term of years (unless the tenancy hereby created shall have been previously determined) the said   may hold, occupy and enjoy the said messuage or tenement and premises from quarter to quarter at the rent and upon and subject to the terms and stipulations hereinbefore mentioned, for so long a time as the said and   shall agree, and that after the expiration of the said term of   years each of the said parties shall be at liberty to determine the said tenancy by giving to the other a quarter's notice or warning in writing, expiring on either of the said quarterly days.

In witness, &c.

Signed, sealed &c.

ARBITRATION DEED.

THIS INDENTURE, made the   day of   A. D. 18   , BETWEEN   of the first part, and of the second part.

WHEREAS disputes and differences have arisen, and are now depending, between the said parties of the first and second parts in reference to   , and in order to put an end thereto, and to obtain an amicable adjustment thereof, the said parties of the first and second parts have respectively agreed to refer the same to the award, order, arbitrament, final end and determination of   and   arbitrators, respectively nominated and chosen, by and on behalf of the said

and   : And in the event of the said two arbitrators hereby appointed not being able to agree within one month from the date of these presents upon their said award, then it shall and may be lawful for them to appoint some fit person as third arbitrator, by a memorandum in writing under their hands, to be endorsed on these presents; and the award of any two of them shall be final and conclusive, both at Law and in Equity, upon both of the said parties hereto, such award to be made in writing on or before the   day of next.

NOW THIS INDENTURE WITNESSETH, that they the said do, and each of them doth, each for himself

F

severally and respectively, and for his and their respective heirs, executors and administrators, covenant, promise and agree, with and to each other, and his and their heirs, executors and administrators, well and truly to stand to, obey, abide by, observe, perform, fulfil and keep the award, order, arbitrament, and final determination of the said arbitrators, hereby appointed; or in the event of it having been necessary to appoint such third arbitrator as aforesaid, to stand, to obey, abide by, observe, perform, fulfil and keep the award, order, arbitrament, and final determination of any two of them of and concerning the premises aforesaid, or anything in any manner relating thereto, so as the said award of the said arbitrators be made in writing under their hands, or under the hands of any two of them (in the event of any such appointment as aforesaid).

AND IT IS ALSO MUTUALLY AGREED by the said and   that the death of either of them shall not operate as a revocation of the power and authority of the said arbitrators appointed by these presents, or to be appointed in pursuance hereof, to make their award, and that such award (in case of such death before the making or publishing such award), in writing under the hands of the said arbitrators, shall be delivered to the respective personal representatives of either of the said and   who shall require the same on or before such day of   as mentioned aforesaid.

AND IT IS HEREBY AGREED, that the said Arbitrators hereby appointed, or in the event of any such appointment being made as aforesaid, any two of them shall be at liberty, by writing under their hands, respectively endorsed on these presents, to enlarge the time for making the said award when and as often and to such times as they shall think fit. And also, that neither of the said parties shall nor will obstruct, delay, impede or prevent in any manner the said arbitrators from making, but will, so far as in them lies respectively, do all such acts and things required to be done, produced or performed by the said arbitrators to enable the said arbitrators to make such award as aforesaid in pursuance hereof. And also, that all the costs and charges attending the said arbitration shall be in the discretion of the said arbitrators hereby appointed, or in the event of such appointment of a third arbitrator as aforesaid, of any two of them so making their award as aforesaid, and shall be paid and satisfied pursuant to their award. And also, that these presents shall be made a Rule of Her Majesty's Court of   at   to the end that the said parties respectively may be finally concluded by the said Arbitration, pursuant to the Statute in such case made and provided.

And for the full performance of such award so to be made as aforesaid, the said parties hereto bind themselves, severally and respectively, their several and respective heirs, executors and administrators, each to the other of them respectively, in the penal sum of   lawful money of Canada, firmly by these presents.

In witness, &c.

Signed, sealed, &c.

ARBITRATION BOND.

KNOW ALL MEN BY THESE PRESENTS, that   of

HELD AND FIRMLY BOUND to   of
in the penal sum of   of lawful money of Canada,
to be paid to the said   or to   certain attorney,
executors, administrators, or assigns ; FOR which payment
to be well and truly made   bind   heirs, executors and administrators for ever firmly by these presents.

SEALED with   Seal DATED this   day of
            A.D. 18

WHEREAS disputes and differences have arisen and are
now pending between the above bounden
and the said   touching and concerning

AND WHEREAS the above bounden   and the
said   have agreed to refer such disputes and differences, as well as all actions, suits, controversies, accounts,
reckonings, matters and things in anywise relating thereto, to the award, arbitrament and determination of
            arbitrators, nominated, appointed and chosen as
well by and on the behalf of the above bounden
            as of the said   and who have consented and
agreed to accept the burden of the said arbitration :

Now THE CONDITION of the above written bond or obligation is such, that if the above bounden   do and
shall well and truly submit to, abide by and perform the
award, arbitrament and determination of the said arbitrators, so nominated, appointed and chosen as aforesaid,
touching and concerning the matters in dispute between
the above bounden   and the said
and so referred to them the said arbitrators as aforesaid
(provided such award be made in writing under the hands
and seals of the said arbitrators, ready to be delivered to

the said parties, or such of them as shall apply for the same, on or before the   day of   A.D. 18 ,
THEN THIS OBLIGATION shall be void, otherwise to be and remain in full force and virtue.

AND IT IS HEREBY AGREED between the said parties in difference, that these presents and the submission hereby made of the said matters in controversy, shall be made a Rule of Her Majesty's Court of Queen's Bench or Common Pleas, at   , pursuant to the Statute in that behalf ; AND that all books, papers, vouchers, entries or memoranda in the power, custody or possession of the said parties shall be produced to the said arbitrators or umpire ; AND that all witnesses produced to the said arbitrators or umpire shall be sworn by them : AND that all costs and charges attending on the drawing of these presents and of the said arbitration and award shall be in the discretion of the said arbitrators or umpire.

Signed, sealed, &c.

APPOINTMENT OF UMPIRE.

WE, the within named   and   do hereby nominate and appoint   of   to be umpire between us in and concerning the matters in difference within referred on condition that he do, within days from the date hereof, by some writing under his hand, accept the umpirage.

Witness our hands this   day of   , A.D. 18
Witness.

ENLARGEMENT OF TIME FOR MAKING AWARD.

WE, the undersigned arbitrators, by virtue of the power to us given for this purpose, do hereby appoint, extend, and [*if a second enlargement,* "further"] enlarge the time for making our award until the   day of   next, on or before which said day our award in writing of and concerning the matters in difference within mentioned and referred to us shall be made and published.

IN WITNESS WHEREOF, we have set our hands the day of   , A.D. 18 .

Witness,

ENLARGEMENT OF TIME BY THE PARTIES.

WE, the within-named   and   for ourselves severally and respectively, and for our several and respective heirs, executors, and administrators, do hereby give, grant, and allow unto the within-named arbitrators further time for making their award of and concerning the several matters within referred to them, until the day of   next.

IN WITNESS WHEREOF, we have hereunto set our hands [*or, if the submission was by bond or deed, say,* "our hands and seals"], the   day of   A.D. 18 .

Witness,

APPOINTMENT OF THIRD PERSON AS ADDITIONAL ARBITRATOR.

WE, the within-named   and   do, by

this *memorandum* under our hands [made before we enter or proceed on the arbitration within mentioned] nominate and appoint   of   , the third person or arbitrator, to whom, together with ourselves, all matters in difference between the said parties within mentioned shall be referred, according to the tenor and effect of the within deed.

WITNESS our hands this   day of   , 18 .
Signed in the presence of

AWARD BY AN UMPIRE.

To ALL TO WHOM THESE PRESENTS SHALL COME, J. P., of   yeoman, sends greeting : WHEREAS, P. Q., of of the one part, and A. B, and C. D. of   of the other part, have mutually entered into, and reciprocally executed bonds or obligations to each other, bearing date the day of   respectively, conditioned, that the said parties should in all things well and truly stand to, abide, observe, perform, fulfil, and keep the award final end and determination of R. S. of   and B. W. of   arbitrators, indifferently chosen by the said parties, of and concerning all and all manner of action and actions, cause and causes of action, suits, bills, bonds, &c. (*reciting the condition of the bond*); And whereas, the said R. S. and B. W. met upon the said arbitration, and did not make their award between the said parties by the time limited in and by the conditions of the said bonds and in pursuance of the said bonds, have chosen and appointed me as umpire, to settle and determine the matters in difference ; now know ye that I, the said J. P., the umpire, named and chosen,

as aforesaid, having taken upon me the burthen of the
said arbitration, and respective witnesses, proofs and allegations on both sides of and concerning the said disputes and differences between them, and fully considered
the same, and the matters to me referred, do make this
my award and umpirage in manner following, that is to
say, I do award and order that the said P. Q., his executors or administrators, do and shall, on the   day of
        between the hours of   and   in the forenoon,
at the house known, &c., pay, or cause to be paid, unto
the said A. B. and C. D. the sum of   in full, for
their damages and costs in a certain action lately commenced by them against the said P. Q., and also, for the
costs of and occasioned by the said .reference ; and upon
payment of the said sum of   I do award and direct,
that the said parties shall duly execute and deliver to
each other, mutual releases in writing, of all and every
action and actions, cause and causes of action, damages,
claims and demands whatsoever, subsisting or depending,
on or before the said   day of   last.

In Witness, &c.

Signed, Sealed, &c.

AWARD BY REFEREES.

(Short Form.)

We, the undersigned, referees appointed by the within
rule of court (or by the within agreement of submission)
having notified and met the parties, and heard their
several allegations, proofs, and arguments, and duly considered the same, do award and determine that the within

named A. B. shall recover of the within-named C. D. the
sum of   together with the costs of suit, to be taxed
by the court, and the costs of this reference, which last
amount to the sum of   and that the same shall be in
full of all matters within referred to us.

In Witness, &c.

Signed, Sealed, &c.

AWARD BY ARBITRATORS.

To ALL TO WHOM THESE PRESENTS SHALL COME, A. A.
of   C. C., of   and D. D., of   send greeting :
WHEREAS divers suits, disputes, controversies, and differences, have happened and arisen, and are now depending, between E. E., of   ·and F. F., of   for pacifying,
composing and ending whereof, the said E. E. and F. F,
have bound themselves each to the other, in the penal
sum of   by several bonds or obligations, bearing date
          last past, before the date hereof, with conditions
thereunder, to stand to, obey, abide, perform and keep the
award, order, arbitrament, final end and determination of
the said A. A., C. C., and D. D., arbitrators indifferently
named, elected and chosen, as well on the part and behalf of the said E. E. as of the said F. F., to arbitrate,
award, adjudge and determine, of and concerning all, and
all manner of action and actions, cause and causes of
actions, suits, bills, bonds, judgments, executions, quar-
rels, controversies, trespasses, damages, and demands,
whatsoever, at any time or times theretofore had, made,
· commenced, sued, prosecuted, or depending, by or between
the said parties, or either of them, so as the said award

should be made in writing, under the hands and seals of the said arbitrators, or any two of them, ready to be delivered unto the said parties, or such of them as should require the same, on or before the   day of   instant, as by the said obligations and conditions thereof it doth and may appear : Now know ye, that the said A. A., C. C., and D. D., taking upon them the charge and burden of the said award, and having deliberately heard the allegations and proofs of both the said parties, do, by these presents, arbitrate, award, order, decree, and adjudge, of and concerning the premises, in manner and form following ; that is to say,

FIRST, they do award, decree and adjudge, that the said F. F., or his heirs, shall and do, on or before the day of   next ensuing the date hereof, make and execute a good and sufficient conveyance of his interest, &c., of and in all those parcels or tracts of land, &c.

And, also, the said arbitrators do further award, decree, and adjudge that the said F. F., his executors or administrators, shall and do, on or before the   day of   next ensuing the date hereof, pay, or cause to be paid, unto the said E. E., his executors, or administrators, at or in the now dwelling-house of the said E. E., in   aforesaid, the sum of   dollars, in full payment, discharge and satisfaction, of and for all moneys, debts, and duties, due or owing unto the said E. E., by the said F. F., upon any account whatsoever, at any time before their entering into the said bonds of arbitration, as aforesaid.

And, also, the said arbitrators do hereby further award, order, decree, and adjudge, that all actions and suits

commenced, brought, or depending between the said E.
E. and F. F., for any matter, cause, or thing whatsoever,
arising or happening at the time of, or before their entering into the said bonds of arbitration, shall, from henceforth, cease and determine, and be no further prosecuted
or proceeded in by them, or either of them, or by their,
or either of their means, consent or procurement.

And lastly, the said arbitrators do hereby further
award, order, adjudge and decree, that the said E. E.
and F. F., shall and do, within the space of two days
next ensuing the date of this present award, seal and
execute unto each other, mutual and general releases of
all actions, cause and causes of actions, suits, controversies, trespasses, debts, duties, damages, accounts, reckonings, and demands whatsoever, for or by reason of any
matter, cause, or thing whatsoever, from the beginning
of the world to the day of the date of the said bonds of
arbitration as aforesaid.

In Witness, &c.

Signed, Sealed, &c.

AWARD WHERE SUBMISSION WAS BY AGREE-
MENT, AND STATING ASSENT FOR EN-
LARGEMENT.

To all to whom these presents shall come, we, A. A.
and T. A., of   send greeting : Whereas on   by a
certain agreement in writing under the hands [and seals]
of A. B., of   and C, D., of   bearing date on or
about the   day of   last, reciting that &c., (*here set
out the recital and such parts of the agreement as bear*

upon the award). And whereas by an endorsement on the said agreement, bearing date on or about the   day of   last past, and under the hands of all the said parties to the said agreement, they the said parties mutually and reciprocally consented and agreed that the time for the said arbitrators making the said award should be enlarged to the   day of   then next, and that they would in all other respects abide by the terms of the said agreement.   Now know ye that we the said arbitrators having taken upon us the burthen of the said reference, and having examined all such witnesses as were produced before us by the said parties respectively, and having fully weighed and considered the allegations, proofs, and vouchers made and produced before us, do award [&c.]

In Witness, &c.

AFFIDAVIT OF EXECUTION OF AWARD.

County of ⎫   I, Y. Z., of, &c., make oath and
    To wit: ⎰ say :

1. That I was present and did see the annexed award duly signed, sealed, and delivered by the therein-named   and that I am the subscribing witness to the execution of the said award.

Sworn before me, at ⎫
in the county of   this ⎬
    day of   18 ⎰

A Commissioner, &c., in B. R., for the County of

[If the affidavit is intended for use in a court of law, it must be entitled in the court.]

APPOINTMENT OF PROXY.

—

I,   , of   , in the county of   , being a member of the   Company, Limited, and entitled to votes, hereby appoint   , of   , as my proxy to vote for me or on my behalf at the [ordinary or extraordinary, *as the case may be*] general meeting of the company to be held on the   day of   , and at any adjournment thereof [or at any meeting of the company that may be held in the year 18   ]. As witness my hand this   day of   A.D. 18 .

Signed, &c.

—

GENERAL FORM OF ASSIGNMENT.

—

KNOW ALL MEN BY THESE PRESENTS, that I, the within-named A. B., in consideration of five dollars to me paid by C. D., have assigned to the said C. D. and his assigns, all my interest in the within-written instrument, and every clause, article, or thing therein contained ; and I do hereby constitute the said C. D. my attorney, in my name, but to his own use, to take all legal measures which may be proper for the complete recovery and enjoyment of the assigned premises, with power of substitution.

Witness my hand and seal, this, &c.

—

ASSIGNMENT OF CROWN LANDS.

—

KNOW ALL MEN BY THESE PRESENTS, that I, of the   of   in the County of   and

Province of   , for and in consideration of   of
lawful money of Canada to   in hand paid by
of the   of   in the County of   and
Province aforesaid,   at or before the date hereof,
the receipt whereof   do hereby acknowledge, HAVE bargained, sold, assigned, transferred and set over, and by
these presents DO bargain, sell, assign, transfer and set
over unto the said   heirs and assigns, all
estate, right, title, interest, claim and demand whatsoever
both at law and in equity, of, in and to th   certain parcel   or tract of land and premises, situate lying and
being in the Township of   in the County of
and Province aforesaid, containing by admeasurement
          acres, be the same more or less, and being com-
posed of   Lot number   in the   Concession
          of the Township of   aforesaid.

To HAVE AND TO HOLD the same, with all and every the
benefit that may or can be derived from the said
acres of land, unto the said   heirs and assigns,
FOREVER.

IN WITNESS WHEREOF,   have hereunto set   Hand
and Seal this   day of   A.D. 18 .

'Signed, sealed, &c.

            ONTARIO :   )   I,
County of   }   of the   of
              To WIT :)   in the County of
make oath and say, that I was personally present and did
see the within-named   duly sign and seal, and as
        act and deed, deliver the within Assignment on the
day of the date thereof, and that I, this deponent, am a

subscribing witness thereto, together with   of.
              in the County of   and that the said In-
strument was executed at

SWORN before me at
  in the County of
  this   day of   in the
  year of our Lord, 18   .
    A Commissioner in B. R., &c.

ASSIGNMENT OF PARTNERSHIP PROPERTY IN TRUST TO CLOSE CONCERN, &c.

WHEREAS, a co-partnership has heretofore existed between J. S. and A. B., both of the   of   which
co-partnership has been known under the name of S. & B.,
and which it is the intention of the said co-partners forthwith to dissolve and determine:

Now THIS INDENTURE of two parts, made this   day
of   in the year 18   by and between the said J. S.
of the one part, and the said A. B., of the other part,
witnesseth,

FIRST. That the co-partnership aforesaid is hereby by
the mutual consent of the said parties, dissolved and
determined.

SECOND. The said J. S. doth hereby sell, transfer, assign,
and set over unto the said A. B., his moiety of all the
stock in trade, goods, merchandize, effects and property of
every description belonging to or owned by the said co-
partnership, wherever the same may be, together with all
debts, choses in action, and sums of money due and owing
to the said firm from any and all persons whomsoever, to

hold the same to the said A. B. and his assigns forever, in trust for the following purposes, namely: that the said A. B. shall sell and dispose of all the goods, property, and effects belonging to the said firm, at such time and in such manner as he may think prudent; and shall with reasonable diligence, collect all the debts and sums of money due and owing to the said firm; and shall, out of the proceeds of the said sales, and with the money thus collected, pay and discharge all the debts and sums of money now due and owing from the said firm, as far as the proceeds of said sales and the sums of money collected will go; and, after fully satisfying all demands against the said firm, if there be any surplus, shall pay over one moiety thereof to the said J. S. or his assigns.

THIRD. The said J. S. doth hereby constitute and appoint the said A. B. his attorney irrevocable, in his the said A. B.'s own name, or in the name of the said firm, to demand, collect, sue for and receive any and all debts and sums of money due and owing to the said firm; to institute and prosecute any suits for the recovery of the said debts, or to compound the same as he may judge most expedient; to defend any and all suits against the said firm; to execute all such paper writings and acquittances as may be necessary; and generally to do all such acts and things as may be necessary and proper for the full aud complete settlement of all business and concerns of the said copartnership.

FOURTH. The said A. B., for himself and his heirs, executors, and administrators, hereby covenants to and with the said J. S. and his assigns, that he will sell and dispose of all the partnership property and effects to the best

advantage; that he will use his best diligence and endeavours to collect all debts and sums of money due and owing
to the said firm; and that he will truly and faithfully
apply the proceeds of the said sale, and the moneys collected, to the payment, discharge, and satisfaction of all
debts and demands against the said firm, as far as the same
will go; and, after discharging all such debts, will pay over
to the said J. S. or his assigns one moiety of any surplus
that may remain; and further, that he will keep full and
accurate accounts of all moneys received by him for goods
sold, or debts collected, as well as of moneys paid out,
and will render a just, true and full account therefor to
the said J. S. or his assigns.

FIFTH. The said J. S., for himself, &c., covenants to
and with the said A. B., &c., that, upon settlement of accounts, if it shall be found that the debts due and owing
from the said firm exceed the amount of moneys received
from the sales of the said goods and the debts collected, he
will pay unto the said A. B. or his assigns, one moiety of
any balance that may then be due and owing from the
said firm.

In witness, &c.

_____

ASSIGNMENT OF PARTNERSHIP PROPERTY BY ONE PARTNER TO ANOTHER.

—

THIS INDENTURE, of two parts, made and concluded
this   day of   A.D. 18 by and between W. S. P.
of   of the first part, and J. B. P., of   of the
second part, witnesseth:

THAT WHEREAS that said parties were lately copartners
in the business of   which partnership was dissolved

G

and determined on the   day of   last; and whereas many debts, due and owing to the said parties on account of their said copartnership, are still outstanding, and
-debts due by the said firm are yet unpaid; and whereas
it is agreed that the said party of the second part shall
assign and release to the said party of the first part all
his interest in the stock in trade, goods and effects belonging to the said firm, and in the debts now owing to the
said firm, and that the said party of the first part shall
assume all the debts and liabilities of the said firm, and
shall discharge and indemnify the said party of the second
part from all liabilities and losses arising from the said
partnership.

Now, therefore, in pursuance of the said agreement, and
in consideration of the sum of   paid and secured to the
said J. B. P., he the said J. B. P. doth hereby fully and
absolutely sell, assign, release and make over to the said
W. S. P. all his right, title, interest, and share in and to
all the stock in trade, goods, merchandize, machinery, tools,
books, leasehold premises, and effects belonging to the said
partnership, of whatever kind or nature, and wheresoever
situated; also, all his right, title, and interest in and to
all the debts and sums of money now due and owing to
the said firm, whether the same be by bond, bill, note or
account, or otherwise; and the said J. B. P. doth hereby
make and appoint the said W. S. P., his executors, administrators and assigns, to be his attorney and attorneys, to
receive all and several the debts and sums of money above
mentioned, to his and their own use and benefit; and doth
hereby authorize the said W. S. P., his executors, &c., to
demand, collect, and sue for the said debts and sums of

money, and to use his, the said J. B. P.'s name in any way or manner that the collection, recovery, and realization of the said debts and demands may render necessary, as well in court as out of court, but at their own proper costs and charges, and without cost or damage to the said J. B. P. And the said J. B. P. doth hereby further authorize the said W. S. P. to convey and transfer to his own name, and for his own use and benefit, any and all sums of money and effects, real and personal estate, which may be taken or received in the name of the said firm, and to hold the same free from all claims by the said J. B. P., his executors, administrators, or assigns.

And these presents further witness, that, in pursuance of the said agreement, the said W. S. P., for himself, his executors, and administrators, doth hereby covenant to and with the said J. B. P., his executors and administrators, that he, the said W. S. P., and his, &c., shall pay and discharge, and at all times hereafter save harmless and indemnify the said J. B. P., his, &c., from and against all and every the debts, duties and liabilities, which, at the dissolution and determination of the said partnership, were due and owing by the said firm to any person or persons, for any matter or thing touching the said partnership, and of and from all actions, suits, costs, expenses, and damages, for or concerning the said debts, duties, and liabilities, unless the said J. B. P. shall have contracted any debts or incurred any liabilities in the name and on account of the said firm, which are unknown to the said W. S. B., and do not appear in the books of the said firm; for which, if any such exist, the said W. S. P. does not hereby intend to make himself responsible.

In witness, &c.

ASSIGNMENT OF AGREEMENT TO PURCHASE.

(By Endorsement.)

WHEREAS, the within named C. D. hath duly paid to the within named A. B. the sum of   being the amount of the first two instalments of the purchase money within mentioned, together with all interest upon such purchase money up to the   day of   last, according to the terms and provisions of the within written articles, and there now remains to be paid the sum of   only, by   equal annual instalments of   each with interest from the   day of   last.   And whereas the said C. D. hath contracted and agreed with E. F. of   for the sale to him of the within mentioned premises and the improvements thereon, and all his right and title thereto and estate and interest therein under or by virtue of the within written agreement, at the price or sum of   but subject nevertheless to the payment by him the said E. F., his heirs, executors or administrators, unto the said A. B., his executors or administrators, of the said sum of   residue of the original purchase money aforesaid and interest thereon from the period aforesaid.

Now these presents witness that in pursuance of such agreement and in consideration of the sum of of good and lawful money aforesaid to him the said C. D. in hand paid by the said E. F. at or before the execution hereof, the receipt whereof he the said C. D. doth hereby acknowledge, he the said C. D. doth grant, bargain, sell, assign, transfer, and set over unto the said E. F., his heirs and assigns, all and singular the within mentioned and described parcel or tract of land and premises and therein described as being Lot No.   in the   concession of   together with all the right, title, and interest of him the said C. D. of in and to the within written articles of agreement, covenants, and the lands and premises therein referred to, and all improvements thereon, and all benefit and advantage to arise therefrom, or from the penal sum of   thereby secured ; to have and to hold, receive and enjoy, the said assigned premises unto the said E. F., his heirs, executors, administrators and assigns, from henceforth, for his and their own use and benefit forever.

And the said C. D. doth hereby make, ordain, authorise, constitute and appoint the said E. F., his heirs, executors, administrators and assigns, his true and lawful attorney and attorneys, irrevocable for him the said C. D., and in his name, but for the sole use and benefit of the said E. F., his heirs, executors, and administrators, to demand, sue for, recover and receive of and from the within named A. B., his heirs, executors, or administrators, all such sum or sums of money and damages as shall or may at any time or times hereafter accrue or grow due to him the said C. D., his heirs, executors, administrators, or assigns, under or by virtue of the said recited articles of agreement and covenants, or any matter, clause or thing therein contained, by reason or on account of the breach or default of him the said A. B., his heirs, executors, or administrators, in relation thereto ; the said C. D. hereby also covenanting with the said E. F., his heirs, executors, and administrators, that he hath not done or suffered, nor will he do or suffer any act, matter, or thing whereby the said E. F., his heirs, executors, or administrators, shall or may be.hindered or prevented from commencing, and prosecuting any action or actions, suit or suits at law or in equity for the recovery of any principal money or damages under or by virtue of the said articles of agreement and covenants referred to, or enforcing the performance of the said articles of agreement, or obtaining such other satisfaction as can or may be had or obtained for the same by virtue thereof; and the said E. F. doth hereby for himself, his heirs, executors and administrators, covenant with the said C. D. his heirs, executors, and administrators, that he, the said E. F., his heirs, executors, or administrators, shall and will well and truly pay to the said A. B., his executors or administrators, the aforesaid sum of   residue of the purchase money aforesaid, and all the interest thereon now or hereafter to become due by the instalments and at the times mentioned and provided therefor in and by the said recited articles of agreement, and therefrom shall and will indemnify and forever save harmless the said C. D., his heirs, executors, and administrators, and his and their goods and chattels, lands and tenements by these presents.

In witness, &c.

ASSIGNMENT OF APPRENTICESHIP INDENTURE BY ENDORSEMENT.

KNOW ALL MEN BY THESE PRESENTS, THAT I, the within named   by and with the consent of   my within named apprentice, and   his father (*or as the case may be*), parties to the within Indenture, testified by their signing and sealing these presents, for divers good causes and considerations have assigned and set over, and do hereby assign and set over, the within Indenture, and the said   the apprentice within named, unto   of the   of   his executors, administrators, or assigns, for the residue of the within mentioned term, he and they performing all and singular the covenants therein contained on my part to be kept and performed.

And I, the said   do hereby covenant on my part, with the consent of my father, the said   faithfully to serve the said   as an apprentice for the residue of the term within mentioned, and to perform toward him all and singular the covenants within mentioned on my part to be kept and performed.

And I, the said   for myself, my executors, administrators, and assigns, do hereby covenant to perform all and singular the covenants within mentioned on the part of the said   to be kept and performed toward the said apprentice.

Witness our hands and seals this   day of   18   .

ASSIGNMENT OF ARTICLES OF CLERKSHIP.

THIS INDENTURE, made the   day of   A. D. 18   , between A. A. of   Gentleman, one of the Attorneys of Her Majesty's Courts of Queen's Bench and Common Pleas for   , and a Solicitor of the Court of Chancery of the first part; C. C. of   and D. C. (the clerk), son of the said C. C., of the second part, and E. F. of

Gentleman, one of the Attorneys of Her Majesty's said Courts and a Solicitor of the Court of Chancery of the third part; Whereas by Articles of Clerkship bearing

date the   day of   A. D. 18 , made between the
said A. A. of the one part and the said C. C. and D. C.
his son of the other part, the said D. C. of his own free
will did put, place and bind himself Clerk to the said A. ￩
A. to serve him from the day of the date thereof for, and
during, and unto the full end and term of five years from
thence next ensuing, and fully to be complete and ended,
subject to the several covenants and conditions therein
contained.

And whereas the said D. C. hath served the said A. A.
as his clerk from the day of the date of the said Articles
to the day of the date of these presents ; and whereas it
has been agreed that the said A. A. shall assign to the
said E. F. all benefit and advantage of him the said A. A.
under or by virtue of the said recited Articles of Clerkship for all the residue now to come and unexpired of
the said term of five years ; and it has been further
agreed that the said D. C. shall put, place and bind himself as clerk to the said E. F. from the day of the date
of these presents for the remainder of the said term.

Now THIS INDENTURE WITNESSETH, that in pursuance
of the said agreement he the said A. A., at the request
and with the consent of the said C. C. and D. C. testified
by their respectively being parties to these presents hath
assigned, transferred and set over, and by these presents
doth assign, transfer and set over unto the said E. F. all
benefit and advantage, interest, claim and demand whatsoever of him the said A. A. under the hereinbefore in
part recited Articles of Clerkship, and the service of him
the said D. C. under or by virtue of the same, to have
and to hold all right and interest whatsoever of him the

said A. A. in and to the service of him the said D. C. under or by virtue of the same unto the said E. F. his executors, administrators and assigns.

And this Indenture further witnesseth, that the said D. C. of his own free will and by and with the consent and approbation of the said C. C. testified as aforesaid, hath put, placed and bound himself, and by these presents doth put, place and bind himself clerk to the said E, F., to serve him from the day of the date of these presents for and during the remainder of the said term of five years, and fully to be complete and ended.

And the said C. C. for himself, his heirs, executors, and administrators, doth covenant with the said E. F., his executors, administrators, and assigns, by these presents in manner following, that is to say, that the said D. C. will well and faithfully serve the said E. F. as his Clerk, &c.(*the rest of the form may be taken from that of the original Articles, but confining the service and covenants to the remainder of the term.*)

In witness, &c.

Signed, sealed, &c.

ASSIGNMENT OF A BOND BY ENDORSEMENT.

KNOW ALL MEN, &c., that for and in consideration of the sum of   of good and lawful money of Canada, by E. F., of   to the within mentioned obligee, C. D., in hand well and truly paid at or before the sealing and de- livery of these presents, the receipt whereof is hereby acknowledged, he the said C. D. hath bargained, sold, assigned, transferred and set over, and by these presents doth bargain, sell, assign, transfer and set over unto the said E. F. his executors, administrators, and assigns, the within written bond or obligation, and all principal and interest money thereby secured, and now due, or hereafter to become due thereon, and all benefit and advantage whatever, to be had made, or obtained by virtue thereof, and all the right, title, interest, property, claim and demand whatsoever, both at law and in equity, of him the said C. D. of, in, to, or out of the said bond and moneys, together with the said bond. To have, hold, receive and enjoy the said bond and moneys, unto the said E. F. his executors, administrators and assigns from henceforth, for his and their own use and benefit forever; and the said C. D. doth hereby make, constitute and appoint, and in his place and stead put and place the said E. F. his executors administrators and assigns the true and lawful attorney and attorneys irrevocable of him the said C. D. in his name, but to and for the sole use and benefit of the said E. F. his executors, administrators and assigns, to ask, demand and receive of and from the within named A. B. the obligor in the within written bond or obligation named, his heirs, executors administrators or assigns, all such principal and interest moneys as now are or shall from time to time, or at any time hereafter be due upon the said bond, and to sue and prosecute any action, suit, judgment or execution thereupon, and to acknowledge, make and give full satisfaction, receipts, releases and discharges, for all moneys secured by the said bond, and now due, or at any time hereafter growing due thereon, and generally to do all and every such further and other lawful acts and things, as well for the recovering and receiving as also for the releasing and discharging of all and singular the said hereby assigned bond, moneys and premises, as fully and effectually to all intents and purposes, as the said C. D. his executors, administrators or assigns could or might do if personally present and doing the same. And the said C. D. doth hereby for himself, his executors and administrators covenant with the said E. F., his executors, administrators and assigns, to ratify, allow and confirm all and whatsoever the said E. F., his executors, administrators or assigns shall lawfully do or cause to be done in or about the premises, by virtue of these presents. And the said C. D. for himself, his executors and administrators, doth further covenant promise and agree to and with the said E. F., his executors, administrators and assigns, by these presents, in manner following, that is to say, that the within mentioned sum of   remains justly due and owing upon the said bond, and that he the said C. D. hath not received or discharged all or any of the said moneys due, or to grow due on the said bond, nor shall or will release, nonsuit, vacate or disavow any suit or other legal proceedings to be had, made, or prosecuted by virtue of these presents, for the suing for, recovering, releasing, or discharging of the said moneys, or any of them, without the license of the said E. F. his executors, administrators or assigns, first had and obtained in writing, nor shall or will revoke, invalidate, hinder, or make void these presents, or any authority or power hereby given, without such license as aforesaid.

In witness, &c.

ASSIGNMENT OF COPY-RIGHT IN BOOKS.

—

THIS INDENTURE, made, &c., between　　　of
of the one part, and　　　of　　　bookseller, of the
other part. Whereas the said　　　hath written and
compiled a book entitled, &c. Now this Indenture witnesseth, that the said　for and in consideration of the
sum of　to him in hand paid by the said　. (the receipt whereof is hereby acknowledged), hath bargained,
sold, and assigned, and by these presents doth bargain,
sell, and assign, unto the said　all that the said book,
and all his copy-right, title, interest, property, claim, and
demand whatsoever of, in, and to the same ; to have and
to hold the said book, copy-right, and all the profit, benefit,
and advantage, that shall or may arise, by and from printing, re-printing, publishing, and vending the same, unto
the said　his executors, administrators and assigns, on
the terms and conditions and for the whole period of time
provided and allowed in and by the laws of Canada in
that behalf. Provided always nevertheless, and these presents are upon this express condition, that the number of
copies to be printed of the first and each and every other
edition or impression of the said book, shall not exceed
one thousand, and that the said　his executors, administrators, and assigns, shall and will pay unto the said
his executors, administrators or assigns, the further sum
and sums of　for, at, and upon the re-printing or
making a second and each and every other future and
further edition or impression that shall or may be made
of the said book, for and towards a further reward and
satisfaction to the said　for his writing and compiling

the same ; the said payments to be made before the publication of the said several impressions, or editions (after
the first) and sale of the same, or any part thereof, by the
said   his executors, administrators, or assigns, or any
of them, or by any other person or persons, by, for or
under them, or any of them. And the said   for himself, his executors, administrators, and assigns, doth covenant, promise and agree to and with the said   his executors, administrators and assigns, that he the said
      his executors, administrators, and assigns, shall
and will pay or cause to be paid to the said   his executors, administrators and assigns, the said respective sum
and sums of   at and upon the reprinting, and before
the publication and sale of the said second and every other
future and further edition and impression that shall or
may be made of the said book, according to the proviso
aforesaid, and the true intent and meaning of these presents.

In witness, &c.

_____

ASSIGNMENT OF A DEBT, WITH POWER OF ATTORNEY, &c.

___

KNOW ALL MEN BY THESE PRESENTS, that   in consideration of the sum of   dollars, paid to   by
of   in the county of   (the receipt of which is hereby
acknowledged,) do   hereby sell, assign, and transfer unto
the said   all   claims and demands against   of
for debts due to the said   and all actions against said
      now pending in   favour, and all causes of action
whatsoever against him.

And the said   do   hereby nominate and appoint the

said   his executors and administrators,   attorney or attorneys irrevocable ; and do give him and them full power and authority to institute any suit or suits against said   and to prosecute the same, and any suit or suits which are now pending for any cause or causes of action, in favour of said   against said   to final judgment and execution ; and any executions for the cause or causes aforesaid, to cause to be satisfied by levying the same on any real or personal estate of the said   and the proceeds thereof to take and apply to his or their own use ; and in case of levying said executions on any real estate, the said   hereby empower the said   his executors and administrators, to sell, and execute deeds to convey the same, for such price or consideration, and to such person or persons, and on such terms, as he or they shall deem expedient; or, if he or they prefer it, to execute any conveyances that may be necessary to vest the title thereof in him or them, as his or their own property ; but it is hereby expressly stipulated that all such acts and proceedings are to be at the proper costs and charges of the said   his executors and administrators without expense to the said

And the said   do further empower the said   his executors and administrators, to appoint such substitute or substitutes as he or they shall see fit, to carry into effect the objects and purposes of this authority, or any of them, and the same to revoke from time to time at his or their pleasure ; the said   hereby ratifying and confirming all the lawful acts of the said   his, &c., in pursuance of the foregoing authority.

In witness, &c., this   day of   A.D. 18

Signed, sealed, &c.

ASSIGNMENT OF JUDGMENT-DEBT.

This Indenture made the   day of   A.D. 18   ,
Between   of the first part ; and .   of the
second part :

Whereas the said part   of the first part on or about
the   day of   18   recovered a judgment in the
Court of   against   for the sum of   damages
and   costs, making together the sum of

And whereas the said part   of the first part ha
agreed to assign the said judgment and all benefit to
arise therefrom either at law or in equity unto the said
part   of the second part in manner hereinafter expressed :

Now this Indenture witnesseth that in pursuance of
the said agreement and in consideration of the sum of
of lawful money of Canada to the said part   of the first
part in hand well and truly paid by the said part · · of
the second part, at or before the execution hereof, the
receipt whereof is hereby acknowledged   the said part
   of the first part ha   granted, bargained, sold, assigned,
transferred and set over, and by these presents do
grant, bargain, sell, assign, transfer and set over unto
the said part   of the second part   executors, administrators and assigns   ALL THAT THE
said hereinbefore mentioned judgment, and all and
every sum and sums of money now due, and hereafter to
grow due by virtue thereof, for principal, interest and
costs, and all benefit to be derived therefrom, either at
law or ·in equity, or otherwise howsoever : to have,
hold, receive, take and enjoy the same, and all benefit

and advantage thereof, unto the said part   of the
second part,   executors, administrators and assigns, to
and for   and their own proper use and as and for
        and their own proper moneys and effects absolutely.

AND the said part   of the first part hereby constitute
        and appoint   the said part   of the second part,
        executors and administrators, to be the true and
lawful Attorney and Attorneys in the name   of the
said part   of the first part, or otherwise, but at the
proper costs and charges of the said part   of the second
part,   executors and administrators, to ask, demand
and receive of and from the said   executors or administrators, the said judgment, debt, and premises hereby
assigned, and on nonpayment of the same, or any part
thereof, to obtain any execution or executions, or bring,
commence and prosecute any action or actions, suit or
suits, as well at law as in equity, for the recovery of the
same, and to use all such other lawful remedies, ways and
means, as the said part   of the first part could or
might have used or taken for the recovery of the same,
and on receipt or recovery thereof to sign and give good
and effectual receipt or receipts for the same, with full
power from time to time to appoint a substitute or substitutes for all or any of the purposes aforesaid.

AND the said part   of the first part do   hereby
agree to ratify and confirm whatsoever the said part
of the second part   executors or administrators, shall
lawfully do, or cause to be done, in or about the premises.

AND the said part   of the second part hereby covenant   to indemnify and save harmless the said part   of
the first part   from all loss, costs, charges, damages

and expenses, by reason or on account of any such proceedings as aforesaid.

In witness, &c.

Signed, sealed, &c.

ASSIGNMENT OF LEASE.

THIS INDENTURE, made the   day of   A. D. 18 , between   hereinafter called the Assignor   of the first part and   hereinafter called the Assignee   of the second part.

WITNESSETH that in consideration of   now paid by the said Assignor   to the said Assignee   (the receipt whereof is hereby acknowledged),   the said Assignor do   grant and assign unto the said Assignee   executors, administrators, and assigns, all and singular, the premises comprised in and demised by a certain Indenture of Lease, bearing date the   day of   one thou_ sand eight hundred and and made between   together with the appurtenances to hold the same unto the said Assignee   executors, administrators, and assigns, henceforth for and during the residue of the term thereby granted, and for all other the estate, term and interest (if any) of the said Assignor   therein. Subject to the payment of the rent and the performance of the Lessees covenants and agreements in the said Indenture of Lease reserved and contained.

And the said Assignor for   heirs, executors and administrators, do   hereby covenant with the said Assignee   executors, administrators, and assigns that notwithstanding any act of the said Assignor   he   now

H

ha good right to assign the said Lease and premises in manner aforesaid.

And that subject to the payment of the rent and the performance of the Lessees covenants, it shall be lawful for the Assignee executors, administrators and assigns, peaceably and quietly to hold occupy and enjoy the said premises hereby assigned during the residue of the term granted by the said Indenture of Lease, and receive the rents and profits thereof without any interruption by the said Assignor, or any person claiming under free from all charges and incumbrances whatsoever. And also that the said Assignor and all persons lawfully claiming under will, at all times hereafter, at the request and costs of the said Assignee executors, administrators, or assigns, assign and confirm to and them, the said premises for the residue of the said term as the said Assignee executors, administrators or assigns shall reasonably require.

And the said Assignee for heirs, executors, and administrators, do hereby covenant with the said Assignor executors and administrators, that the said Assignee executors, administrators, and assigns, will, from time to time, pay the rent and observe and perform the Lessees covenants and conditions in the said Indenture of Lease, reserved and contained, and indemnify and save harmless the said Assignor, heirs, executors, and administrators, from all losses and expenses in respect of the non-observance or performance of the said covenants and conditions or any of them.

In witness, &c.

Signed, sealed, &c.

(*Usual Affidavit of Execution.*)

ASSIGNMENT OF LEASE BY ADMINISTRATOR.

KNOW ALL MEN BY THESE PRESENTS, that A. B., of
administrator of all and singular the goods and chattels,
rights and credits of the within named C. D., deceased,
for and in consideration of the sum of   of good and
lawful money of Canada, to him in hand well and truly
paid by E. F. of   at or before the sealing and delivery
of these presents, the receipt whereof is hereby acknowledged, hath (by and with the consent of the within
named A. B. testified by his executing these presents)
bargained, sold, assigned, transferred and set over, and
by these presents doth (by and with such consent as
aforesaid) bargain, sell, assign, transfer and set over unto
the said E. F., his executors, administrators, and assigns,
all and singular the parcel or tract of land and premises,
comprised in the within written indenture of lease, and
all the estate, right, title and interest which he the said
A. B., as administrator of the said C. D. as aforesaid, or
otherwise, now hath, or at any time hereafter shall or may
have, claim, challenge, or demand of, in, or to, all or any
of the said premises, by virtue of the said indenture of
lease or otherwise, as administrator of the said C. D.   To
have and to hold the said parcel or tract of land, and all
and singular other the premises, with their and every of
their appurtenances, unto the said E. F., his executors,
administrators and assigns, for and during all the rest,
residue and remainder yet to come and unexpired, of the
within mentioned term of   years, subject nevertheless,
to the yearly rent of   in and by the said indenture of
lease reserved and contained, and to become due and

payable, and to all and every the covenants, clauses, provisoes and agreements therein contained.   And the said
A. B. for himself, his heirs, executors and administrators,
doth hereby covenant and declare to and with the said
E. F., his executors and administrators, and assigns, that
he the said A. B. hath not at any time heretofore made,
done, committed, or executed, or wittingly or willingly
permitted, or suffered, any act, deed, matter, or thing
whatsoever, whereby or wherewith, or by means whereof,
the said parcel or tract of land and premises hereby
assigned, are, is, can, shall, or may be any ways impeached, charged, affected, or incumbered in title, estate or
otherwise, howsoever.

In witness, &c., this   day of   A. D. 18 . ·
Signed, sealed, &c.

ASSIGNMENT OF MORTGAGE.

THIS INDENTURE made (in duplicate) the   day of
     A. D. 18   , BETWEEN   hereinafter called
the "ASSIGNEE" of the   part

WHEREAS, by a mortgage dated on the   day of
18   did grant and mortgage the land and premises therein and hereinafter described to   heirs
and assigns for securing the payment of   and
there is now owing upon the said mortgage

NOW THIS INDENTURE WITNESSETH, that, in consideration of   of lawful money of Canada now paid by the
said Assignee , to the said Assignor (the receipt whereof
is hereby acknowledged) THE said Assignor DO HEREBY
ASSIGN and set over unto the said Assignee   executors,
administrators and assigns ALL that the said before in

part recited mortage, and also the said sum of now owing as aforesaid together with all moneys that may hereafter become due or owing in respect of said mortgage and the full benefit of all powers and of all covenants and provisoes contained in said mortgage. And also full power and authority to use the name or names of the said Assignor heirs, exe utors, administrators or assigns for enforcing the performance of the covenants and other matters and things contained in the said mortgage. AND the said Assignor DO HEREBY GRANT and CONVEY unto the said Assignee heirs and assigns, ALL AND SINGULAR TO HAVE AND TO HOLD the said mortgage and all moneys arising in respect of the same and to accrue thereon, and also the said land and premises thereby granted and mortgaged TO THE USE of the said Assignee heirs, executors, administrators and assigns absolutely forever; but subject to the terms contained in such mortgage.

AND THE SAID ASSIGNOR for heirs, executors, administrators and assigns do hereby covenant with the said Assignee heirs, executors, administrators and assigns, THAT the said mortgage hereby assigned is a good and valid security and that the sum of is now owing and unpaid, AND THAT ha not done or permitted any act matter or thing whereby the said mortgage has been released or discharged either partly or in entirety; AND that will upon request do perform and execute every act necessary to enforce the full performance of the covenants and other matters contained therein.

In witness, &c. Signed, sealed, &c.

*RECEIVED on the day of the date of this Indenture from

(Usual Affidavit of Execution.)

ASSIGNMENT OF MORTGAGE.
(By Indorsement.)

—

THIS INDENTURE made the   day of   in the year of our Lord 18 , BETWEEN   within named, of the first part, and   of   of the second part, WITNESSETH. that the party of the first part, for divers good considerations, him thereunto moving, and for the further consideration of the sum of five shillings to him in hand well and truly paid by the party of the second part at or before the sealing and delivery of these presents, the receipt whereof is hereby acknowledged, hath granted, bargained, sold and assigned, and by these presents doth grant, bargain, sell and assign to the party of the second part, his heirs, executors, administrators and assigns, all the right, title, interest, claim and demand whatsoever, of him the party of the first part, of, in and to the lands and tenements mentioned and described in the within mortgage, and also to all sum and sums of money secured and payable thereby and now remaining unpaid, to have and to hold the same, and to ask demand, sue for and recover the same, as fully to all intents and purposes as he the party of the first part now holds and is entitled to the same.

In witness, &c.

Signed, sealed, &c.

———

ASSIGNMENT OF A POLICY OF INSURANCE BY ENDORSEMENT.

—

KNOW ALL MEN BY THESE PRESENTS, that I, the within named A. B., for and in consideration of the sum of to me paid by C. D., of, &c., (the receipt whereof is hereby acknowledged) have granted, sold, assigned, transferred, and set over, and by these presents I do absolutely grant, sell, assign, transfer, and set over to him, the said C. D., all my right, property, interest, claim, and demand in and to the within policy of insurance, which have already arisen, or which may hereafter arise thereon, with full power to use my name so far as may be necessary to enable him fully to avail himself of the interest herein assigned, or hereby intended to be assigned. The conveyance herein made, and the powers hereby given, are for myself and my legal representatives to said C. D. and his legal representatives.

In witness, &c., this   day of   18 .

AUCTION AGREEMENT BY AUCTIONEER.

I HEREBY acknowledge that A. B. has been this day declared by me the highest bidder, and purchaser of (*describe the land*) at the sum of   (*or* at the sum of   per acre, or foot,) and that he has paid into my hands the sum of   as a deposit and in part payment of the purchase money; and I hereby agree, that the vendor, C. D., shall in all respects fulfil the conditions of sale hereto annexed.

WITNESS my hand, at   on the   day of   A. D. 18.

AUCTION AGREEMENT BY PURCHASER.

I HEREBY acknowledge, that I have this day purchased at public auction all that (*describe the land*) for the sum of   (*or*, for the price of   per acre, or per foot,) and

have paid into the hands of J. S., the auctioneer, the sum
of   as a deposit, and in part payment of the said purchase money ; and I hereby agree to pay the remaining
sum of   unto C. D., the vendor, at   on or before
the   day of   and in all other respects on my part
to fulfil the annexed conditions of sale.

WITNESS my hand, this   day of   A. D. 18 .

BILLS OF EXCHANGE AND PROMISSORY NOTES.

FOREIGN BILLS OF EXCHANGE.

No —   BANK OF BRITISH NORTH AMERICA,
                  (*Incorporated by Royal Charter.*)
                  Toronto Branch, 1st January, 18 .

For £100   Sterling.

Three days after sight pay this first of exchange (second
and third not paid) to the order of   one hundred
pounds sterling, value received.

                                        Manager.
                        Entered   *Accountant.*

To the Court of Directors of the Bank of British North
America, London.

                  BANK OF BRITISH NORTH AMERICA,
                  (*Incorporated by Royal Charter.*)
No —   Toronto Branch, 1st January, 18 .

For £100   Sterling.

Three days after sight pay this second of exchange

(first and third not paid) to the order of   one hundred pounds sterling, value received.

Manager.

Entered   *Accountant.*

To the Court of Directors of the Bank of British North America, London.

BANK OF BRITISH NORTH AMERICA,

(Incorporated by Royal Charter.)

No —   Toronto Branch, 1st January, 18   .

For £100   Sterling.

Three days after sight pay this third of exchange (first and second not paid) to the order of   one hundred pounds sterling, value received.

Manager.

Entered   *Accountant.*

To the Court of Directors of the Bank of British North America, London.

INLAND BILL OF EXCHANGE.

No. —   Toronto, 1st January, 18   .

$100   Three months after date pay to   or order the sum of one hundred dollars for value received.

(Signed)   A. B.

To C. D.   *Endorsed.*

Accepted payable at the Bank of

C. D.

PROMISSORY NOTE.

$100.   Toronto, 1st January, 18   .

Three months after date I (or we jointly and severally)

promise to pay to ·   or order at the Bank of   Toronto, the sum of one hundred dollars value received.

(Signed)¹   A. B. or $\left\{\begin{array}{l} \text{A. B.} \\ \text{C. D.} \end{array}\right.$

BILL OF SALE (CHATTELS).

THIS INDENTURE, made the   day of   A. D. 18 , BETWEEN

WHEREAS the said part   of the first part is possessed of the   hereinafter set forth, described, and enumerated, and hath contracted and agreed with the said part   of the second part for the absolute sale to   of the same, for the sum of   NOW THIS INDENTURE WITNESSETH, that in the pursuance of the said agreement, and in consideration of the sum of   of lawful money of Canada paid by the said part   of the second part to the said part   of the first part, at or before the sealing and delivery of these presents, (the receipt whereof is hereby acknowledged)   the said part   of the first part ha bargained, sold, assigned, transferred and set over, and by these presents do   bargain, sell, assign, transfer and set over unto the said part   of the second part, executors, administrators and assigns,   ALL THOSE the said   and all the right, title, interest, property, claim and demand whatsoever, both at law and in equity, or otherwise howsoever, of   the said part of the first part, of, in, to, and out of the same, and every part thereof ; TO HAVE AND TO HOLD the said hereinbefore assigned   and every of them and every part thereof, with the appurtenances, and all the right, title and interest of the said part   of the first part thereto and therein, as aforesaid, unto and to the use of the said part of the second part,   executors, administrators and assigns, to and for   sole and only use FOR EVER : AND the said part   of the first part do   hereby, for heirs, executors and administrators, COVENANT, PROMISE and agree with the said part   of the second part, executors and administrators, in manner following, that is to say : THAT   the said part   of the first part, now rightfully and absolutely possessed of and entitled to the said hereby assigned   and every of them, and every part thereof ; AND that the said part   of the first part, now ha in   good right to assign the same unto the said part   of the second part,   executors, administrators and assigns, in manner aforesaid, and according to the true intent and meaning of these presents ; AND that the said part   hereto, of the second part, executors, administrators and assigns, shall and may from time to time, and at all times hereafter, peaceably and quietly have, hold, possess and enjoy the said hereby assigned   and every of them, and every part thereof, to and for   own use and benefit, without any manner of hindrance, interruption, molestation, claim or demand whatsoever of from or by   the said part   of the first part, or any person or persons whomsoever : AND that free and clear, and freely and absolutely released and discharged, or otherwise, at the cost of the said part of the first part, effectually indemnified from and against all former and other bargains, sales, gifts, grants, titles, charges and encumbrances whatsoever : AND moreover, that   the said part   of the first part, and all persons rightfully claiming or to claim any estate, right, title or interest of, in or to the said hereby assigned · and every of them, and every part thereof, shall and will from time to time, and at all times hereafter upon every reasonable request of the said part of the second part, executors, administrators or assigns, but at the cost and charges of the said part of the second part, make, do and execute, or cause or procure to be made, done and executed, all such further acts, deeds and assurances for the more effectually assigning and assuring the said hereby assigned unto the said part of the second part, executors, administrators and assigns, in manner aforesaid, and according to the true intent and meaning of these presents, as by the said part of the second part, executors, administrators or assigns, or his counsel shall be reasonably advised or required.

In witness, &c.

Signed, sealed, &c.

———

COUNTY OF

     To WIT : } I

in the foregoing bill of sale named, make oath and say : THAT the sale therein made is *bona fide*, and for good consideration, namely :— and not for the purpose of holding or enabling me, this deponent, to hold the goods mentioned therein against the creditors of the said bargainor.

SWORN *before me at*
in the County of .
this day of
A. D. 18 .

    A Commissioner in B. R. &c.

AFFIDAVIT OF EXECUTION.

CANADA.

County of

TO WIT :

      make oath and say that I was personally present and did see the annexed Bill of Sale   duly signed, sealed and delivered by   the part   thereto ; and that I, this deponent, am a subscribing witness to the same, and that the name   set and subscribed as a witness to the execution thereof, is of the proper handwriting of me, this deponent ; and that the same was executed at

  Sworn before me, at
in the County of
this   day of
-A.D. 18   .

      A Commissioner &c.,

BILL OF SALE OF VESSEL.

KNOW ALL MEN BY THESE PRESENTS, that I, A. B. of, &c., owner of the brig or vessel, called the of the burden of   tons, or thereabouts, now lying at the port of   for and in consideration of the sum of   dollars, lawful money of Canada, to me paid by C. D., of the place aforesaid, the receipt whereof I hereby acknowledge, have bargained and sold, and by these presents do bargain, and sell unto the said C. D., his executors, administrators, and assigns, all the hull or body of said brig, or vessel, together with the masts, bowsprit, sails, boats, anchors, cables, spars, and all other neces-

saries thereunto appertaining and belonging : the certificate
of the registry of which said brig, or vessel, is as follows,
to wit : [copy certificate of registry.] To have and to
hold the said brig or vessel, and appurtenances thereunto
belonging, unto the said C. D. his executors, administrators and assigns, to his and their proper use, benefit, and
behoof, forever. And I do, for myself, my heirs, executors, and administrators, covenant and agree, to and with
said C. D., his executors, administrators and assigns, to
warrant and defend the said brig, or vessel, and all the
before-mentioned appurtenances, against all and every person and persons whomsoever.

In Witness, &c., this   day of   A.D. 18 .
      [*Affidavit &c., as in last Form.*]

BOND BLANK (WITHOUT CONDITION).

KNOW ALL MEN BY THESE PRESENTS, that   held
and firmly bound unto   in the penal sum of   of
lawful money of Canada, to be paid to the said   or
to   certain attorney, executors, administrators, or
assigns, for which payment well and truly to be made
      bind   heirs, executors, and administrators
and every of them, for ever, firmly by these Presents.
Sealed with   Seal. Dated this   day of   A.D.
18 .

Signed, Sealed &c.

MONEY BOND

KNOW ALL MEN BY THESE PRESENTS, that   held
and firmly bound unto   in the penal sum of

of lawful money of Canada to be paid to the said
or to   certain attorney, executors, administrators or
assigns, for which payment well and truly to be made
bind   heirs, executors and administrators for ever
firmly by these presents. SEALED with   seal. DATED
this   day of   A.D. 18 .

THE CONDITION of the above written bond or obligation
is such that if the above bounden   . heirs, executors
or administrators do and shall well and truly pay or cause
to be paid unto   executors, administrators or assigns, the just and full sum of   of lawful money
of Canada with interest thereon at the rate of   per cent.
per annum, on the days and times and in the manner following, that is to say: without
any deduction, defalcation or abatement whatsoever, THEN
the said bond or obligation to be void, otherwise to be and
remain in full force and virtue.

Signed, sealed, &c.

BOND TO CONVEY LAND.

KNOW ALL MEN BY THESE PRESENTS, that   held
and firmly bound to   in the penal sum of
to be paid to the said   or to   certain attorney,
executors, administrators or assigns, for which payment
well and truly to be made   bind   heirs, executors
and administrators, firmly by these presents. SEALED
with   seal and DATED this   day of   A.D. 18 .

WHEREAS the above bounden ,   ha   contracted
and agreed to sell, and also to convey to the said
in fee simple absolute the following lands and heredita-

ments, namely   IN CONSIDERATION of the
sum of   AND the said   ha   agreed to purchase from the said   the said lands, upon the
conditions aforesaid.

NOW THE CONDITION OF THIS OBLIGATION is such, that
if the above bounden   shall at the request of the
said   heirs or assigns, on or before the   day of
in the year of our Lord one thousand eight hundred and
          absolutely convey to the said   heirs or as-
signs, or to such person or persons as the said
shall direct or appoint, the said hereditaments hereinbefore mentioned, conformably to the said agreement : PRO-
VIDED the said   shall have duly paid the sum of
in the manner hereinbefore mentioned in the said agreement, THEN THIS OBLIGATION shall be null and void ;
OTHERWISE to remain in full force virtue and effect.

Signed, sealed, &c.

(Usual Affidavit of Execution.)

BOND FOR PAYMENT OF PURCHASE MONEY.

—

KNOW ALL MEN by these presents that   held and
firmly bound unto   in the penal sum of
of lawful money of Canada to be paid to the said
or to   certain attorney, executors, administrators, or
assigns, for which payment well and truly to be made
     bind   heirs, executors, and administrators and
every of them, for ever, firmly by these presents

SEALED with   seal. DATED this   day of
A.D. 18 .

WHEREAS the above bounden   h   contracted
with the said   for the absolute purchase in fee
simple, free from all incumbrances of the following parcel or tract of land hereditaments and premises that is
to say :   AND WHEREAS the above bounden
     ha   agreed to pay therefor the sum of   of law-
ful money of Canada at the times and in the manner
following that is to say :   AND WHEREAS
upon the treaty for the said purchase it was agreed that
the above bounden   should enter into the above bond
or obligation for payment of the said purchase money or
unpaid part thereof, and interest, in manner aforesaid and
be let into possession of the said lands and premises and
receipt of the rents and profits thereof from the day of
the date hereof.

Now the condition of the above obligation is such that
if the above bounden   heirs, executors, administrators, or assigns, shall well and truly pay or cause to be
paid to the said   executors, administrators, or
assigns, the whole of the said purchase money, and interest
thereon as aforesaid at the times and in the manner aforesaid, without making any deduction, defalcation, or abatement thereout on any account whatsoever, then the above
obligation shall be void OTHERWISE to be and remain in full
force and virtue.

Signed, sealed, &c.

(Usual Affidavit of Execution.)

BOND OF INDEMNITY.

KNOW ALL MEN BY THESE PRESENTS, that   held
and firmly bound unto   in the penal sum of

I

of lawful money of Canada, to be paid to the said
or to   certain attorney, executors, administrators or
assigns, for which payment well and truly to be made
    bind   heirs, executors, and administrators, 'and
every of them, for ever, firmly by these presents, SEALED
with   seal. DATED this   day of A.D. 18

THE CONDITION of the above written bond or obligation
is such that if the above bounden obligor, his heirs, executors and administrators, do and shall, from time to
time, and at all times hereafter, well and truly save, defend
and keep harmless, and fully indemnified the said obligee,
his heirs, executors, and administrators, and his and their
lands and tenements, goods, chattels, and effects of from,
and against all loss, costs, charges, damages and expenses
which the said obligee, his heirs, executors, or administrators, or any of them, may at any time, or times, hereafter
bear, sustain, suffer, be at or be put unto, for or by reason,
or on account of (*Here state the particular matter or thing,
against which the obligee is to be indemnified*) or anything
in any manner relating thereto, THEN the above written
bond or obligation to be void, otherwise to be and remain
in full force, virtue and effect.

Signed, sealed, &c.

BOND OF INDEMNITY UPON PAYING A LOST NOTE.

KNOW ALL MEN BY THESE PRESENTS, that I,   of
    am held and firmly bound unto   of
in the sum of   of lawful money of Canada, to be paid
to the said   or his certain attorney, executors, administrators or assigns; for which payment, well and

truly to be made I bind myself, my heirs, executors, and administrators, and each and every of them, firmly by these
presents. Sealed with my seal. Dated this   day of
    A.D. 18 .

WHEREAS the above-named   by his promissory
note signed by him, and dated   day of   A.D. 18   ,
did promise to pay unto   or order   six months
after date, for value received, and such note was afterwards endorsed by the said   and others, and became the property of   of   as the said
avers; and whereas the said   alleges that he sent
the said note by mail, on the   day of   last to the
above-named   to be by him received for the use
of said   which said note, it is apprehended, was
stolen out of the mail, [or *as the case is*,] or otherwise
lost. And whereas the said   has, on the day of
the date hereof, at the request as well of the said
as of the said   and upon his, the said
promising to indemnify the said   and deliver up
the said note to be cancelled when found, paid the said
        the said sum of   in full satisfaction and
discharge of the said note, the receipt whereof the said
        doth hereby acknowledge; The condition, there-
fore, of the above-named obligation is such, that if the
said   his heirs, executors, or administrators, or
any of them, do and shall, from time to time, and at all
times hereafter, save, defend, keep harmless, and indemnify
the said   his executors and administrators, and
the goods, chattels, lands, and tenements of the said
of, from, and against the said note of   and of and from
all costs, charges, damages, and expenses, that shall, or

may happen or arise therefrom, and also to deliver or cause to be delivered up the said note, when and so soon as the same shall be found, to be cancelled, then this obligation to be void; otherwise to be and remain in full force and virtue.

Signed, sealed, &c.

BOND FOR FIDELITY OF CLERK.

KNOW ALL MEN BY THESE PRESENTS, that we of   and   of   and each of us, our, and each of our heirs, executors, and administrators, are firmly bound unto   of   and   of   their executors, administrators and assigns, for the payment to them of the penal sum of   Sealed with   seal. Dated this   day of   A.D. 18 .

WHEREAS the said   and   have ageed to admit   into their service as clerk, and to continue him in such service, subject to three months notice in writing on either side, on our becoming sureties for his faithfully serving and accounting to them, and the suvivor of them, their and his executors and administrators, and other the person or persons who shall have become partner or partners with them or either of them, and his or their executors and administraters in manner hereinafter mentioned, so long as the said   continues in such service; and whereas by the above-written obligation, we have become sureties accordingly;

Now, the above-written obligation is conditioned to be void if the said   shall faithfully serve, and from time to time, and at all times account for, and pay over to the said   and   or the survivor of them, their and his executors and administrators, and other the person or persons who shall have become partner or partners with them, or either of them, and his and their executors and administrators, all moneys, securities for money, goods and effects whatsoever, which he, the said   shall receive for their or any of their use, or for the use of any person or body politic, to whom they or either of them shall be accountable or which shall be intrusted to his care by them, or either or any of them, or by or for any person or body politic to whom they or either of them shall be accountable. And shall not embezzle, withhold, destroy, or anywise injure any such moneys, securities for money, goods and effects as aforesaid, or any books, papers, writings, goods, or effects of them, or either or any of them, provided always that each of the said sureties is not to be separately liable, nor are his executors administrators for more than half of the penal sum secured by the above-written obligation. and also that each of said sureties may put an end to his liability on the above written obligation, by giving to the said   and   their executors or administrators, six months notice in writing of his intention so to do, and shall be free from liability for any event or default happening after the expiration of such notice.

Signed, sealed, &c.

BOND FROM LESSEE AND SURETY TO PAY RENT.

KNOW ALL MEN BY THESE PRESENTS, that we, C. D., of   in the County of   and Province of

Carpenter, and E. F. of the same place, Butcher, are held and firmly bound unto A.B., of   in the County of   and Province of   , Esquire, in the penal sum of   of lawful money of   , to be paid to the said A.B. or to his certain attorney, executors, administrators or assigns, for which payment well and truly to be made, we bind ourselves, and each of us by himself, our and each of our heirs, executors and administrators, for ever firmly by these presents. Sealed with our seals. Dated this   day of   A.D. 18   .

WHEREAS, the above named A.B. by his Indenture of Lease, bearing even date with and executed before the above written obligation, for the consideration in the said lease mentioned, hath demised to the above bounden C. D.. a certain saw mill, situate at, &c. To hold unto the said C D., his executors, administrators and assigns, for the term of   years, from thence next ensuing, determinable, nevertheless, at the end of the first   years of the said term, if the said C. D., his executors, administrators, or assigns, shall give   months notice thereof, in manner therein mentioned, at and under the yearly rent of   payable quarterly, in manner as therein expressed, as by the said lease will more fully appear. Now the condition of the above-written obligation is such that if the above bounden C. D. and E. F., or either of them, their or either of their heirs, executors or administrators, shall and do, during the continuance of the said recited lease, well and truly pay, or cause to be paid, the said yearly rent or sum of   unto him the said A. B., his heirs or assigns, by four equal quarterly payments, of   each, on the several days following, that is to say, the

day of , the   day of   the   day of
and the   day of   in each and every year
during the said demise, or within   days next after
every of the said days or times of payment, according to
the true intent and meaning of the said recited lease, the
first quarterly payment to be made on the   day of
next ; then the above-written obligation shall be void and
of no effect, but if default shall happen to be made of or
in any of the said quarterly payments, then the same
shall remain in full force.

Signed, sealed, &c.

BOND FOR MINOR TO CONVEY WHEN OF AGE.

KNOW ALL MEN BY THESE PRESENTS, that   held and
firmly bound unto   in the penal sum of   of lawful
money of Canada, to be paid to the said   or to
certain attorney, executors, administrators or assigns, for
which payment, well and truly to be made,   bind
heirs, executors, and administrators or assigns, for ever
firmly by these presents. Sealed with   seal. Dated
this   day of   A. D. 18 .

WHEREAS   of, &c., deceased, by his last will and
testament, in writing, dated the   day of   and duly
proved in the Surrogate Court for the County of   on
the   day of   A. D. 18 did, among other things,
give, devise, and bequeath, all that messuage or tenement situated at   described as follows, to wit,
which was then in the occupation of   to be divided
equally between his two sons,   and   their heirs

and assigns ; and whereas   the above-named obligee, has agreed with the said   and   for the absolute purchase of the tenement and premises, so devised to them as aforesaid, at and for the sum of   but the said   not being yet of the age of twenty-one years, cannot join in conveying the same to the said And whereas the said   has, at the request of the above-bound   and on his promise and undertaking that the said   should, when, and as soon as he shall have attained the age of twenty-one years, at the cost and charge of the said   convey and assure to him the said   his heirs and assigns, his undivided moiety or half part of the said messuage or tenement and premises, paid into the hands of the said   the whole of the said purchase money ; and the said   has, by his deed of even date herewith, duly made, sealed, and delivered, conveyed his undivided moiety or half part of said messuage or tenement and premises to the said   his heirs and assigns ; Now, the condition of this obligation is such, that if the said   do and shall, when and as soon as he shall have attained the age of twenty-one years, at the cost and charge of the said convey and assure unto him the said   his heirs and assigns, by such deeds and conveyances as the counsel of the said   shall advise, his undivided moiety or half part of and in the said messuage or tenement and premises, devised to him and the said   as aforesaid, and that without any consideration to be paid to him by the said   , and also, if, and in case the said his heirs, executors, and administrators, do and shall, in the mean time, and until the said   shall have executed such conveyance as aforesaid, save, defend, keep harmless and indemnified the said his heirs executors, administrators, and assigns, and the said messuage or tenement and premises, so to be conveyed by the said to the said as aforesaid, and the rents, issues, and profits thereof, of and from all claim and demand to be made thereto, by or on behalf of the said ; then, &c. ; otherwise, &c.

Signed, sealed, &c.

CHATTEL MORTGAGE.

THIS INDENTURE, made (in duplicate) the day of one thousand eight hundred and ,
BETWEEN hereinafter called the Mortgagor of the first part ; and hereinafter called the Mortgagee of the second part

WITNESSETH that the Mortgagor for and in considera-tion of dollars of lawful money of Canada to in hand well and truly paid by the Mortgagee at or before the sealing and delivery of these presents (the receipt whereof is hereby acknowledged) hath grant-ed bargained sold and assigned and by these presents doth grant bargain sell and assign unto the Mortgagee executors administrators and assigns all and singular the goods chattels furniture and household stuff hereinafter particularly mentioned and described all which said goods and chattels are now lying and being on the premises situate

TO HAVE AND TO HOLD all and singular the said goods and chattels furniture and household stuff unto the

Mortgagee   executors administrators and assigns
to the only proper use and behoof of the Mortgagee
executors administrators and assigns for ever :

PROVIDED ALWAYS and these presents are upon this
express condition that if the Mortgagor
executors or administrators do and shall well and truly
pay or cause to be paid to the Mortgagee
executors administrators or assigns the full sum of
dollars with interest for the same at the rate of
per centum per annum :

THEN THESE PRESENTS and every matter and thing
herein contained shall cease determine, and be utterly
void to all intents and purposes anything herein contained
to the contrary thereof in anywise notwithstanding :

And the Mortgagor   for   executors and administrators shall and will warrant and for ever defend by
these presents all and singular the said goods chattels and
property unto the Mortgagee   executors administrators
and assigns against   the Mortgagor   executors
and administrators and against all and every other person
or persons whomsoever

And the Mortgagor   doth hereby for   executors
and administrators covenant promise and agree to and
with the Mortgagee   executors administrators and
assigns that the Mortgagor   executors or administrators or some or one of them shall and will well and
truly pay or cause to be paid unto the Mortgagee
executors administrators or assigns the said sum of money
in the above proviso mentioned with interest for the
same as aforesaid on the day   and time   and in the
manner above limited for the payment thereof: And also

in case default shall be made in the payment of the said
sum of money in the said proviso mentioned or of the
interest thereon or any part thereof or in case the Mortgagor shall attempt to sell or dispose of or in any way
part with the possession of the said goods and chattels or
any of them or to remove the same or any part thereof
out of the   or suffer or permit the same to be
seized or taken in execution without the consent of
the Mortgagee   executors administrators or assigns to such sale removal or disposal thereof first
had and obtained in writing then and in such case
it shall and may be lawful for the Mortgagee
executors administrators or assigns with   or their
servant or servants and with such other assistant or assistants as   may require at any time during the day
to enter into and upon any lands tenements houses and
premises wheresoever and whatsoever where the said
goods and chattels or any part thereof may be and for
such persons to break and force open any doors locks
bars bolts fastenings hinges gates fences houses buildings
enclosures and place for the purpose of taking possession
of and removing the said goods and chattels : And upon
and from and after the taking possession of such goods
and chattels as aforesaid it shall and may be lawful and
the Mortgagee   executors administrators or assigns
and each and any of them is and are hereby authorized
and empowered to sell the said goods and chattels or any
of them or any part thereof at public auction or private
sale as to them or any of them may seem meet : And
from and out of the proceeds of such sale in the first
place to pay and reimburse   or themselves all such

sums and sum of money   as may then be due by
virtue of these presents and all such expenses as may
have been incurred by the Mortgagee   executors
administrators or assigns in consequence of the default
neglect or failure of the Mortgagor   executors administrators or assigns in payment of the said sum of
money with interest thereon as above mentioned or
in consequence of such sale or removal as above mentioned and in the next place to pay unto the Mortgagor   executors administrators and assigns all
. such surplus as may remain after such sale and after payment of all such sum or sums of money and interest
thereon as may be due by virtue of these presents at the
time of such seizure and after payment of the costs
charges and expenses incurred by such seizure and sale as
aforesaid :

PROVIDED ALWAYS nevertheless that it shall not be incumbent on the Mortgagee   executors administrators
or assigns to sell and dispose of the said goods and chattels but that in case of default of payment of the said
sum of money with interest thereon as aforesaid it shall
and may be lawful for the Mortgagee   executors
administrators or assigns peaceably and quietly to have
hold use occupy possess and enjoy the said goods and
chattels without the let molestation eviction hindrance or
interruption of   the Mortgagor   executors
administrators or assigns or any of them or any other
person or persons whomsoever : and the Mortgagor doth
hereby further covenant promise and agree to and with
the Mortgagee   executors administrators and assigns
that in case the sum of money realized under any such

sale as above mentioned shall not be sufficient to pay the whole amount due at the time of such sale that the Mortgagor   executors or administrators shall and will fortwith pay or cause to be paid unto the Mortgagee executors administrators and assigns all such sum or sums of money with interest thereon as may then be remaining due :

And the Mortgagor   doth put the Mortgagee   in the full possession of said goods and chattels by delivering to   in the name of all the said goods and chattels at the sealing and delivery hereof :

And the Mortgagor   covenant   with the Mortgagee that   he   will during the continuance of this mortgage and any and every renewal thereof insure the chattels hereinbefore mentioned against loss or damage by fire in some insurance office (authorized to transact business in Canada) in the sum of not less than   dollars and will pay all premiums and moneys necessary for that purpose as the same becomes due and will on demand assign and deliver over to the said Mortgagee   executors and administrators the policy or policies of insurance and receipts thereto appertaining : provided that if on default of payment of said premium or sums of money by the Mortgagor the Mortgagee   executors or administrators may pay the same and such sums of money shall be added to the debt hereby secured (and shall bear interest at the same rate from the day of such payment) and shall be repayable with the principal sum hereby secured.

In witness whereof, &c.

Signed, sealed, &c.

ONTARIO :
County of
          To WIT : ⎰

in the foregoing Bill of Sale by way of Mortgage named make oath and say : That   the Mortgagor   in the the foregoing   bill of sale by way of mortgage named is justly and truly indebted to   th   depon- ent   the Mortgagee   therein named in the sum of   dollars mentioned therein :

That the said bill of sale by way of mortgage was exe- cuted in good faith and for the express purpose of secur- ing the payment of the money so justly due or accruing due as aforesaid and not for the purpose of protecting the goods and chattels mentioned in the said bill of sale by way of mortgage against the creditors of the said the Mortgagor   therein named or preventing the creditors of such Mortgagor   from obtaining payment of any claim against

Sworn before me at
in the County of   this
          day of   in the
year of our Lord 18

(*A Commissioner for taking Affidavits in the Queen's Bench, &c.*)

ONTARIO :   I,
County of   of the   in the
          To WIT :   County of   make oath and say :

That I was personally present, and did see the within bill of sale by way of mortgage duly signed sealed and de- livered by   the parties thereto and that the name   set and subscribed as a witness to the execution thereof is of the proper handwriting of me this deponent

and that the same was executed at the   of   in the
said County of

Sworn before me at
in the County of   ⎫
this   day of   ⎬
in the year of our Lord 18   ⎭

    *(A Commissioner for taking Affidavits in the Queen's
      Bench, &c.)*

RECEIVED on the day of the date of this Indenture,
from &c.

CHATTEL MORTGAGE (BILL OR PROMISSORY NOTE).

THIS INDENTURE made the   day of   in the
year of our Lord one thousand eight hundred and   ,
  BETWEEN   (hereinafter called the Mortgagor), of
the first part ; and   (hereinafter called the Mortgagee), of the second part ;

  WHEREAS the said Mortgagee ha   endorsed the
of the said Mortgagor , for the sum of   of lawful money
of Canada, for the accommodation of the said Mortgagor ,
which   is in the words and figures following, that is
to say :—

  AND WHEREAS the said Mortgagor   ha   agreed to
enter into these Presents for the purpose of indemnifying
and saving harmless the said Mortgagee of and from
the payment of the said   or any part thereof, or
any ·   ʼ hereafter to be endorsed by the said Mortgagee   for the accommodation of the said Mortgagor ,
by way of renewal of the said recited   so that,
however, said renewal shall not extend the time for pay-

ment of said   beyond the period of one year
from the date hereof, nor increase the amount of said
liability beyond the amount of said interest accruing
thereon.

Now THIS INDENTURE WITNESSETH that the said Mortgagor for and in consideration of the premises and of
the sum of one dollar of lawful money of Canada, to
in hand well and truly paid by the said Mortgagee ,
at or before the sealing and delivery of these Presents,
(the receipt whereof is hereby acknowledged,) ha granted, bargained, sold, and assigned, and by these presents
do grant, bargain, sell, and assign unto the said Mortgagee   executors, administrators, and assigns, all
and singular the goods and chattels hereinafter particularly mentioned and described, that is to say :—

To HAVE AND TO HOLD all and singular the goods and
chattels   hereinbefore granted, bargained, sold and
assigned, or mentioned, or intended so to be, unto the
said Mortgagee   executors, administrators, and
assigns, to the only proper use and behoof of the said
Mortgagee   executors, administrators, and assigns,
for ever ; provided always, and the presents are upon this
condition, that if the said Mortgagor   executors or
administrators, do and shall well and truly pay, or cause
to be paid the said   so as aforesaid endorsed by
the said Mortgagee a copy of which said   is set
out in the Recital to this Indenture ; and do and shall
well and truly pay or cause to be paid all and every other
        which may hereafter be endorsed by the said
Mortgagee   for the accommodation of the said Mortgagor by way of renewal of the said   in the said

Recital to this Indenture set forth, and indemnify, and save harmless the said Mortgagee   heirs, executors, and administrators, from all loss, costs, charges, damages, or expenses, in respect of the said   or Renewals, as hereinbefore set forth,

THEN THESE PRESENTS and every matter and thing herein contained, shall cease, determine, and be utterly void to all intents and purposes, anything herein contained to the contrary thereof in anywise notwithstanding ; and the said Mortgagor   for   executors and administrators, shall and will warrant and forever defend by these Presents all and singular the said goods, chattels, and property by these Presents unto the said Mortgagee   executors, administrators, and assigns, against   the said Mortgagor   executors, and administrators, and against all and every other person and persons whomsoever.

And the said Mortgagor do hereby for   executors and administrators, covenant promise and agree, to and with the said Mortgagee   executors, administrators, and assigns, that the said Mortgagor   executors or administrators, or some or one of them, shall and will well and truly pay, or cause to be paid, the said in the above Recital and Proviso mentioned, and all future and other   which the said Mortgagee   shall hereafter endorse for the accommodation of the said Mortgagor as aforesaid, and indemnify and save harmless the said Mortgagee   heirs, executors, and administrators, from all loss, costs, charges, damages, or expenses in respect thereof.

And also, that in case default shall be made in the pay-

K

ment of the said	or any future	as in the said
Proviso mentioned, or the interest thereon, or any part
thereof, or otherwise as aforesaid, or in case the said
Mortgagor shall attempt to sell or dispose of, or in any
way part with the possession of the said goods and
chattels, or any of them, or remove the same or any part
thereof, out of the	without the consent of the said
Mortgagee	executors, administrators, or assigns, to
such sale, removal or disposal thereof first had and obtained in writing, or in case said Mortgagor shall not
pay the taxes on said premises, or said goods, as they become due, or within ten days thereafter, or in case said
goods be seized either for rent or taxes, then and in any
of such cases all the moneys hereby secured shall become
due and payable, and it shall and may be lawful for the
said Mortgagee	executors, administrators, or assigns,
with	or their servant or servants, and with such other
assistant or assistants as	or they may require, at any
time during the day, to enter into and upon any lands,
tenements, houses, and premises wheresoever and whatsoever, where the said goods and chattels or any part
thereof may be, and for such persons to break and force
open any doors, locks, bars, bolts, fastenings, hinges,
gates, fences, houses, buildings, encloseures, and places,
for the purpose of taking possession of and removing the
said goods and chattels; and upon and from and after
the taking possession of such goods and chattels as aforesaid, it shall and may be lawful, and the said Mortgagee
		executors, administrators, or assigns, and each or
any of them, is and are hereby authorized and empowered
to sell the said goods and chattels, or any of them, or any

part thereof, at public auction or private sale, as to
or them or any of them may seem meet; and from and
out of the proceeds of such sale in the first place to pay
and reimburse   or themselves all such sums and sum
of money as may then be due by virtue of these Presents,
on the said   or any future   as aforesaid, and
all such expenses as may have been incurred by the said
Mortgagee   executors, administrators, or assigns, in
consequence of the default, neglect or failures of the said
Mortgagor   executors, administrators, or assigns, in
payment of the said   as above mentioned, or in
consequence of such sale or removal, or otherwise, as
above mentioned, and in the next place to pay unto the
said Mortgagor   executors, administrators, or assigns,
all such surplus as may remain after such sale, and after
payment of all such sum and sums of money and interest
thereon, as   the said Mortgagee   shall be called upon
to pay by reason of endorsing the said   in the said
Recital and Proviso mentioned, or any future   to
be endorsed by the said Mortgagee   for the said
Mortgagor   as aforesaid, at the time of such
seizure, and after payment of the costs, charges, and
expenses incurred by such seizure and sale, or otherwise, as aforesaid; provided always, nevertheless, that it
shall not be incumbent on the said Mortgagee   executors, administrators, and assigns, to sell and dispose of
the said goods and chattels; but that in case of default in
payment of the said   as aforesaid, it shall and may
be lawful for the said Mortgagee   executors, administrators, and assigns, peaceably and quietly to have, hold,
use, occupy, possess and enjoy the said goods and chattels,

without let, molestation, eviction, hindrance, or interruption of ⁂   the said Mortgagor   executors, administrators, or assigns, or any of them, or any other person or
persons whomsoever ; and the said Mortgagor   do
hereby for   heirs, executors, and administrators, further covenant, promise, and agree, to and with the said
Mortgagee   executors, administrators, and assigns,
that in case the sum of money realized under any such
sale as above mentioned shall not be sufficient to pay the
whole amount due at the time of such sale, that   the
said Mortgagor   executors or administrators, shall
and will forthwith pay, or cause to be paid unto the said
Mortgagee   executors, administrators, and assigns,
all such sum or sums of money, with interest thereon as
may then be remaining due upon or under the said
and the said Mortgagor   do   put the said Mortgagee
in full possession of the said goods and chattels by delivering to   in the name of all the said goods and
chattels at the sealing and delivery hereof

And the said Mortgagor   covenant   with the said Mortgagee   that he will during the continuance of this Mortgage, and any and every renewal thereof, insure the
chattels hereinbefore mentioned against loss or damage by
fire in some insurance office (authorized to transact business in Canada) in the sum of not less than   dollars, and will pay all premiums and moneys necessary for
that purpose, as the same become due ; and will on demand assign and deliver over to the said Mortgagee
executors and administrators, the policy or policies of insurance and receipts thereto appertaining ; provided, that
if on default of payment of said premium or sums of

money by the said Mortgagor , the said Mortgagee executors or administrators, shall pay the same; then such sums of money shall be added to the debt hereby secured, and shall bear interest at the same rate, from the day of such payment, and shall be repayable with the sum hereby secured.

In witness whereof, &c.

Signed, sealed, &c.

ONTARIO:
County of

To WIT: I   of   in the foregoing Bill of Sale by way of Mortgage named, make oath and say : That such Mortgage truly sets forth the agreement entered into between   and the said Mortgagor therein named, and truly states the extent of the liability intended to be created by such agreement, and covered by such Mortgage, and that the said Bill of Sale by way of Mortgage was executed in good faith and for the express purpose of securing   the said Mortgagee therein named against the payment of the amount of such   liability for the said Mortgagor   as therein set out, and not for the purpose of securing the goods and chattels mentioned therein against the Creditors of the Mortgagor   nor to prevent such Creditors from recovering any claims which they may have against such Mortgagor.

Sworn before me, at
in the County of
            this
day of   in the year
of our Lord 18 .

A Commissioner for taking Affidavits in the Queen's Bench, &c.

ONTARIO:
County of
              To WIT: } I,   of   make oath and
say: That I was personaly present and did see the within
Bill of Sale by way of Mortgage duly signed, sealed, and
delivered by   the parties thereto, and that I, this
deponent, am a subscribing witness to the same ; That the
name   set and subcribed as a witness to the execution thereof, is of the proper handwriting of me this
deponent ; and that the same was executed at   in
the said County of

Sworn before me, at
in the County of
this   day of
in the year of our Lord 18 .

*A Commissioner for taking Affidavits in the Queen's
    Bench, &c.*

CHATTEL MORTGAGE. (FUTURE ADVANCES.)

THIS INDENTURE, made the   day of   in the
year of our Lord one thousand eight hundred and   .

BETWEEN   , of the first part ; and
of the second part.

WITNESSETH, that whereas
Now, therefore, the said party of the first part
for the consideration hereinbefore recited, and in pursuance of the said agreement, hath granted, bargained,
sold and assigned, and by these presents doth grant, bargain, sell and assign unto the said party of the second

part,   executors, administrators, and assigns, all
and singular, the goods, chattels, furniture and household
stuff hereinafter particularly mentioned and described in
the schedule hereunto annexed marked A., to have and to
hold, all and singular, the said goods, chattels, furniture
and household stuff hereinbefore granted, bargained, sold
and assigned or mentioned, or intended so to be, unto the
said party of the second part   executors, administrators and assigns, to the sole and proper use and
behoof of the said party of the second part
executors, administrators and assigns for ever ; provided
always, and these presents are upon this condition, that
if the said party of the first part,   executors or
administrators do and shall well and truly   and
do and shall well and truly save harmless the said party
of the second part from

Then these presents, and every matter and thing herein
contained, shall cease, determine and be utterly void to
all intents and purposes, anything herein contained to
the contrary thereof in anywise notwithstanding.   And
the said party of the first part, for   executors
and administrators, all and singular the said goods, chattels and property by these presents   unto the
said party of the second part,   executors, administrators and assigns, against   the said party of the
first part,   heirs, executors and administrators,
and against all and every other person and persons
whomsoever claiming under him, shall and will warrant
and forever defend by these presents ; and the said party
of the first part doth hereby for   heirs, executors
and administrators, covenant, promise and agree to and

with the said party of the second part,   executors, administrators and assigns,   or in case the said party of the first part shall attempt to sell or dispose of or in any way part with the possession of the said goods and chattels, or any of them, or to remove the same or any part thereof out of the county of   without the consent of the said party of the second part, executors, administrators or assigns, to such sale, removal or disposal thereof first had and obtained in writing, then and in such case it shall and may be lawful for the said party of the second part,   executors, administrators or assigns, with   or their servant or servants, and with such other assistant or assistants as

or they may require at any time during the day to enter into and upon any lands, tenements, houses and premises wheresoever the said goods and chattels or any part thereof may be, and for such persons to break and force open any door, locks, bolts, bars, fastenings, hinges, gates, fences, houses, buildings, enclosures and places, for the purpose of taking possession of and removing the said goods and chattels ; and upon and from and after taking possession of such goods and chattels as aforesaid, it shall and may be lawful for the said party of the second part,   executors, administrators or assigns, and each or any of them is and are hereby authorized and empowered to sell the said goods and chattels, or any of them, or any part thereof, at public auction or private sale, as to them or any of them may seem meet, and from and out of the proceeds of such sale in the first place to pay and reimburse   and themselves all such sums and sum of money as may be due by virtue of these

presents, and all such expenses as may have been incurred by the said party of the second part,
executors, administrators or assigns, in consequence of the default, neglect or failure of the said party of the first part, executors, administrators or assigns, in payment of the said sum of money with interest thereon as above mentioned; and in the next place to pay unto the said party of the first part, executors or administrators, all such surplus as may remain after such sale, and after payment of all such sum and sums of money and interest thereon as may be due by virtue of these presents at the time of such seizure, and after payment of the costs and charges and expenses incurred by such seizure and sale as aforesaid;

PROVIDED ALWAYS, nevertheless, that it shall not be incumbent on the said party of the second part, executors, administrators or assigns, to sell and dispose of the said goods and chattels, but that in case of default it shall and may be lawful for the said party of the second part executors, administrators or assigns, peaceably and quietly to have, hold, use, occupy possess and enjoy the said goods and chattels, without the let, molestation, eviction, hindrance or interruption of the said party of the first part, executors or administrators, or any of them, or any other person or persons whomsoever:

And the said party of the first part doth hereby further covenant, promise and agree, to and with the said party of the second part, executors administrators and assigns, that in case the sum of money realized under any such sale as above mentioned shall not be sufficient to

pay the whole amount due at the time of such sale, that
       the said party of the first part,   executors
or administrators, shall and will forthwith pay or cause
to be paid unto the said party of the second part,
executors, administrators or assigns all such sum and
sums of money, with interest thereon, as may then be
remaining due.

And the said party of the first part doth put the said
party of the second part in full possession of the said
goods and chattels, by delivering to   in the name
of all the said goods and chattels, at the sealing and
delivery hereof.

In witness whereof, &c.

Signed, sealed, &c.

———

ONTARIO,   ⎫
County of   ⎬
      To wit : ⎭ I,   make oath and say :

That the foregoing mortgage truly sets forth the
agreement entered into between myself and
therein named, and truly states the extent of the liability
intended to be created by such agreement, and covered
by the foregoing mortgage.

That the foregoing mortgage is executed in good faith,
and for the express purpose of securing me   against
the payment of the amount of my liability, for the
said

That the foregoing mortgage is not executed for the
purpose of securing the goods and chattels mentioned in
the Schedule attached hereto marked A. against the
creditors of the said   or to prevent such creditors

from recovering any claim which they may have against the said

Sworn before me, at
in the County of
this   day of
A. D. 18   .

A Commissioner in B. R., &c.

———

ONTARIO,
County of
         To WIT : I,   of   make oath and say :

That I was personally present and did see the within Chattel Mortgage duly signed, sealed and executed by the parties thereto, and that the name
set and subscribed as a witness to the execution thereof is my proper handwriting, and that the same was executed at the   of   in the County of

Sworn before me, at the
of   in the County
of   the
day of   A. D. 18 .

A Commissioner in B. R., &c.

———

CHATTEL MORTGAGE ASSIGNMENT.

———

THIS INDENTURE, made the   day of   one thousand eight hundred and   , BETWEEN
hereinafter called the Assignor of the first part
hereinafter called the Assignee of the second part

WHEREAS, by a certain chattel mortgage dated on the   day of   one thousand eight hundred and
and duly filed in the County Court of the County of

one   mortgaged the goods and chattels therein mentioned unto the said assignor   executors, administrators and assigns for securing the payment of
dollars and interest thereon at the rate of   per cent.
per annum, from

And whereas there is now owing upon the said mortgage the sum of   dollars and interest thereon at the rate aforesaid from the   day of

Now THIS INDENTURE WITNESSETH, that in consideration of   dollars of lawful money of Canada now paid by.the said Assignee   to the said Assignor   (the receipt whereof is hereby acknowledged) the said Assignor do   hereby assign and set over unto the said Assignee executors administrators and assigns all that the said hereinbefore in part recited mortgage, and also the said sum of   dollars and the interest thereon now owing as aforesaid together with all moneys that may hereafter become due or owing in respect of the said mortgage and the full benefit of all powers and of all covenants and provisoes contained in said mortgage, and the said Assignor do   hereby grant bargain sell and assign unto the said Assignee   heirs and assigns all and singular the said goods and chattels therein and hereinafter more particularly mentioned and described, that is to say :
And all the right title interest property claim and demand whatsoever, both at law and in equity, or otherwise howsoever of him the said Assignor of in to and out of the same and every part thereof.

To HAVE AND TO HOLD the said hereinbefore recited mortgage and the moneys secured thereby, and also the said goods and chattels and every of them with their ap-

purtenances unto the said Assignee   executors administrators and assigns absolutely ; Subject to the proviso
for redemption contained in the said mortgage.

And the said Assignor for   executors and administrators do   hereby covenant with the said Assignee
      executors administrators and assigns that the said
sum of   dollars and interest thereon at the rate aforesaid from the '   day of   is now justly due owing
and unpaid upon and by virtue of the said mortgage and
that   ha   not done or permitted any act matter
or thing whereby the said mortgage has been released or
discharged, or the said goods and chattels in any wise encumbered or whereby the said goods and chattels or any
of them have been or may be removed from the said
and that .   executors and administrators will upon the
request and and at the cost of the said assignee
executors administrators and assigns do perform and
execute every act necessary for further assuring the said
mortgage and money goods and chattels and for enforcing
the performance of the covenants and other matters contained in the said mortgage.

In witness whereof, &c.

Signed, sealed, &c.

_____

ONTARIO :   ⎫ I,
County of   ⎬ of the   of
      To WIT : ⎭ in the County of   make oath and say :

That I was personally present and did see the foregoing
assignment of chattel mortgage duly signed sealed and
executed by   the parties thereto ; and that I this
deponent am a subscribing witness to the same : and that
the name   set and subscribed as a witness to the

execution thereof is of the proper handwriting of me this
deponent and that the same was executed at

Sworn before me at   ⎞
in the County of   ⎬
this   day of   ⎟
in the year of our Lord 18   ⎠

  *(A Commissioner for taking Affidavits in the Queen's
    Bench, &c.)*

     ONTARIO :   ⎞ I
County of   ⎬
        TO WIT : ⎠

    in the foregoing assignment named, make oath and
say : that the sale therein made is *bona fide*, and for good
consideration, namely :   and not for the purpose
of holding or enabling me this deponent to hold the goods
mentioned therein against the creditors of   therein
named.

Sworn before me at   ⎞
in the County of   ⎬
this   day of   ⎟
in the year of our Lord 18   ⎠

    (A Commissioner in B. R., &c.)

CHATTEL MORTGAGE RENEWAL.

(Statement " B.")

THE INTEREST OF   the mortgagee in the goods
and chattels described in the chattel mortgage of which
the annexed paper writing marked "A," is a true copy,
made by   to   and dated the   day of
one thousand eight hundred and   is as follows:

    The said mortgage was made by the said mortgagor to

said mortgagee to secure the due payment of   for
which said mortgage has   been assigned.

The amount still due and payable for principal and
interest is   according to the following particulars :

_____

ONTARIO :
County of   ⎞   I
                             ⎟   of the   of
                             ⎬   in the County of
              TO WIT: ⎠.   make oath and say :

1. I am the mortgagee mentioned in the chattel mortgage of which the annexed paper writing marked "A," is
a true copy.

2. That the said chattel mortgage has not been nor is
kept on foot for any fraudulent purpose.

3. That the foregoing statement marked "B," is true.

SWORN before me at   ⎞
        in the County of   ⎬
this   day of   A.D. 18 .⎠

A Commissioner in B. R., &c.

_____

CHATTEL MORTGAGE DISCHARGE.

—

DOMINION OF CANADA, ⎞
  Province of Ontario. ⎠

To the Clerk of the County Court of the   Count
of   I   do certify, that   ha   satisfied all
money due on or to grow due on a certain CHATTEL
MORTGAGE made by   to   which Mortgage bears
date the   day of   A.D. 18 , and was   registered   in the Office of the Clerk of the County Court of
the   Count   of   on the   day of   A.D. 18,

as No,   that such Chattel Mortgage has
been assigned,   and that I am the person entitled
by law to receive the money, and that such Mortgage is
therefore discharged.   Witness my hand this
day of   A.D. 18
Witness

Residence. }
Occupation. }

ONTARIO :   } I
County of   }
          To WIT : } make oath and say :

1. That I was personally present and did see the within Certificate of Discharge of Chattel Mortgage duly
signed, sealed and executed by   one of the parties
thereto.   2. That the said certificate was executed
at the   . 3. That I know the said   . 4. That
I am a subscribing witness to the said certificate.

Sworn before me, at   }
in the County of   }
this   day of   }
in the year of our Lord 18   .   }

A Commissioner for taking Affidavits in B. R., &c.

WARRANT UNDER CHATTEL MORTGAGE.

To   }
my bailiff in this behalf   }

You are hereby authorized and required to seize and
take all the goods and chattels mentioned in the mortgage,
a   whereof is hereunto annexed wherever the same may
be found and the same to sell and dispose of as provided
by the said mortgage so as to realize the sum of

now due and owing to   by virtue of the provisions
therein contained, and the said sum or so much thereof as
may be realized to pay over to   executors, administrators or assigns, and proceed thereupon to obtain possession of such goods and chattels and for the recovery of
the last mentioned sum as the law directs, and the said
indenture permits, and for your so doing this shall be
your sufficient warrant and authority.

Witness   hand   and seal   this   day of
A.D. 18 .

Witness,

WARRANT UNDER CHATTEL MORTGAGE.
(Another form.)

To   my bailiff in this behalf

You are hereby authorized and required to seize and
take all the goods and chattels mentioned in a certain chattel mortgage made by   a duplicate of which said mortgage is hereunto annexed and marked with the letter A,
wherever the same may be found, and the same to sell
and dispose of as provided by the said mortgage so as to
realize the sum of   now due and owing to
by virtue of the provisions therein contained, and the said
sum, or so much thereof as may be realized, to pay over
to   executors, administrators or assigns, and proceed
thereupon to obtain possession of such goods and chattels
and for the recovery of the last mentioned sum as the law
directs, and the said indenture permits, and for your so
doing this shall be your sufficient warrant and authority.

Witness   hand and seal this   day of   18 .

L

CHARTER PARTY.

—

THIS CHARTER PARTY, indented, made, concluded, and and agreed upon, the   day of   A. D. 18   BE-TWEEN A.B. of   master and owner of the ship or vessel called   of the burthen of   of the one part, and C. D. of   of the other part, witnesseth : That the said A. B., for the consideration hereinafter mentioned, hath granted and to freight letten, and by these presents doth grant and to freight let, unto the said C. D., his executors, administrators, and assigns, the whole tonnage of the hold, stem, sheets, and half deck of the said ship or vessel, from the port of   to the port of   in a voyage to be made with the said ship in the manner following (that is to say :) the said A. B. is to sail with the first fair wind and weather that shall happen next after the   day of   or before the   day of next, from the said port of   with the goods and mer-chandize of the said C. D., his factors or assigns on board to   aforesaid, there to be delivered and dis-charged of her said cargo, within fifteen days next after her arrival to the end of the said voyage : In considera-tion whereof, the said C. D., for himself, his heirs, exe-cutors, and administrators, doth covenant, promise, and agree, to and with the said A. B., his executors, admin-istrators, and assigns, and every of them, by these pres-ents, that the said C. D., his executors, administrators, factors, or assigns, shall and will well and truly pay, or cause to be paid, unto the said A. B., his executors, ad-ministrators, and assigns, for the freight of the said ship or goods, the sum of   [or thus, 20 dollars a ton for loading or unloading and taking in goods at   and ports,] within one and twenty days after the said ship's arrival, and goods discharged at   aforesaid, for the end of the voyage ; and also shall and will pay for demurrage, if any shall be by default of him the said C. D., his factors or assigns, the sum of two dollars a day, daily and every day, as the same shall grow due ; and the said A. B., for himself, his heirs, executors, and administrators, doth covenant, promise, grant, and agree, to and with the said C. D., his executors, administrators, and assigns, and every of them, by these presents, that the said ship or vessel shall be ready at the said port of

at   wharf, to take in goods, by the said   day of next coming ; and within ten days after the said ship shall be ready at the said wharf as aforesaid, the said C. D. doth grant, promise, and agree, to have his goods ready and put on board of said ship, in order that she may proceed on her said voyage. And the said A. B. doth also covenant, promise, grant, and agree, to and with the said C. D., his executors, administrators, and assigns, that the said ship or vessel now is, and at all times during the said voyage shall be at the best endeavour of the said A. B., his executors and administrators, at his and their own proper costs and charges, in all things made and kept stiff, staunch, and strong, and well furnished, and provided as well with men and mariners sufficient and able to sail, guide, and govern the said ship as with all manner of rigging, boats, tackle, apparel, furniture, provision, and appurtenances, fitting and necessary for the said men and mariners, and for the said ship, during the voyage aforesaid.

In Witness, &c.

CLERKSHIP, ARTICLES OF, TO AN ATTORNEY

ARTICLES OF AGREEMENT made the   day of
A.D. 18 .   BETWEEN A. B. of   gentleman, one of
the attorneys of Her Majesty's Courts of Queen's Bench
and Common Pleas for Ontario, and a solicitor of the Court
of Chancery of the one part, and C. D. of   and E. F.
son of the said C. D. of the other part, WITNESS that the
said E. F. of his own free will and by and with the consent and approbation of the said C. D. hath placed and
bound himself, and by these presents doth place and bind
himself clerk to the said A. B. to serve him from the day
of the date hereof, for and during, and until the full end
and term of five years from hence next ensuing, and fully
to be complete and ended.   And the said C. D. doth
hereby for himself, his heirs, executors, and administrators, covenant with the said A. B., his executors, administrators, and assigns, that the said E. F. shall and will
well and faithfully, and diligently serve the said A. B. as
his clerk in the business, practice, or profession of an
attorney at law and solicitor in chancery, from the day
of the date hereof, for and during, and unto the full end
of the said term of five years, and that he the said E. F.
shall not at any time during such term, cancel, obliterate,
injure, spoil, destroy, waste, embezzle, spend, or make
away with, any of the books, papers, writings, documents,
moneys, chattels, or other property of the said A. B., his
executors, administrators, or assigns, or his partner or
partners, or any of his clients or employers. And that in
case the said E. F. shall act contrary to the last mentioned
covenant, or if the said A. B., his executors, administra-

tors, or assigns, or his partner or partners, shall sustain or suffer any loss or damage by the misbehavior, neglect, or improper conduct of the said E. F., the said C. D., his heirs, executors, or administrators, shall indemnify the said A. B. and make good and reimburse him the amount or value thereof. And further, that the said E. F. will at all times keep the secrets of the said A. B. and his partner or partners, and will at all times during the said term, readily and cheerfully obey and execute his or their lawful and reasonable commands, and shall not depart or absent himself from the service or employ of the said A. B. at any time during the said term without his consent first had and obtained, and shall, from time to time, and at all times during the said term, conduct himself with all true diligence, honesty, and sobriety. And that the said C. D., his executors, and administrators, will from time to time, and at all times during the said term, find and provide the said E. F. with all necessary and becoming apparel, and also medicine and surgery in case of illness. [*This latter covenant may be extended to other things as for the support and maintenance of the Clerk, &c.*] And the said E. F. doth hereby for himself covenant with the said A. B., his executors, administrators, and assigns, that he, the said E. F. will truly, honestly and diligently serve the said A. B. at all times for and during the said term, as a faithful clerk ought to do in all things whatsoever in the manner above specified.

IN CONSIDERATION WHEREOF and of five shillings of lawful money by the said C. D. to the said A. B. paid at or before the sealing and delivery of these presents (the receipt whereof is hereby acknowledged) the said A. B. for himself, his heirs, executors and administrators, doth covenant with the said C. D. his executors and administrators, that he the said A. B. will accept and take said E. F. as his clerk. And also that the said A. B. will, by the best ways and means he may or can, and to the utmost of his skill and knowledge, teach and instruct or cause to be taught and instructed, the said E. F. in the said practice or profession of an attorney-at-law and solicitor-in-chancery, which he said A. B. now doth, or shall at any time during the said term, use or practice. (Other covenants may if within the object of the clerkship be inserted here. Sometimes, especially if the clerk has been sometime in the profession, the attorney covenants to pay him a salary.) And also will at the expiration of the said term use his best means and endeavours, at the request, costs and charges of the said C. D. and E. F. or either of them, to cause and procure him, the said E. F. to be admitted and sworn an attorney of Her Majesty's said Courts of Queen's Bench and Common Pleas, or either of them, and a solicitor of the Court of Chancery, or any other of Her Majesty's Courts of Law or Equity, provided the said E. F. shall have well, faithfully, and diligently served his said intended clerkship.

In witness, &c.

Signed, sealed, &c.

————

If the intended clerk be of full age, there will be no necessity for the father to be made a party.

CONDITIONS OF SALE OF LAND.

(Special form.)

1. The highest bidder shall be declared the purchaser; and if any dispute shall arise as to the last or best bidder, the property shall be immediately put up again at the former bidding.

2. No person shall advance at any one bidding less than   dollars, or retract his or her bidding; and the vendors, by themselves or their agent, shall be at liberty to bid once for the property.

3. The purchaser shall pay, immediately after the sale, to the vendor's solicitor, a deposit of   per cent in part of the purchase money and sign an agreement for the payment of the remainder on or before the   day of   , 18 . The premises will be sold subject to all defects or imperfections of title   subsisting before the commencement of the   title of the present vendors, and not occasioned by any act done by them or any person claiming under or in trust for them (and subject also to the several mortgages outstanding appearing on the certificate of the registrar of the county of   which will be produced at the time of the sale.)

4. The purchaser shall accept a conveyance from the vendors, to be prepared at his own expense, on payment of the remainder of the purchase money; and possession will be given on completion of the purchase; from which time the purchaser shall be entitled to the rents and profits.   But if, from any cause, the remainder of the purchase money shall not be paid on the   day of   , 18   , the purchaser shall pay interest for the same at the

rate of   per cent. from that day to the day of payment; but, nevertheless, this stipulation to be without prejudice to the vendor's right to insist on the performance of this last condition.

5. If any mistake be made in the description of the property, or there be any other error in the particulars of sale, the same shall not annul the sale, but a compensation or equivalent shall be given, or taken, as the case may require, according to the average of the whole 'purchase money (on such error or misstatement being proved): such compensation or equivalent to be settled by two referees or their umpire—one referee to be chosen by each party, within ten days after notice given of the error, and the umpire to be chosen by the referees immediately after their appointment.

6. The purchaser shall not be entitled to the production of any title deeds other than such as are in the vendor's hands, or in the hands of the several mortgagees.

7. Lastly, upon failure of complying with the above conditions, the deposit shall be forfeited, and the vendors shall be at full liberty (with or without notice) to re-sell the estate by public auction or private sale; and if, on such resale, there should be any deficiency, the purchaser shall make good such deficiency to the vendors, and all expenses attending such re-sale; the same to be recoverable as liquidated damages.

CONDITIONS OF SALE.

(Another form—Court of Chancery.)

1. No person shall advance less than $ at any

bidding under $ nor less than $ an any bidding over $ and no person shall retract   h bidding.

2. The highest bidder shall be the purchaser, and if any dispute arise as to the last, or highest bidder, the property . shall be put up at a former bidding.

3. The parties to the suit, with the exception of the vendor are to be at liberty   to bid

4. The purchaser shall at the time of sale, pay down a deposit in the proportion of $ for every $ of his purchase money, to the vendor   , or   Solicitor and shall pay   and upon such payment the purchaser shall be entitled to the conveyance, and to be let into possession, the purchaser at the time of sale to sign an agreement for the completion of the purchase.

5. The purchaser shall have the conveyance prepared at h   own expense, and tender the same for execution.

6. If the purchaser shall fail to comply with the conditions aforesaid, or any of them, the deposit, and all other payments made thereon shall be forfeited, and the premises may be re-sold, and the deficiency (if any) by such re-sale, together with all charges attending the same or occasioned by the defaulter, are to be made good by the defaulter.

Dated the   day of   A.D. 18

I agree to purchase   mentioned in the annexed particulars for the sum of   and upon the terms mentioned in the above conditions of sale.

Dated the   day of   A.D. 18

Witness :

CONDITIONS OF SALE OF GOODS.

1. The highest bidder to be the purchaser; and if any dispute shall arise as to the last or best bidder, the property shall be immediately put up again at the former bidding.

2. No person to advance less than   cents at a bidding.

3. The purchasers to give in their names, and place of residence *(if required)*, and pay down a deposit of per cent. in part payment of purchase money; in default of which, the lot or lots so purchased will be immediately put up again and re-sold.

4. The lots to be taken away at the buyer's expense, within three days after, and the remainder of the purchase money to be paid on or before delivery.

5. Upon failure of complying with these conditions, the deposit money shall be forfeited; and all lots uncleared within the time aforesaid shall be re-sold by public auction or private sale, and the deficiency, if any, on such re-sale shall be made good by the defaulter.

CONTRACT TO DO WORKS, &c.

THIS INDENTURE, made the   day of   A.D. 18 , BETWEEN

WITNESSETH that the said part   of the first part, in consideration of the sum of   of lawful money of Canada to be paid to   therefor, do hereby for   heirs, executors and administrators, covenant and agree with the said part   of the second part and   executors, administrators and assigns,

that,   the said part of the first part   heirs,
executors and administrators, shall and will execute
and perform ALL the   of every kind required in the
erection and finishing of   which said Works are
represented and specified in certain Plans and Specifications prepared therefor, and signed by   Architect, and the said part   of the first part, which said
Plans and Specifications are hereby expressly declared to
be incorporated in and to form part of this Indenture as
if the same had been embodied therein, and the said
Works shall in all things be performed according to the
same plans and specifications after the manner therein set
forth and explained, and shall be   in all things to
the entire satisfaction of the said   or   other
person who may succeed   .   as Architect, in charge of
the said Works, under a penalty of   as liquidated
damages for every   ' beyond the said time, the said
Works shall remain incomplete, and that the said part
of the first part   heirs, executors, and administrators, and every one of   workmen, agents and servants, shall, in all things concerning the performance of
the said Works, obey, abide by and keep all the several
conditions set forth in the said Specifications, and particularly in that portion of said Specifications entitled conditions, and numbered from one to   inclusive. AND
it is hereby expressly declared and agreed on by and
between the said parties of the first and second parts
that all detailed drawings and specifications to be furnished by the Architect during the progress of the
Work, as mentioned in the Specification hereinbefore
mentioned, shall be equally considered as incorporated in

and forming part of this Indenture, as if the same had
been embodied therein. AND the said parties of the first
and second parts, do hereby interchangeably covenant
and agree, the one with the other of them, that all differences or disputes which shall or may during the continuance of this contract arise as to the meaning or
intention of any part of the Plans, drawings or specifications already or hereafter to be provided, or which shall
or may in anywise arise or be caused between the said
parties by reason of this contract during the continuance
thereof, when and so often as the same shall happen
shall be referred to the award, order and determination of
said   or other person who may succeed   as
architect in charge of the said works, whose award in
writing under   hand concerning all matters so to
          referred shall be final, so as the said arbitrator do
make and publish   award in writing, within the
space of   days after   shall have been requested
by either party in writing, to decide concerning the matter in difference, and that this submission, and reference
in respect of the same may be made a rule of Her
Majesty's Court of Queen's Bench, at Toronto, if such
Court shall so please according to the statute in such
case made and provided.

In Witness, &c.

Signed, Sealed &c.

CONTRACT TO BUILD A HOUSE.

—

BE IT REMEMBERED, that on this   day of   ,
A. D. 18   , it is agreed by and between A. B. of   ,
and C. D. of   , in manner and form following, viz.:

The said C. D., for the considerations hereinafter mentioned, doth for himself, his executors and administrators, promise and agree to and with the said A. B., his executors, administrators, and assigns, that he, the said C. D., or his assigns, shall and will, within the space of next after the date hereof, in good and workmanlike manner, and according to the best of his art and skill, at , well and substantially erect, build, set up, and finish one house or messuage, according to the draught or scheme hereunto annexed, of the dimensions following, viz., &c., and to compose the same with such stone, brick, timber and other materials as the said A. B., or his assigns, shall find and provide for the same : in consideration whereof, the said A. B. doth for himself, his executors and administrators, promise and agree to and with the said C. D., his executors, administrators, and assigns, well and truly to pay or cause to be paid, unto the said C. D., or his assigns, the sum of in manner following, that is to say, the sum of , part thereof, at the beginning of the said work ; the sum of more, another part thereof, when the same shall be completely finished ; and also that he, the said A. B., his executors, administrators, or assigns, shall and will, at his and their own proper expense, find and provide all the stone, brick, tile, timber, and other materials necessary for making and building the said house. And for the performance of all and every the articles and agreements above mentioned, the said A. B. and C. D. do hereby bind themselves, their executors, &c., each to the other, in the penal sum of , firmly by these presents.

In witness whereof, &c.

SUB-CONTRACT BETWEEN BUILDER AND CARPENTER.

—

AN AGREEMENT made the   day of   , in the
year of our Lord 18   , between T. G., of   builder,
and C. D., of   , carpenter.

WHEREAS, the said T. G. hath entered into a contract
with J. B., of &c, to erect a dwelling house and offices
according to certain plans, elevations, and specifications
referred to in the said contract, under the superintend-
ance of W. M. or other surveyor of the said J. B., and
which contract is dated the   day of   . Now
it is hereby agreed, that in consideration of the sum of ·
     to be paid by the said T. G. to the said C. D., as
hereinafter mentioned, the said C. D. shall do all the
carpenter's work necessary to be done for the completion
of the said contract, and referred to in the said plans and
specifications, and provide all materials, tools, and implements necessary for the performance of such work, and
shall do the same in all things according to the said contract and specifications, and shall in all things abide by,
perform, fulfil and keep the said terms and stipulations
of the said contract, so far as the same are or shall be
applicable to such carpenter's work; and that in case the
said T. G. shall become liable to pay any penalties under
the said contract in consequence of the delay of the said
C. D. in the performance of the work agreed to be performed by him, the said C. D. shall pay to the said T. G.
the amount of such penalties; and that in case the said
W. M. or other surveyor appointed to superintend the
works under the said contract shall disapprove of the

work done by the said C. D., or the materials used by
him, or the manner in which such work is done, it shall
be lawful for the said T. G. to dismiss and discharge the
said C.-D. from the further performance of such work,
and employ some other person to complete the same; and
that in such case the money which the said T. G. shall
pay to the said other person for the completion of the
said works shall be deducted from the sum which would
otherwise be payable to the said C. D. under this agreement Xand that for the consideration aforesaid, the said
T. G. shall pay to the said C. D. the sum of   in
manner following : 75 per cent, on the price and value of
the work done by the said C. D. during any week, to be
paid to him on the Saturday in every week during the
continuance of the said works, and the balance within
one month after the completion of the said dwelling
house and offices.

In witness, &c.

The foregoing form may be easily adapted to any particular work on a building, as bricklayers, painters, &c.

CONTRACT TO DO REPAIRS, &c.

AN. AGREEMENT made the   day of   , in the year
of our Lord 18   , between A.B., of, &c., and C.D., of &c.
The said A.B. agrees to do all the works hereunder specified, in the best and most workman-like manner, and to
provide for such works all necessary materials and things
of the best quality, and to complete and finish the said
works on or before the   day of   next; and in case

the works shall not be finished on or before the said
day of   to pay or allow to the said C. D., out of the
moneys payable under this agreement, the sum of   for
each day during which the said works shall remain unfin-
ished after the said   day of ; and that in case the said
C. D. shall require any additions 'or alterations to be
made to the works hereunder specified, to execute such
additions and alterations in the best and most workman-
like manner, with materials of the best quality : And it is
hereby agreed, that in case any additional works shall be
required by the said C. D., or in case the said C. D. shall
delay the execution of the said works, the said A. B. shall
have such additional time for the performance of the said
works, after the said   day of   as shall have been
consumed in the execution of such additional works, or as
the time during which the said C. D. shall have delayed
the said works, and that the payments for delay shall not
be payable until after the expiration of such additional
time : And it is hereby further agreed, that materials
brought upon the premises of the said C. D. for the purpose of being used in the said works, shall, if of proper
description and quality, immediately become the property
of the said C. D. ; And the said C. D. agrees to pay to the
said A. B. for the said works the sum of   within one
week after the same shall be finished : And it is hereby
agreed, that in case of any additions or alterations being
made in or to the said works, the price of such additions
or alterations shall be estimated in proportion to the said
sum of   for the whole of the said works, and such
price so estimated shall be either added to or deducted
from the sum of

In witness, &c.

CONTRACT FOR SALE OF STOCK.

THIS AGREEMENT, made the   day of   , A.D. 18 , between A. B., of, &c., merchant, of the one part, and C. D., of, &c., merchant, of the other part.

The said A. B. agrees to sell, and the said C. D. agrees to buy, all the stock of goods, wares, and merchandise now being in and upon the store occupied by the said A. B., at   aforesaid, at the invoice price thereof (or at the sum of $, or otherwise as agreed on), an account of such goods, wares, and merchandise being taken by the parties hereto in the presence of each other. And it is hereby agreed that any of the said goods, wares, or merchandise which may be damaged, shall be appraised and valued by three disinterested persons; each of the parties hereto selecting one of such persons and the two so selected appointing the third; and that the price set upon such damaged goods, wares, and merchandise by the said three persons shall be substituted for the invoice price thereof; and that within ten days after the value of the said goods, wares, and merchandise shall have been ascertained as aforesaid, the said C. D. is to pay the valuation thereof to the said A. B. And the said A. B. agrees to make, execute, and deliver unto the said C. D. a good and sufficient bill of sale and conveyance thereof, and to give to the said C. D. quiet and peaceable possession thereof upon payment to him, the said A. B., by the said C. D., within the time before specified, of the invoiced or appraised value as aforesaid.

In witness, &c.

If desired the form for appraising damaged goods can be made applicable to the entire stock.

M

CONTRACT FOR SALE OF GRAIN.

—

It is AGREED, this   day of   A.D. 18   by and between A. B., of, &c., and C. D., of, &c., as follows: The said
A. B. agrees to sell to the said C. D. five thousand bush-
els of wheat, to be delivered to the said C. D., at   .
on or before 'the first day of January next, free of all
charges, at the price or sum of   per bushel.   And the
said C. D., agrees to purchase the said wheat, and to pay
therefor at the rate aforesaid, upon delivery as aforesaid.
And the said A. B. hereby guarantees and warrants the
said wheat to be good, clean, and merchantable grain.

Witness our hands.

Signed, sealed, &c.

CONTRACT FOR SALE ON COMMISSION.

—

This AGREEMENT, made this   day of   , A.D.
18 , between A. B., of   manufacturer of   and
C. D., of   traveller on commission.

1. The said A. B. for himself, his executors and administrators agrees that upon receiving a written order
from the said C. D., the A. B. his executors and administrators, will, from time to time, at his warehouse aforesaid, and according to such order, supply·to the said C. D.
the   as now manufactured by the said A. B.

2. The said   is to be invoiced to the said C. D. at
      and the said C. D. is to account for the same at
that price every three months, beginning from the date
hereof.

3. The said A. B., his executors and administrators
shall not be bound to supply more than   on any one

day, nor more than   in any one week, without a week's notice in writing with a written order from the said C. D. nor shall the said A. B., his executors or administrators be bound to continue supplying   as aforesaid after   shall have been delivered and shall remain unaccounted for, whether the said period of three months shall have elapsed since such delivery or not.

4. This agreement shall continue in force for seven years from the date hereof but subject to determination at any time by six months' previous notice in writing from either of the said parties or the executors or administrators of the said A. B. to the other of them and delivered at his usual or last known place of abode.

5. During the continuance of this agreement the said A. B., his executors and administrators shall not employ, nor shall knowingly suffer any other person than the said C. D. to sell on commission for them the said   beyond a radius of   miles from   and in case of a breach of this clause the said A. B.. for himself his executors and administrators undertakes to pay the said C. D. the sum of   by way of agreed and liquidated damages.

In witness, &c.

Signed, sealed, &c.

———

CONTRACT FOR SERVICE AS CLERK.

—

IT IS AGREED, this   day of   A.D. 18   , BETWEEN   and   both of   in manner following, to wit :

The said   covenants and agrees, faithfully and diligently to serve and act as the clerk, or salesman, of

the said   in his store in   from the day of the
date hereof, for and during the space of one year, if both
parties shall so long live, without absenting himself from
the same; during which time he, the said   will in
the store of the said   faithfully, honestly and diligently attend, doing and performing all matters pertaining
to his duties as clerk or salesman aforesaid, and in all
respects complying with the request and desire of the said
        relative to the discharge of such duties.

In consideration of which services so to be performed
by the said   he, the said   covenants and
agrees to allow and pay to the said   the yearly
sum of   by four equal quarterly payments, or oftener,
if required; provided nevertheless that payment for all
time during which the said   may be absent from
the store of the said   is to be deducted from the sum,
otherwise by this agreement due from, and payable by, the
said   to the said

Witness our hands and seals, the day and year first
written.

Signed, sealed, &c.

DEED WITH DOWER.

THIS INDENTURE, made (in duplicate) the   day of
    A.D. 18   , in pursuance of the Act respecting Short
Forms of Conveyances:

BETWEEN   of the first part; wi   of the said
part   of the first part of the second part; and
of the the third part

WITNESSETH, that in consideration of   of lawful

money of Canada, now paid by the said part   of the
third part, to the said part   of the first part, (the receipt whereof is hereby by   acknowledged),   the
said part   of the first part do   grant unto the said
part   of the third part,   heirs and assigns, for
ever :

All and singular th   certain parcel   or tract   of land
and premises, situate, lying and being

To HAVE AND TO HOLD unto the said part   of the
third part,   heirs and assigns, to and for   their
sole and only use for ever : subject, nevertheless, to the
reservations, limitations, provisoes and conditions expressed in the original grant thereof from the Crown.

The said part   of the first part covenant   with the
said part   of the the third part, that   ha   the
right to convey the said lands to the said part   of the
third part notwithstanding any act of the said part   of
the first part.

And that the said part   of the third part shall have
quiet possession of the said lands, free from all incumbrances.

And the said part   of the first part, covenant   with
the said part   . of the third part, that   will execute
such further assurances of the said lands as may be requisite.

And the said part   of the first part covenant   with
the said part   of the third part. that   ha   done no
act to encumber the said lands.

And the said part   of the first part release   to the
said part   of the third part all   claims upon the said
lands.

And the said part   of the second part, wi   of the
said part   of the first part, hereby bar   dower in
the said lands.

In witness whereof, &c.

Signed, sealed, &c.

RECEIVED on the day of the date of this Indenture, &c.

(Usual Affidavit of Execution.)

STATUTORY DEED.

THIS INDENTURE, made (in duplicate) the   day of
     A.D. 18   , in pursuance of the Act respecting
Short Forms of Conveyances: BETWEEN

WITNESSETH, that in consideration of   of lawful
money of Canada, now paid by the said part   of the
     part, to the said part   of the first part, (the receipt
whereof is hereby by   acknowledged),   the said
part   of the first part do   grant unto the said part
of the   part,   heirs and assigns, for ever:

All and singular th   certain parcel   or tract   of
land   and premises, situate, lying and being

To HAVE AND TO HOLD unto the said part   of the
part,   heirs and assigns, to and for   .   their sole and
only use for ever: subject nevertheless, to the reservations, limitations, provisoes and conditions expressed in
the original grant thereof from the Crown.

The said part   of the first part covenant   with the
said part   of the   part, that   ha   the right to
convey the said lands to the said part   of the   part
notwithstanding any act of the said part   of the first
part.

And that the said part   of the   part shall have quiet possession of the said lands, free from all incumbrances.

And the said part   of the first part covenant   with the said part   of the   part, that   will execute such further assurances of the said lands as may be requisite.

(DÈEDS.)

And the said part   of the first part covenant   with the said part   of the   part, that   ha   done no act to encumber the said lands.

And the said part   of the first part release   to the said part   of the   part all   claims upon the said lands.

(DOWER.)   ,

In witness whereof, &c.

Signed, sealed, &c.

RECEIVED on the day of the date of this Indenture from, &c.

(Usual Affidavit of Execution.)

DEED OF BARGAIN AND SALE.

(Full Covenants.)

—

THIS INDENTURE, made in duplicate the   day of A.D. 18   , BETWEEN

WITNESSETH, that the said part   or the first part, in consideration of the sum of   dollars of lawful money of Canada, to   paid by the said part   of the

part (the receipt whereof is hereby acknowledged),
do by these presents, grant, bargain, sell, convey and
confirm unto the said part of the part heirs
and assigns, all and singular th certain parcel or
tract of land and premises situate, lying and being in
the

Together with all and singular the rights, members,
easements privileges and appurtenances thereto belonging
or appertaining;and all reversions, remainders, rents, issues
and profits thereof : and all the estate, right, title, interest,
both at law and in equity, of the said part of
the first part of, in, to, or out of the said lands, hereditaments and premises, and every part thereof : to have and
to hold the hereditaments and premises, and all and
singular the premises hereby conveyed unto the said part
· of the part, heirs and assigns, to the sole
and only use of the said part of the part, heirs
and assigns for ever. Subject, nevertheless, to the reservations, limitations, provisoes and conditions expressed
in the original grant thereof from the Crown :

And the said part of the first part do hereby for
heirs, executors and administrators, covenant, promise and agree, to and with the said part of the part,
heirs and assigns, in manner following, that is to
say : that the said part of the first part, at the
time of the ensealing and delivery hereof stand
solely, rightfully and lawfully.seized of a good, sure, perfect, absolute and indefeasible estate of inheritance, in
fee simple, of and in the hereditaments and premises
hereinbefore described, with their and every of their
appurtenances, and of and in every part and parcel thereof,

without any manner of reservations, limitations, provisoes, or conditions (other than as aforesaid), or any
other matter or thing, to alter, charge, change, encumber
or defeat the same ; and also, that   the said part
of the first part, now ha   in   good right, full power,
and lawful and absolute authority, to grant and convey
the said hereditaments and premises, and every part and
parcel .thereof with the appurtenances, unto the said
part* of the   part   heirs and assigns, in manner
and form aforesaid

And also, that the said part   of the first part
hath not, at any time heretofore, done, executed, committed, or suffered any act, deed, matter, or charge whereby these hereditaments and premises hereby conveyed
have been or may be in anywise impeached, charged or
encumbered.

And also, that it shall and may be lawful to and for
the said part   of the   part,   heirs and assigns,
peaceably and quietly to enter into, occupy, possess, and
enjoy the aforesaid hereditaments and premises, with the
appurtenances, without the let, interruption, or denial of
      the said part   of the first part   heirs or assigns,
. or any other person or persons whomsoever, and free and
clear, exonerated, and discharged of and from all arrears
of taxes, and assessments whatsoever, due or payable upon
or in respect of the said hereditaments and premises, or
any part thereof, and of and from all former conveyances,
mortgages, rights, annuities, debts, judgments, executions,
and recognizances, and of and from all manner of other
charges and encumbrances whatsoever ; and, lastly, that
      the said part   of the first part,   heirs and

assigns, and all and every other person or persons whomsoever, having or lawfully claiming, or who shall or may
have or lawfully claim any estate, right, title, interest or
trust, of, in, to, or out of the lands, hereditaments, and
premises, hereby conveyed, with their appurtunances, or
any part thereof, by, from, or under, or in trust for
the said part   of the first part   heirs or assigns,
shall and will from time to time, and at all times hereafter, at the proper costs and charges in the law of the
said part   of the   part,   heirs and assigns,
make, do, suffer, and execute, or cause or procure to be
made, done, suffered, and executed, all and every such
further reasonable acts, deeds, conveyances, and assurances in the law, for the further and the more perfectly
and absolutely conveying and assuring of the said hereditaments and premises, with the appurtenances, unto the
said part   of the   part,   heirs, or assigns as
by the said part   of the   part   heirs or assigns or
their counsel learned in the law, shall be lawfully and
reasonably devised, advised, or required.

AND THIS INDENTURE FURTHER WITNESSETH, that the
said   wife of the said   for and in consideration
of the sum of one dollar of lawful money of Canada, to
her in hand paid by the said   at or before the sealing and delivery of these presents, the receipt whereof is
hereby acknowledged, hath granted, remised, and released,
and by these presents doth grant, remise, and release
unto the said   his heirs and assigns, all her dower,
and right and title to dower which she now hath, or
which, in the event of her surviving her said husband,
she might or would have to dower, in, to, or out of the

the lands and premises hereby conveyed or intended
so to be.

In witness, &c.

Signed, sealed, &c.

RECEIVED on the day of the date of this Indenture
from, &c.

(Usual Affidavit of Execution.)

EXECUTOR'S DEED.

THIS INDENTURE, made in Duplicate the   day of
          A.D. 18   , BETWEEN   the Execut
of the Last Will and Testament   of   late of
deceased, of the First part, and   of the Second part;

WHEREAS, the said   was at the time of
decease seized in free simple, or otherwise well entitled to
the Real Estate and Premises hereinafter specified and
described ; and before   decease did duly make and
publish in writing   Last Will and Testament, bearing date the   day of   in the year of our Lord,
one thousand, eight hundred, and   thereby auth-
orising and empowering   said Execut   to
execute and give Deeds of Conveyance for his Real
Estate.

AND WHEREAS the said   departed this life on the
          day of   in the year of our Lord, one thous-
and, eight hundred and   without revoking or
otherwise cancelling or altering the said Will.

NOW THIS INDENTURE WITNESSETH, that in pursu-
ance of the powers vested in   the said part   of
the First part, by virtue of the said Will   and in

consideration of the sum of   of lawful money
of Canada to   in hand paid by the said part   of the
Second part, the receipt whereof is hereby acknowledged,
        the said part   of the first part in   fiduciary
character aforesaid do   grant, bargain, sell, assign,
convey and confirm unto the said part   of the
Second part, and to   heirs and assigns for ever

ALL AND SINGULAR, th   certain parcel   or tract
of land and premises situate lying and being

TOGETHER with all the Estate, Right, Title and Interest
of the said part   of the First Part, in   character
aforesaid therein.

TO HAVE AND TO HOLD the same unto the said part
of the Second part   heirs and assigns forever.

AND the said part   of the First part for   do
hereby covenant, promise, and agree to and with the said
part   of the Second part   heirs and assigns, that
        the said part   of the First part ha   not
at any time heretofore made, done, committed or executed, or wittingly or willingly suffered any act, deed,
matter or thing whatsoever, whereby or by means whereof, the said parcel   or tract of land and premises hereinbefore mentioned and described, or any part or parcel
thereof are, is or shall or may be in any wise impeached,
charged, affected or incumbered, in title, charge, estate,
or otherwise howsoever. And that   will, in
fiduciary character aforesaid, execute such further assurances of the said lands as may be requisite.

In witness, &c.

Signed, sealed, &c.

(Usual Affidavit of Execution.)

DEED UNDER POWER OF SALE.

THIS INDENTURE, made (in duplicate) the   day of
       18 , in pursuance of the Act respecting Short
Forms of Conveyances (and being chapter one hundred
and two of the Revised Statutes of Ontario).

BETWEEN   hereinafter called " the grantor," of
the first part   hereinafter called "the grantee,"
of the second part.

WHEREAS one   by indenture of bargain and
sale, by way of mortgage, made the   day of   18
and duly registered in the registry office of the
under number   did grant and convey the lands,
hereditaments and premises hereinafter particularly described unto   (herein called the grantor) for securing payment of the sum of   and interest as therein
mentioned.

AND WHEREAS in said mortgage there is contained a
a proviso that in case the said   should make default in payment of principal or interest for   month
       the said grantor   giving   ' notice to the
said   might enter on and lease or sell the said
lands.

AND WHEREAS it is further provided in and by the said
mortgage that on any default in the payment of interest,
the whole of the principal should at once become due and
payable.

AND WHEREAS default has been made in payment of the
said sum of

And notice of   intention to sell the said lands and premises has been duly given to the said

AND WHEREAS the said lands have been advertised for sale pursuant to the said power coutained in said mortgage, by public auction, at   by advertisement thereof inserted ln the   newspaper and by posters, &c., for the space of

AND WHEREAS the said lands being put up and offered for sale at public auction, pursuant to such advertisement thereof as aforesaid, the said grantee was the highest bid der, and became the purchaser of said lands at and for the sum or price of

Now this indenture witnesseth, that in pursuance of the premises, and in consideration of the said sum of of lawful money of Canada now paid by the said grantee to the said grantor (the receipt whereof is hereby by acknowledged). The said grantor by virtue and in exercise of the aforesaid power of sale and of all other powers thereunto enabling, do   grant unto the said grantee heirs and assigns for ever :

All and singular, th. certain parcel or tract of land and premises, situate lying and being To hold unto the said grantee   heirs and assigns to and for   their sole and only use for ever.

The said grantor covenants with the said grantee that the said mortgage security is now in full force unprejudiced and unreleased in whole or in part, and that default has so happened as aforesaid in the payment of the money due thereby.

And the said grantor covenants with the said grantee

that he has done no act to incumber the said mortgaged premises, or the said lands.

And the said grantor releases to the said grantee all claims upon the said lands.

In witness, &c.

Signed, sealed, &c.

RECEIVED from the said grantee the sum of dollars, being the full amount of the purchase money payable by him on the sale of the said lands to him, under and in pursuance of the powers and provisos contained in the hereinbefore mentioned mortgage.

Witness :

(Usual Affidavit of Execution.)

DEED BY BUILDING SOCIETY UNDER POWER OF SALE.

THIS INDENTURE, made the day of A.D. 18 , in pursuance of the Act respecting Short Forms of Conveyances, BETWEEN the Loan and Savings Society, of the city of in the county of of the first part, and of in the county of of the second part.

WHEREAS, by indenture of mortgage dated the day of A. D, 18 , and made between of in the county of of the first part his wife of the second part, and the said Society of the third part, the said for and in consideration of

the sum of   advanced and paid to him by the said
Society, did convey and assure unto the said Society the
land and premises hereinafter described and set out.   To
hold the same with the appurtenances unto the said
Society, their successors and assigns.   To the use of the
said Society, their successors and assigns for ever, and in
which said Indenture of Mortgage is contained an express
condition that if the said   should well and truly
pay to the said Society their successors or assigns the
said sum of money, interest and charges in equal instalments of   on the first day of each month during
the term of   months until the said sum of money,
interest, and charges should be fully paid, and also during
the whole time aforesaid pay to the said Society, their
successors and assigns all other monthly payments and
contributions for upon or in respect of the shares therein
mentioned, and also all fines and other charges whatsoever imposed or thereafter to be imposed by the said
Society and their successors upon the said   his
heirs, executors, administrators, and assigns, as a member
or members of the said Society, or upon the   shares
therein mentioned, or for upon or in respect of any
default or neglect or breach of any of the rules and regu-
lations or by-laws of the said Society by the said
his heirs, executors, administrators, and assigns, without
any deduction or abatement whatsoever, and also all
taxes, assessments, premiums of insurance, interest
thereon, and other charges for upon or in respect of the
said premises and every part thereof, then the said presents and everything therein contained should be void.
And whereas, it was in and by the said Indenture of

Mortgage agreed that if default should happen to be made for the space of six months in payment of the said monthly subscriptions, fines, and forfeitures, or of any of them, or of any part thereof at the days and times at which the same were thereinbefore covenanted to be paid contrary to the true intent and meaning of the said proviso, it should and might be lawful for the said Society, their successors or assigns without any previous demand of possession, peaceably and quietly to enter in and take possession of the lands and premises thereinbefore described with their appurtenances or of any part thereof, and to collect, have, receive, and take the rents, issues, and profits thereof, and without any notice to the said

his heirs or assigns, and at the discretion of the said Society to sell and absolutely dispose of the said lands and premises or any part thereof, either altogether or in parcels or lots, and either by public sale or private contract, or partly by each of these means, and on such terms as should seem to the said Society, its successors or assigns, most advantageous for the interests of the said Society, and for such price or prices as could be reasonably obtained for the same.

AND WHEREAS, the said ⸍ hath made default in payment for six months, and more of the said instalments of as are in and by the said hereinbefore in part recited Indenture of Mortgage covenanted to be paid as aforesaid. And whereas, the said Society under and by virtue of the said hereinbefore recited Power of Sale, did on the day of A. D. 18 , sell by public auction at the of the lands and premises hereinafter described to the said at and for the

N

price or sum of   he being declared the highest
bidder therefor.

Now THIS INDENTURE WITNESSETH, that in consideration of the premises and of the sum of   of lawful
money of Canada, now paid by the said party of the
second part to the said Society, (the receipt whereof is
hereby, by the said Society acknowledged) they, the said
Society, do grant unto the said party of the second part,
his heirs and assigns for ever, all th   certain parcel of
land and premises situate in the

To HAVE AND TO HOLD unto the said party of the
second part,   his heirs and assigns, to and for his and
their sole and only use for ever.

The said Society covenant with the said party of the
second part, that they have the right to convey the said
lands to the said party of the second part   notwithstanding any act of the said Society.   .

And that there has been default made for six months
and more, in payment of the instalments mentioned in
the said hereinbefore in part recited Indenture of Mortgage. And that they, the said Society, will execute all
such further assurances of the said lands as may be
requisite at the costs and charges of the said party of the
second part. And that they, the said Society, have done
no act to incumber the said lands.

In witness, &c.

Signed, sealed, &c.

INSTRUCTIONS FOR EXECUTING AND ATTESTING DEEDS.

(To accompany Documents going abroad.)

Parties to sign their names where the same are written in pencil, and after signing to touch the seal and say, " *I deliver this as my act and deed.*" Dates to be filled in. Witness to sign where the word *witness* is written in pencil, both to Attestation and Receipt. The Christian names and surname, place of residence and addition occupation or calling *in full* of subscribing witness, and the place of execution and name or names of party or parties whose execution he attests to be filled in Affidavit of Execution.

The Affidavit if made in Ontario, shall be made before the Registrar or Deputy Registrar of the County in which the lands lie, or before a Judge of any of the Superior Courts of Law or Equity, or before any Judge of a County Court within his County, or before a Commissioner authorised by any of the Superior Courts to take Affidavits.

The Affidavit if made in Quebec, shall be made before a Judge or Prothonotary of the Superior Court, or Clerk of the Circuit Court, or before a Commissioner authorised by any of the Superior Courts of Common Law for ontario to take affidavits in Quebec, or before any Notary Public in Quebec certified under his Official Seal.

The Affidavit if made in Great Britain or Ireland, to be made before a Judge of the Superior Courts, or of the County Courts within the County, or the Mayor or Chief

Magistrate of any City, Borough, or Town Corporate therein, certified under the Common Seal of such City, Borough, or Town Corporate, or before a Commissioner for taking Affidavits in and for any of the Courts of Record for the Province of Ontario, or before any Notary Public certified under his Official seal. If made in any British Colony or possession, the Affidavit to be made before a judge of the Court of Record, or the Mayor of any City, Borough, or Town Corporate certified under the Common Seal of such City, Borough, or Town, or before any Notary Public, certified under his Official Seal. If made in the British Possessions in India, before any Magistrate or Collector certified to have been such under the hand of the Governor of such Possession. If made in any foreign country, before the Mayor of any City, Borough, or Town Corporate of such Country, and certified under the Common Seal of such City, Borough or Town Corporate ; or before any Consul or Vice-Consul of Her Majesty resident therein ; or before a Judge of a Court of Record, or a Notary Public, certified under his Official Seal.

The Duplicate to be an exact counterpart of the Original.

DEED OF COVENANT CONCERNING LIGHT.

THIS INDENTURE, made the   day of   A.D. 18 ,

BETWEEN A. B., of the one part, and C. D., of the other part.

WHEREAS the said C. D. is seized in fee of a house, messuage and garden, No. 1,   street, in and the said A. B. is possessed of an adjoining house, messuage and garden, No. 2,   street, aforesaid, for an unexpired term of about   years; and whereas the said C. D. has recently opened three windows in a portion of No. 1, overlooking and deriving their light over a portion of the garden and yard of No. 2; and whereas the said A. B. does not desire that the said C. D., his heirs or assigns, should acquire an indefeasible right to derive light for the said windows over any part of No. 2, during the residue of the said term, but does not desire to obstruct such light for   in order to prevent such right accruing; and whereas the said C. D. only desires that he, his heirs and assigns, shall enjoy the said light till an interruption thereof should arise from new buildings, or other permanent improvements. Now, this Indenture witnesseth as follows:

1. The said A. B., for himself, his heirs, executors, administrators and assigns, covenants with the said C. D., his heirs and assigns, that the said A. B., his executors, administrators and assigns, will not obstruct the light to the said windows, save by new buildings or other permanent improvements.

2. And the said C, D., for himself, his heirs and assigns, covenants with the said A. B., his executors, administrators and assigns, that the said C. D., his executors, administrators or assigns, may, at any time hereafter, by buildings or other permanent improvements, obstruct the light to the said windows, without let or hindrance on the part of the said A. B., his heirs and assigns.

In witness whereof, &c.

Signed, sealed, &c.

DEED OF A WATERCOURSE.

—

THIS INDENTURE, made, *(here insert the date, parties, &c.,)*. WHEREAS the said   and   at the time of the sealing and delivery of these presents, are respectively seized in fee, of and in two contiguous tracts, pieces or parcels of land, with the appurtenances, in the township of   aforesaid : And whereas there is a dam and race or watercourse built, erected and made, in and upon a certain run or stream of water (called   ) within the land of the said   for watering, overflowing and improving meadow ground thereon.   Now this Indenture witnesseth that the said   , for divers good causes and considerations, and more especially for and in consideration of the sum of one dollar, to him in hand paid by the said   at or before the sealing and delivery hereof, the receipt whereof he doth hereby acknowledge, hath granted, bargained, sold, released and confirmed, and by these presents doth grant, bargain, sell, release and confirm unto the said   and to his heirs and assigns, all the water of the said run or stream of water, to be led and conveyed from the said dam along the race or watercourse aforesaid into the said land of the said for the space of four days in every week, to wit : from Tuesday evening at sunset, to Saturday evening at sunset, from the first day of April to the first day of October, yearly and every year, for the watering, overflowing and improving of meadow ground on the land of the said together with free ingress, egress and regress to and for the said   his heirs and assigns, and his and their workmen, with horses, carts and carriages, at all conven-

ient times and seasons, through the land of the said
his heirs and assigns, in and along the banks of the said
dam and race or watercourse, for the amending, cleansing
and repairing the same, with liberty and privilege, for
that purpose, to dig and take stones and earth from the
adjacent land of the said   when and as often as
need be or occasion require : To have and to hold all and
singular the premises and privileges hereby granted, or
mentioned, or intended so to be, with the appurtenances,
unto the said   to the only proper use and behoof
of the said   his heirs and assigns for ever, he or
they paying one moiety or half part of the expenses which
from time to time may accrue, in supporting, cleansing
and repairing the dam and watercourse aforesaid.

In witness, &c.

Signed, sealed, &c.

DEED OF RIGHT OF WAY.

THIS INDENTURE, made this   day of   A.D 18 ,
BETWEEN   of   of the one part, and   of
      aforesaid, of the other part ; WITNESSETH, that the
said   for and in consideration of the sum of
lawful money of Canada, unto him well and truly paid by
the said   at and before the ensealing and delivery
hereof, the receipt whereof is hereby acknowledged, hath
granted, bargained and sold, and by these presents doth
grant, bargain and sell unto the said   his heirs
and assigns, the free and uninterrupted use, liberty and
privilege of, and passage in and along a certain alley or
passage, of   feet in breadth by   feet in depth, ex-

tending out and from (describing the direction of the way); together with free ingress, egress and regress to and for the said   his heirs and assigns, and his and their tenants, under-tenants (if for a carriage-way, here add, "with carts, vehicles, carriages, horses or cattle, as by him or them shall be necessary and convenient"), at all times and seasons forever thereafter, into, along, upon and out of the said alley or passage-way, in common with him the said   his heirs and assigns, and his and their tenants or under-tenants : To have and to hold all and singular the privileges aforesaid to him the said   his heirs and assigns, to his and their only proper use and behoof, in common with him, the said   his heirs and assigns, as aforesaid. (Here add, if desired, " subject, nevertheless, to the moiety or equal half part of all necessary charges and expenses, which shall from time to time accrue, in paving, amending, repairing and cleansing the said alley or passage-way.")

In witness, &c.

Signed, sealed, &c.

DEED OF EXCHANGE.

THIS INDENTURE, made the   day of   A. D. 18 .

BETWEEN   of   of the one part, and of   of the other part, WITNESSETH, that the said   hath given and granted, and by these presents doth give and grant, unto the said   one field or close of freehold land, called or known by the name of   &c. with all and every of their appurtenances, situate, lying, and being in   in the county of

J. Parker Thomas

CONVEYANCER. 4/2/82 201

for and in exchange of and for all the lands, tenements, and hereditaments of the said   called or known by the name of   in   aforesaid, in the said county of   to have and to hold the said field or close to the said   heirs and assigns for ever, for and in exchange of and for the said lands, tenements, and hereditaments, called   in aforesaid with the appurtenances. And the said doth covenant, &c.: (against incumbrances) And the said hath likewise, on his part, given and granted, and by these presents doth fully, freely, and absolutely give and grant, unto the said   his heirs and assigns, all those lands, tenements, and hereditaments, aforesaid, with the appurtenances, called or known by the name of situate, lying, and being in   aforesaid, in the said county of   to have and to hold the said lands, tenements, and hereditaments, &c. to the said   his heirs and assigns, forever, for and in exchange of and for the said field or close of land &c. And the said doth covenant, &c. (against incumbrances.) Provided always, nevertheless, and these presents are upon this condition, and it is the true intent and meaning of the parties hereunto, that if it shall happen that either of the said parties to these presents, their executors, administrators, or assigns, shall at any time hereafter during the said respective terms above granted, by colour or means of any former or other gift, grant, bargain, or sale, or otherwise howsoever, be ousted or evicted of and from the possession of either of the said messuages or tenements, and other the premises, so respectively granted in exchange, as aforesaid, or any part thereof, then and in such cases, these presents, and every matter and thing therein contained, shall be utterly void and of none effect, and then and thenceforth it shall and may be lawful to and for the party or parties so ousted or evicted, into his or their said former messuage or tenement and premises, with all and singular the appurtenances to re-enter, and the same to have again, repossess, and enjoy, as of his and their former estate or estates : anything herein contained to the contrary thereof in any wise notwith-standing.

In witness, &c.

Signed, sealed, &c.

DEED OF EXCHANGE.

(Another form.)

THIS INDENTURE, made the   day of   A.D. 18 ,

BETWEEN A. B., of   yeoman, of the one part, and E. F., of   yeoman, of the other part,

WITNESSETH that the said A. B., hath given, granted and confirmed, and by these presents doth give, grant and confirm unto the said E. F. all that parcel and tract of land, &c. (*describing the premises.*)

To HAVE AND TO HOLD, the said parcel or tract of land and premises, with their appurtenances, to the said E. F. and his heirs forever, in exchange for certain lands of the said E. F. hereinafter granted to the said A. B. And the said E. F. hath given, granted, and confirmed, and by these presents doth give, grant and confirm unto the said A. B., all that parcel or tract of land, &c. (*describing the premises.*)

To HAVE AND TO HOLD the said last mentioned premises with their appurtenances, to the said A. B. and his heirs for ever, in exchange for the lands and premises hereinbefore granted by the said A. B. to the said E. F. and his heirs.

In witness, &c.

Signed, sealed, &c.

DEED OF PARTITION.

THIS INDENTURE, made the   day of   A.D. 18   ,

BETWEEN A. B., of   spinster, one of the two daughters and coheiresses of G. B., of   deceased, of the first part, and E. B., of   spinster, the other of the two daughters and coheiresses of the said G. B. of the second part, and C. D., of   of the third part;

WHEREAS, the said A. B. and E. B. are desirous of making an equal partition of the lands and hereditaments which descended to them upon the decease of their said late father G. B. deceased, as his coheiresses at law, and they have accordingly agreed to divide the same, in the manner hereafter mentioned : Now this Indenture witnesseth, that in consideration of the premises, and for making a perfect partition of all the said hereditaments and premises, and in consideration of the sum of one dollar a piece to them, the said A. B. and E. B. in hand paid, by the said C. D. at or before the sealing and delivery of these presents (the receipt whereof is hereby acknowledged) they the said A. B. and E. B. have, and

each of them hath granted, bargained, sold, released and
confirmed, and by these presents do, and each of them
doth grant, bargain, .sell, release and confirm unto the
said C. D. his heirs and assigns, all that, &c. (*here insert
the whole of the premises*) and all ways, waters, water-
courses, trees, woods, under-woods, commodities, advantage, hereditaments and appurtenances whatsoever, to the
said several parcels or tracts of land, hereditamemts and
premises, or any of them, belonging, or in any wise,ap-
pertaining ; and the reversion and reversions, remainder
and remainders, rents, issues and profits thereof, and of
every part thereof ; and also all the estate, right, title, interest, trust, property claim and demand whatsoever, both
at law and in equity, of them the said A. B. and E. B.,
of, in, to, or out of the said several parcels or tracts of
land, hereditaments and premises, or any of them, or any
part, or parcel thereof.

To HAVE AND TO HOLD the said several parcels, or
tracts of land, hereditaments an·l premises, with their
and every of their appurtenances, unto the said C. D.
his heirs and assigns for ever, to and for the uses hereinafter mentioned and declared, of and concerning the
same respectively, that is to say, as to the said parcel or
tract of land, being lot No.   in the   concession
of the said township of   and hereinbefore more particularly described, with the appurtenances, to the use and
behoof of the said A. B. her heirs and assigns forever ;
and as to the said parcel or tract of land, being lot No.
in the   concession of the said township of
and hereinbefore more particularly described, with the
appurtenances, to the use and behoof of the said E. B.

her heirs and assigns for éver ; and the said A. B. for herself, her heirs, executors and administrators, doth hereby covenant with the said E. B. her heirs and assigns, that she, the said A. B. hath not at any time heretofore done any act whereby the said parcel or tract of land, hereditaments and premises, so limited to the use of her, the said E. B. her heirs and assigns, as aforesaid, is, are, shall, or may be impeached or incumbered in title, charge, estate or otherwise howsoever. (*Add a similar covenant for E. B. with A. B.*)

In witness, &c.

Signed, sealed, &c.

DEED OF PARTITION.

(*Another form.*)

THIS INDENTURE, made, &c., (*here insert the parties.*)

WHEREAS the said A. B. and C. D. now stand seized in fee simple, as tenants in common, of, and in a certain tract or parcel of land, situate in   township aforesaid, adjoining lands of   containing one hundred acres, with the appurtenances : Now this indenture witnesses, that the parties to these presents have agreed to make, and by these presents do make, a full, just, and equal partition and division between them, of and in the aforesaid tract of land, according to their respective shares and interests therein, in manner following ; that is to say, that the said A. B. and his heirs shall have all that piece or allotment of land, part of the said tract, beginning   containing,   together with the messuages, edifices, buildings, and improvements, on the said described piece of land, and all the rights, privileges, and appurtenances whatsoever, thereunto belonging, or in any wise appertaining, and the profits thereof. And the said C. D. does by these presents, for himself and his heirs, give, grant, allot, assign, set over, release, and confirm unto the said A. B. and to his heirs and assigns for ever, the said described piece or allotment of land, with the appurtenances.

To HAVE AND TO HOLD to him the said A. B., his heirs and assigns, to the only proper use and behoof of him the said A. B., his heirs and assigns forever, in severalty, as his and their full part thereof.

And that the said C. D. and his heirs shall have all that piece or allotment of land (residue of the said tract) beginning, &c., containing, &c., together, &c., (*the same as before.*)

And the said C. D., for himself, his heirs, executors, and administrators, does covenant, promise, and grant, to and with the said A. B., his heirs and assigns, by these presents, that he the said A. B., his heirs and assigns, shall or lawfully may, from time to time, and at all times hereafter, forever, freely, peaceably and quietly, have, hold, occupy, possess or enjoy, the said first-described piece or allotment of land, containing, &c., with the appurtenances, and receive and take the rents, issues, and profits thereof, without any molestation, interruption, or denial, of him the said C. D., his heirs or assigns, or of any other or persons whatsoever, lawfully claiming, or to claim by, from, or under him or them, or by or with his or their act, privity, or procurement.   And the said

A. B., for himself, &c. *(Here insert thė same covenant from A. B. to C. D.)*

In witness whereof, &c.

Signed, sealed, &c.

DEED BY CO-HEIRS.

To all to whom these presents shall come :

 of yeoman, eldest son and heir-at-law of late of deceased ; of another of the sons of said deceased; and of and his wife, late daughter of the said deceased, (who are the only heirs of said deceased,) send greeting : Whereas, by Indenture, bearing date the day of A.D. 18 , of and his wife, for the consideration therein mentioned, did grant and confirm unto the said deceased, and to his heirs and assigns for ever, as in and by the said in part recited Indenture, recorded in the Registry Office in and for the said County of relation being there-unto had, more fully and at large appears, a certain messuage or tract and parcel of land, situate in and bounded and described as follows : *(describing the premises.)* Now know ye, that the said and his wife, for and in consideration of the sum of lawful money of Canada, to them in hand paid by of at and before the sealing and delivery hereof, (the receipt whereof they do hereby acknowledge,) have grant-ed, sold, released and confirmed, and by these presents do grant, bargain, sell, release, and confirm unto the said his heirs and assigns, all the above messuage or tract of land, ·situate and bounded and described as aforesaid ;

together with all and singular the buildings improvements, rights, liberties, privileges, hereditaments, and appurtenances whatsoever, thereunto belonging, or in any
wise appertaining, and the reversions and remainders,
rents, issues, and profits thereof ; and also all the estate
right, title interest, property, claim, and demand whatsoever of them, the said   and   and   his wife,
in law or equity, or otherwise howsoever, of in, to, or out
of, the same ; To have and to hold the said messuage or
tract and parcel of land, hereditaments, and premises
hereby granted, or mentioned, or intended so to be, with
the appurtenance, unto the said   heirs and assigns,
to his and their sole use and behoof for ever.

In witness, &c.

Signed, sealed, &c.

DEED OF GIFT OF PERSONAL PROPERTY.

THIS INDENTURE, made the   day of   A.D. 18   ,

BETWEEN A. B., of, &c., of the one part, and C. B., of,
&c., of the other part.

WHEREAS, the said A. B., being the father of the said
C. B., by reason of his age and infirmities, is not capable
of attending to his estate and affairs as formerly, and has
therefore agreed, for advancement of the said C. B., to
make over his property to the said C. B,, so that the said
C. B. should pay the debts of the said A. B., and afford
him a maintenance, as hereinafter mentioned : Now this
indenture witnesseth, that the said A. B., in order to carry
the said agreement into effect, and in consideration of the
natural love and affection which he hath for and towards

his son, the said C. B., and of the provisoes, covenants, and agreements, hereinafter mentioned, by the said C. B., to be observed and performed, hath given, granted, bargained, sold, and assigned, and by· these presents doth give, grant, bargain, sell, and assign, unto the said C. B., his executors, administrators, and assigns, all and singular, his household goods and implements of trade, stock in trade, debts, rights, credits, and personal estate, whereof he is now possessed, or any ways interested in or entitled unto, of what nature or kind soever the same are, or wheresoever or in whosoever hands they be, or may be found, with their and every of their rights, members, and appurtenances.

To HAVE AND TO HOLD, the said goods, household stuff, stock in trade, debts, rights, and personal estate, and other the premises, unto the said C. B., his executors, administrators, and assigns, forever, without rendering any account or being in any wise accountable to the said A. B., his heirs, executors, or administrators, for the same.

And the said C. B., for himself, his heirs, executors, and administrators, doth covenant, promise,· grant, and agree, to and with the said A. B., his executors, administrators, and assigns, in manner and form following, that is to say : that he, the said C. B., his heirs, executors, and administrators, shall and will settle pay, discharge, and satisfy, or cause to be settled, paid, discharged, and satisfied, all accounts, debtes, judgments, and demands, of every nature and kind whatsoever, now outstanding against, or now due from, or payable by, the said A. B., or for the payment of which the said A. B. shall be liable, or be held liable, either at law or in equity, on account of

o

any matter, cause, or thing heretofore had, suffered, done, or performed, and at all times hereafter, free, discharge, and keep harmless, and indemnified, the said A. B., his heirs, executors, and administrators, from all and every such accounts, debts, judgments, and demands, and from all actions, suits, and damages, that may to him or them arise, by reason of the non-payment thereof ; and, moreover, that he, the said C. B., his heirs, executors, and administrators, shall and will, yearly, and every year, during the term of the natural life of the said A. B., by four equal quarterly payments, the first to begin on the day of   next, well and truly pay, or cause to be paid, to the said A. B., or his assigns, the sum of   for, or towards his support or maintenance, and find or provide for him sufficient meat, drink, washing, lodging, apparel, and attendance, suitable to his state and situation, at the choice and election, from time to time, of the said A. B.

PROVIDED ALWAYS, and upon this condition, and it is the true intent and meaning of these presents, that if the said C. B., his heirs, executors, and administrators, shall neglect or refuse to pay the said accounts, debts, judgments, and demands, according to his covenant, aforesaid, or shall suffer the said A. B. to be put to any cost, charge, trouble, or expense, on account of the same, or shall neglect or refuse to pay the said annual sum, in manner aforesaid, or to find and provide for the said A. B., as aforesaid, that then, in all, any or either of the cases aforesaid, it shall and may be lawful to and for the said A. B., all and singular the premises hereby granted to take, repossess, and enjoy, as in his former estate.

In witness, &c.

Signed, sealed, &c.

DEED OF GIFT OF PERSONAL PROPERTY.
(Another form.)

KNOW ALL MEN BY THESE PRESENTS, that I, A. B., of the   of   in the Province of   merchant, for and in consideration of the natural love and affection which I bear unto my daughter C. B., and for her better preferment in marriage, and the increase of her portion ; and also in consideration of the sum of one dollar to me paid by my said daughter C. B., at and before the sealing and delivery hereof (the receipt whereof I do hereby acknowledge), have given, granted, bargained, sold, and by these presents do give, grant, bargain, and sell, unto my said daughter C. B., all the goods and chattels following, to wit, &c., (or, all those goods and chattels mentioned and expressed in the schedule or writing hereunto annexed.)

To have and to hold, all and singular, the premises hereby given and granted unto the said C. B., my daughter, her executors and administrators forever, as her and their own proper goods and chattels.

In witness whereof I have hereunto set my hand and seal this   day of   18 .

Witness,

DEED OF GIFT OF LANDS.

THIS INDENTURE, made the   day of   A.D. 18 ,
BETWEEN A. B., of the township of   in the county of   yeoman, of the one part, and C. D. (eldest son and heir apparent of 'the said A. B.) of the other part,

WITNESSETH, that the said A. B., as well for and in consideration of the natural love and affection which he hath and beareth unto the said C. D., as also for the better maintenance, support, livelihood, and preferment of him the said C. D., hath given, granted, aliened, enfeoffed and confirmed, and by these presents doth give, grant, alien, enfeoff and confirm unto the said C. D., his heirs and assigns, all that parcel or tract of land, &c., *(describing the premises,)* together with all and singular, houses, out-houses, edifices, buildings, barns, stables, courts, curtilages, gardens, orchards, woods, underwoods, ways, waters, water-courses, advantages and appurtenances, whatsoever, to the said parcel or tract of land and premises belonging, or in anywise appertaining, and the reversion and reversions, remainder and remainders, rents, issues and profits of the same, and all the estate, right, title, interest, property, claim and demand whatsoever, of him the said A. B., of, in and to the said parcel or tract of land and pre-premises, and of, in and to every part and parcel thereof, with their and every of their appurtenances, and all deeds, evidences and writings, concerning the said premises. To have and to hold the said parcel and tract of land, and all and singular other the premises hereby granted and confirmed unto and to the only proper use and behoof of the said C. D. his heirs and assigns for ever. *(Add covenant against incumbrances and otherwise as the donor pleases.)*

In witness whereof, &c.

Signed, sealed, &c.

DEED POLL BY EXECUTORS.

To ALL PERSONS TO WHOM THESE PRESENTS SHALL COME, we,   and   both of, &c., executors of the last will and testament of   late of, &c., deceased, send greeting.

WHEREAS the said   in order to enable his said executors fully to carry into effect his intentions, did, in and by his last will and testament, authorize and empower his said executors, in any manner which they should deem proper, to make sale of, and execute and deliver deeds to convey, all his the said testator's real estate ;—

NOW THEREFORE KNOW YE, that, by virtue and authority to us given by said   in his last will and testament, we, the said   and   executors as aforesaid, in consideration of the sum of   to us paid by   of, &c., (the receipt whereof is hereby acknowledged,) have given, granted, bargained, sold, and conveyed, and by these presents   do give, grant, bargain, sell, and convey, unto the said   his heirs and assigns, the following described parcel of real estate, which was the property of the said   situated in   and bounded and described as follows, to wit, &c.

To HAVE AND TO HOLD the afore-granted premises to him the said   his heirs and assigns, to his and their use and behoof forever. And we the said A. B. and C. D., do covenant with the said   his heirs and assigns, that we are lawfully the executors of the last will and testament of said   and that we have not made or suffered any incumbrance on the hereby-granted premises, since we were appointed executors of said   and that we have in all respects acted, in making this conveyance, in pursuance of the authority granted to us in and by the said last will and testament of the said

In testimony whereof, &c.

Signed, sealed, &c.

DEED OF CONFIRMATION.

THIS INDENTURE, made the   day of   A.D. 18 .

BETWEEN C. D., of, &c., a son, and one of the heirs of E. D., deceased, of the one part, and A. B., of, &c., of the other part.

WHEREAS, by a certain deed of bargain and sale, bearing date on or about, &c., and made between E. F. and the said C. D., of the one part, and the said A. B., of the other part, for the consideration of   the several messuages or tenements therein mentioned, and hereinafter intended to be released and confirmed, are thereby granted and conveyed, or intended so to be, unto and to the use of the said A. B., his heirs and assigns forever, as by the said indenture of bargain and sale, relation being thereunto had, may more fully appear : And whereas, the said C. D., at the time of the date and making the said in part recited Indenture of bargain and sale, was not of the age of twenty-one years, but hath since attained to such his age of twenty-one years, and hath this day   before the execution of these presents, duly sealed and delivered the said in part recited Indenture of bargain and sale.

NOW THIS INDENTURE WITNESSETH, that as well in performance of a covenant for further assurance in the said Indenture of bargain and sale contained, as also for and

in consideration of the sum of   to him the said C.
D. in hand paid by the said A. B., at and before the ensealing, &c., being his full part and share of, and in the
before mentioned sum of   agreed to be paid for the
purchase of the said messuage, tenements, and hereditaments, the receipt whereof he the said C. D. doth hereby
acknowledge, he the said C. D. hath remised, released,
aliened, and quit-claimed, and by these presents doth remise, release, alien, and for ever quit-claim, and confirm
unto the said A. B., in his actual possession now being
by virtue of the before mentioned Indenture of bargain
and sale, and to his heirs and assigns, all, &c.

To HAVE AND TO HOLD unto and to the use of the said
A. B., his heirs and assigns forever. *(Insert a covenant
that he has done no act to encumber, except, &c., and for
further assurance, &c.)*

In witness, &c.

Signed, sealed, &c.

DEED OF TRUST FOR MARRIED WOMAN.

THIS INDENTURE, made the   day of   A.D. 18 ,
BETWEEN   of   of the one part, and   of
the other part :

WITNESSETH, that the said   for and in consideration of the sum of   to him in hand paid by the said
    for the uses and upon the trusts hereinafter men-
tioned, at and before the ensealing and delivery hereof,
the receipt whereof he does hereby acknowledge, has
granted, bargained, sold, aliened, enfeoffed, released and
confirmed, and by these presents doth grant, bargain, sell,

alien, enfeoff, release and confirm unto the said   his heirs and assigns forever, all that certain piece or parcel of land, situate, &c, (describe the premises); together with all and singular the buildings and improvements to the same belonging, or in any wise appertaining, and reversions and remainders, rents, issues and profits thereof :

To HAVE AND TO HOLD, the said piece or parcel of land, with the appurtenances, hereby granted, or intended so to be, unto the said   his heirs and assigns forever : In trust, nevertheless, and for the uses following, and, none other, that is to say, for the sole and separate use of the wife of   of   for and during her natural life, and so as she alone, or such person as she shall appoint, shall take and receive the rents, issues and profits thereof, and so as her said husband shall not in any wise intermeddle therewith ; and, from and after the decease of the said   in trust for the use of the heirs of the body of the said   by the said   begotten, or to be begotten, forever ; with power to the said   to sell and convey, in fee simple, the whole or any part of the aforesaid premises and appurtenances, to any person or persons, and for such sum or sums of money as the said   by writing under her hand and seal, and duly executed at any time during her natural life may appoint and direct : And the said   for himself, his heirs executors and administrators, doth covenant and agree to and with the said · his heirs and assigns, by these presents, that he the said   and his heirs, the said above-mentioned and described piece or parcel of land, with the appurtenances, unto the said   his heirs and assigns, against him, the said   and his heirs, and against all and every other person and persons whomsoever, lawfully claiming or to claim the same, or any part thereof (if a special warranty is desired, add here, "by, from, or under him, them or any of them"), shall and will warrant and forever defend by these presents.

In witness, &c.

Signed, sealed, &c.

_____

DECLARATION OF TRUST OF PURCHASE MONEY.

—

To all to whom, &c. : I, A. B., &c. [*as described in the purchase deed*,] send greeting.

WHEREAS, by indenture of, &c., bearing date, &c., made between C. D., of, &c., [*as described in the deed*,] of the one part, and me the said A. B., of the other part; he the said C. D., for and in consideration of   therein mentioned, to be paid to him by me the said A. B., has granted, and did grant, &c., all that, &c., to hold the same to me the said A. B., my, &c., for, &c., which said premises were heretofore the estate of *or* in the possession of   of   : Now, know ye, that I, the said A. B., do hereby acknowledge, testify, and declare, that the sum of   above mentioned to be paid to the said C. D. by me the said A. B., as aforesaid, was and is the proper money of E. F., of, &c. ; and that the name of me the said A. B., in the said indenture, of, &c., is used only in trust for him the said E. F., his, &c. ; and that I and my heirs, &c., shall, at all times hereafter, upon the request, and at the cost and charge of the said E. F., convey and assure unto him the said E. F., his, &c., by a good quit-claim deed, warranting against all claiming under me, the said premises so bargained and sold to me by the said C. D., and all the interest therein that he so conveyed to me.

In witness, &c., this   day of   A.D. 18 .

Signed, sealed, &c.

DECLARATION OF TRUST OF A BOND.

WHEREAS, in and by an obligation bearing even date with these presents. C. D., of, &c., stands bound and obliged to me, A. B., of, &c., in the sum of one thousand dollars, conditioned for the payment of five hundred dollars, with interest, in one year from the date hereof, as in and by said obligation appears : Now, know all men by these presents, that I, the said A. B., do hereby acknowledge and declare, that the said sum of five hundred dollars, loaned upon said obligation, was the proper money of E. F., of, &c., and not of me the said A. B. ; and that the name of me, the said A. B., was used and and inserted as obligee in said obligation, only as trustee, and in trust and for the use and benefit of him the said E. F. [*A power of attorney may be inserted from A. B. to E. F. to receive the money, and a covenant that A. B. will not discharge the bond, or do anything to prevent E. F. from receiving the amount.*]

In witness, &c., this   day of   A.D. 18 .

Signed, sealed, &c.

DECLARATION OF TRUST OF STOCK.

MEMORANDUM. I, A. B., of, &c., do hereby acknowledge and declare, that I am possessed of   shares in the cap-

ital stock of   Company, numbered from   to   inclusive, and that the same were transferred to me in trust
for the only use, benefit, and advantage of   of, &c.,
and his legal represectatives ; and that the same stock was
purchased with money which belonged solely to said
and that the certificate of said shares of said stock were
taken in the name of me the said A. B. from motives of
temporary convenience ; and that the said stock and all
dividends and advantages accruing thereon, are and shall
be held by me and my legal representatives only for the
convenience, use, benefit and advantage of him the said
        and his legal representatives ; and on demand from
him or them I will, and my legal representatives shall,
assign the same to him or them, and account to and pay
over to him or them all dividends and profits that shall
by me or them have been received thereon.

In witness whereof, &c. this   day of   A.D. 18   ,
Signed, sealed, &c.

DISTRESS WARRANT.

To   , my bailiff,   Greeting.

DISTRAIN the goods and Chattels of   the tenant in
the house   he now dwells in or upon the premises in h
possession situated   for the sum of   being the
amount of   rent due to me on the same, on the
day of   18 . , and for your so doing this shall be
your sufficient warrant and authority.

Dated the   day of .   A.D. 18   .

UNDERTAKING TO DELIVER GOODS.

We, the undersigned, acknowledge to have received from   bailiff, the following property, seized under and by virtue of a   for   against the goods and chattels of   at the instance of   which said property we undertake to deliver to him, the said bailiff, whenever demanded, in as good a condition as they now are.

Witness our hands the   day of   18 .

Witness:

APPRAISEMENT.

Memorandum, that on the   day of   in the year of our Lord 18   ,   of   sworn appraisers, were sworn upon the Holy Evangelists, by me   of   well and truly to appraise the goods and chattels mentioned in the Inventory, according to the best of your judgment.

Present at the time of swearing }
　　the said   , as above, }
　　and witness thereto.   }   *Constable.*

I, the above named   being sworn upon the Holy Evangelists, by   the Constable above named, well and truly to appraise the goods and chattels mentioned in this Inventory, according to the best of my judgment, and having viewed the said goods and chattels, do appraise the same at the sum of

As witness my hand the   day of   18 .

APPRAISEMENT.
(Another form.)

WE, the above named   and   being duly sworn on the Holy Evangelists by   constable, above named, well and truly to appraise the goods and chattels mentioned in this inventory according to the best of our ability, and having viewed the said goods and chattels, do appraise and value the same at the sum of

As witness our hands this   day of   18 .

TENANT'S CONSENT TO LANDLORD CONTINU-ING IN POSSESSION.

To A. B.

I desire you to keep possession of the goods and chattels which on the   day of   A.D. 18 , you distrained for rent due from me to you in the places where they are now lying for the space of   days from the date hereof, on your undertaking to delay the sale for that time to enable me to defray the rent and charges, and I will pay the man for keeping possession.

Dated the   day of   A.D. 18 .

OATH TO BE ADMINISTERED TO APPRAISERS BY CONSTABLE.

You, and each of you shall well and truly appraise the goods and chattels mentioned in this inventory, according to the best of your judgment. So help you God.

MEMORANDUM TO BE INDORSED ON THE INVENTORY.

—

MEMORANDUM : That on the   day of   in the year
of our Lord 18 ,   of   , and   of   , were
sworn on the Holy Evangelists by me,   of   ,
constable, truly to appraise the goods and chattels mentioned in this inventory, according to the best of their
judgment.   As witness my hand.

Constable.

Present at the swearing of the
    said . and   as above, and
    witness thereto.

INVENTORY.

—

AN INVENTORY of the several goods and chattels distrained by me   the   day of   in the year 18
in the house, outhouses and lands of   situate
by authority and on behalf of   your landlord, for
the sum of   being   rent due to the said
on the   day of   18 .

In the dwelling-house :

On the premises :

Mr.   Take notice, that as the bailiff to
your landlord, I have this day distrained on the premises
above mentioned the several goods and chattels specified
in the above inventory, for the sum of   being
rent due to the said   the   day of   18   for
the said premises ; and that unless you pay the said rent,
with the charges of distraining for the same, or replevy

within five days from the date hereof, the said goods and chattels will be appraised and sold according to law.

Given under my hand, the   day of   A.D. 18 .
Witness:

***

BAILIFF'S SALE.

NOTICE IS HEREBY GIVEN, that the cattle, goods, and chattels, distrained for rent on the   day of   18 , by me   as bailiff to   the landlord of the premises of   the tenant, will be sold by public auction, on the   day of   18 , at   o'clock, which cattle, goods and chattels are as follows, that is to say :

Toronto,   day of   18 .

***

GRANT OF ANNUITY.

THIS INDENTURE, made the   day of   A.D. 18 , BETWEEN A. B., of   of the one part, and C. D., of   of the other part.

WITNESSETH, that the said A. B., for, and in consideration of the sum of   to him in hand well and truly paid, by the said C. D., at or before the sealing and delivery of these presents, (the receipt whereof the said A. B. doth hereby acknowledge,) hath given, granted, and confirmed, and by these presents doth give, grant, and confirm unto the said C. D. and his assigns, one annuity of   to be received, taken, had, and to be issuing out of, all that messuage, &c., with all and singular the appurtenances thereunto belonging, and every part and parcel thereof, unto the said C. D. and his assigns, for, and during the natural life of him, the said C. D., payable, and to be paid at and upon   yearly, by even and equal portions; the first payment to begin and be made at or upon   . And if it shall happen that the said annuity of   or any part thereof, be behind or unpaid, in part or in all, by the space of twenty-one days next after either of the said days or times of payment thereof, whereupon the same should or ought to be paid, as aforesaid: that then, and so often, at any time thereafter, it shall and may be lawful to, and for the said C. D., and his assigns, into, and upon the said messuage and premises above mentioned, or any part thereof, to enter and distrain, and the distress and distresses then and there found, to take, lead, drive, carry away, and impound, and the same impound to take, hold and keep, until the said annuity and the arrears thereof, (if any there shall be,) together with all costs and charges thereabout, or concerning the same, shall be fully paid and satisfied. And the said A. B., for himself, his heirs, executors, and administrators, doth covenant, grant, and agree, to and with the said C. D., his executors, administrators, and assigns, that he, the said A. B., his heirs, executors, or administrators, shall and will, well and truly pay, or cause to be paid unto the said C. D., his executors, administrators, or assigns, the said annuity, or yearly rent-charge, &c., at the days and times, and in the manner and form, as above expressed, and limited for payment thereof, according to the true intent and meaning of these presents. And also that the said messuage, &c., above-mentioned, to be charged and chargeable with the said annuity hereby granted, shall, from time to time, be, and continue, over and sufficient for the payment of the said annuity of   yearly, during the life of the said C. D.

    In witness, &c.

    Signed, sealed, &c.

ANNUITY BOND.

KNOW ALL MEN BY THESE PRESENTS, that I, A. B., of, &c., am held and firmly bound unto C. D., of, &c., in the penal sum of   of lawful money of Canada, to be paid to the said C. D. or to   certain attorney, executors, administrators or assigns. For which payment, well and truly to be made,   bind   heirs, executors, and administrators, forever, firmly by these presents. Sealed with   seal. Dated this   day of   A.D. 18 .

WHEREAS the above bound A. B., on the day of the date of the above written obligation, has had and received to his own use, of and from the above named C. D., the sum of   (the receipt whereof is hereby acknowledged) in consideration whereof the said A. B. has agreed to pay the said C. D. an annuity or clear yearly sum of   for and during his natural life, to be paid in the manner hereinafter mentioned; Now, the condition of this obligation is such, that if the above bound A. B., his heirs, executors and administrators, or any of them, do and shall yearly, and every year during the natural life of the said C. D., well and truly pay or cause to be paid to him the said C. D., or his assigns, the clear yearly sum of   in half-yearly payments of   each, payable on the   days of each and every   in each and every year which shall occur during the natural life of the said C. D., then this

P

obligation shall be void; but if default be made in any of
said half-yearly payments, or any part of them, then the
same shall remain and be in full force and virtue.

Signed, sealed, &c.

GROUND RENT DEED.

THIS INDENTURE, made the   day of   A.D. 18   ,
BETWEEN   of   and   his wife, of the one part,
and   of the same place, of the other part :

WITNESSETH, that the said   and   his wife, as
well for and in consideration of the sum of one dollar,
lawful money of Canada, unto them, at or before the
sealing and delivery hereof, by the said   ,   well and
truly paid, the receipt whereof is hereby acknowledged,
as of the payment of the yearly rent and taxes, and performance of the covenants and agreements hereinafter
mentioned, which, on the part of the said   his heirs
and assigns, is and are to be paid and performed, have
granted, bargained, sold, aliened, enfeoffed, released, and
confirmed, and by these presents do grant, bargain, sell,
alien, enfeoff, release, and confirm, unto the said   his
heirs and assigns, all that certain lot or piece of ground,
situate and being [*describing the premises*], together with
all and singular the improvements, ways, streets, water-
courses, rights, privileges, hereditaments, and appurtenances whatsoever, unto the same belonging, or in anywise
appertaining, and the reversion and reversions thereof.

To HAVE AND TO HOLD, the above-described lot or piece
of ground, with the appurtenances unto the said   his
heirs and assigns, to his and their sole use and behoof

forever. Yielding and paying therefor and thereunto, unto the said   his heirs and assigns, the yearly rent or
sum of   lawful money of Canada, in half-yearly payments, on the first day of the months of July and January, in each and every year hereafter, forever, without
any reduction or abatement whatever, for, or by reason
of, any charges, taxes, or assessments whatsoever, to be
assessed on the said lot hereby granted, or on the said
yearly rent hereby, therefrom and thereout reserved and
made payable; the first half-yearly payment to be made
on the first day of July, in the year of our Lord one
thousand eight hundred and   And upon default of
paying the said yearly rent on the days and times and in
the manner aforesaid, it shall and may be lawful for the
said   his heirs and assigns, to enter into and upon the
said hereby granted premises, or any part or parcel thereof, and into the buildings thereon to be erected, and
to distrain for such yearly rent so then in arrear and unpaid, and to proceed with and sell such distrained goods
and effects according to the usual course of distresses for
rent-charges. But, if sufficient distress for the purposes
afore-named and the payment of the charges attendant
upon such levy cannot be found upon the said premises,
it shall and may be lawful for the said   his heirs and
assigns, wholly to re-enter upon the said lot and all its
improvements, and the same to have again, repossess and
enjoy, as fully and completely as though this indenture
had never been executed.

    And the said   for himself, his heirs, executors, ad-
ministrators, and assigns, doth covenant, promise, and
agree to and with the said   his heirs and assigns, by

these presents, that he, the said   the said yearly rent
or sum of   lawful money as aforesaid, shall and will
well and truly pay or cause to be paid, on the days and
times hereinbefore mentioned and appointed for such
payment, without any deduction or abatement for or by
reason of any charges, taxes, or assessments whatsoever;
it being the express agreement of the parties hereto, that
the said   ·   his heirs and assigns, shall pay all taxes
whatsoever that shall hereafter be laid or assessed, by
virtue of any law whatsoever, upon the herein granted
lot or the buildings thereon to be there erected, or the
said yearly rent charged thereon, or upon either or all of,
them ; also that he, the said   his heirs or assigns,
shall and will, within one year from the date hereof, erect
and build on the said hereby granted lot, a good and sub-
stantial brick or stone building, of sufficient value to secure the said yearly rent hereby reserved.

PROVIDED ALWAYS, nevertheless, that if the said
his heirs or assigns, shall and do, at any time hereafter,
pay, or cause to be paid, unto the said   his heirs or
assigns, the sum of   lawful money as aforesaid, and
all arrearages of the said yearly rent to the time of such
payment, then the same shall forever thereafter cease and
be extinguished, and the covenant for payment thereof
shall become void : and then he, the said   his heirs or
assigns, shall and will, at the proper costs and charges in
law of the said grantor, his heirs and assigns, seal and
execute a sufficient release and discharge of the said hereby reserved yearly rent, to the said   his heirs and
assigns, forever, anything hereinbefore to the contrary
contained notwithstanding. And the said   for him-

self, his heirs, executors and administrators, doth covenant, promise and agree, to and with the said   his
heirs and assigns, by these presents, that he the said
his heirs and assigns, paying the said rearly rent, or ex-
tinguishing the same, together with the taxes, and performing the covenants and agreements aforesaid, shall
and may, at all times hereafter forever, freely, peaceably,
and quietly have, hold and enjoy, all and singular the
premises hereby granted, with the appurtenances, and
take and receive the rents and profits thereof, without
any molestation, interruption, or eviction, of the said
his heirs, or any other person or persons whomsoever,
lawfully claiming, or to claim, by, from, or under, him,
them, or any of them.

In witness, &c.

Signed, sealed, &c.

GUARANTEES.

GUARANTEE FOR A CERTAIN AMOUNT.

To Messrs.   ,—If you will supply   with
such goods as he may require, I hereby guarantee that
you shall be paid for them to the extent of $. But
this is not to be a continuing guarantee.   Dated the
day of   A.D. 18 .

CONTINUING GUARANTEE.

To Messrs.   ,—If you will supply   with
such goods as he may require from time to time, I hereby
guarantee that you shall be paid for them to the extent
of $.   This guarantee is to continue for
Dated the   day of   A.D. 18 .

GUARANTEE FOR FIDELITY OF CLERK.

To Messrs.   ,—In consideration of your taking into your employ as clerk, and so continuing him, subject to three months' notice on either side, I guarantee that he shall faithfully serve you, and truly account to you for all property, writings, and securities belonging to you, or to any one on your behalf, or to any one to whom you are accountable, and shall take due care of all such property while in his possession. This guarantee is made to your firm, including any future partners, and is to continue as long as   is in the employ of such firm, but subject to a determination by six calendar months' notice in writing on my part. Dated the day of   A.D. 18 .

LEASE OF HOUSE.

THIS INDENTURE, made the   day of   A.D. 18 ,
BETWEEN
WITNESSETH, that in consideration of the rents, covenants and agreements hereinafter reserved and contained on the part of the said part   of the second part, executors, administrators and assigns, to be paid, observed and performed   the said part of the first part ha demised and leased, and by these presents do   demise and lease unto the said part   of the second part,   executors, administrators and assigns, all that messuage or tenement situate, lying and being   together with all houses, outhouses, yards and other appurtenances thereto belonging or usually known as part or parcel thereof, or as belonging thereto :

To have and to hold the said messuage or tenement and premises unto the said part   of the second part   executors, administrators and assigns, for and during the term of   to be computed from the   day of   one thousand eight hundred and   and from thenceforth next ensuing, and fully to be complete and ended : yielding and paying therefor yearly and every year during the said term hereby granted, unto the said part   of the first part,   heirs, executors, administrators or assigns, the sum of   to be payable   on the following days and times, that is to say :

The first of such payments to become due and be made on the   day of   next, and the last of such payments to be made in advance, on the   day of   preceding the expiration of the said term

PROVIDED ALWAYS, and these presents are upon this express condition, that if the said yearly rent hereby reserved or any part thereof, shall at any time remain unpaid for the space of twenty-one days, next over or after any of the days on which the same shall become due and payable, or if a breach or default shall be made in any of the covenants hereinafter contained by the said part   of the second part,   executors, administrators or assigns, then and in every such case it shall be lawful for the said part   of the first part,   heirs, executors, administrators or assigns, into and upon the said premises or any part thereof in the name of the whole, to re-enter, and the same to have again, re-possess and enjoy, as if these presents had never been executed : And the said part   of the second part, for   heirs, executors, administrators or assigns, do   hereby covenant promise, and agree

to and with the said part   of the first part,   heirs,
executors, administrators and assigns; that   the said
part   of the second part,   executors, administrators
and assigns, shall and will well and truly pay or cause to
be paid to the said part   of the first part,   heirs,
executors, administrators or assigns, the said yearly rent
hereby reserved, at the times and in the manner hereinbefore appointed for the payment thereof : And also, shall
and will, from time to time, and at all times during the
said term, keep in good and sufficient repair the said premises hereby demised, reasonable wear and tear and accidents by fire and tempest excepted : And the same, so
kept in repair, shall and will at the end, expiration or
other sooner termination of the said term, peaceably and
quietly yield and deliver up to the said part   of the first
part,   heirs, executors, administrators or assigns ; And
also shall and will well and truly pay or cause to
be paid all taxes, rates, levies, duties, charges, assessments and impositions whatsoever, whether parliamentary, local or otherwise, which now are or which during
the continuance of this demise shall at any time be rated,
taxed or imposed on or in respect of the said demised
premises, or any part thereof ; And also, that it shall be
lawful for the said part   of the first part,   heirs, executors, administrators and assigns, and their agents respectively, either alone or with workmen or others, from
time to time, at all reasonable times in the daytime during the said term, to enter upon the' said demised premises, and every part thereof, to view and examine the
state and condition thereof, and in case any want of reparation, or amendment be found on any such examina-

tion,   the said part   of the second part,
executors, administrators or assigns, shall and will from
time to time cause the same to be well and sufficiently
repaired, amended and made good within one month next
after notice in writing shall have been given to   or
left at or upon the said hereby demised premises for that
purpose ; And if the said part   of the second part,
executors, administrators or assigns, shall fail in making
the necessary repairs in manner hereinbefore described,
that it shall be lawful for the said part   of the second
part,   heirs, executors, administrators and assigns, and
          agents, to enter into and upon the said hereby de-
mised premises, and have the same repaired in a proper
manner, and to render the account for such repairs to the
said part   of the second part,   executors, administrators and assigns, and demand payment for the same, and
if default is made, to sue for the same in any court of
law, having jurisdiction over the same :

And the said part   of the second part,   executors, administrators or assigns, shall not nor will at any
time or times during the continuance of this demise,
sell, assign, let or otherwise part with this present lease,
or the said premises hereby demised, or any part thereof,
to any person or persons whomsoever, for the whole or
any part of the said term, nor alter, change or remove
any part of the said premises, yards or offices, externally
or internally, without the license or consent in writing
of the said part   of the first part,   heirs, executors,
administrators or assigns, from time to time first had and
obtained :

And the said part   of the first part, for   heirs, executors, administrators and assigns: covenant with the said part   of the second part,   executors, administrators and assigns, that   the said part   of the second part,   executors, administrators and assigns, well and truly paying the rent hereinbefore reserved, and observing, performing and keeping all the covenants hereinbefore contained, shall and may from time to time, and at all times during the said term, peaceably and-quietly enjoy the said premises hereby demised, without molestation or hindrance:

And if the term hereby demised shall at any time be seized or taken in execution, or in attachment by any creditor of the party of the second part, or if the said party of the second part shall make any assignment for the benefit of creditors, or being bankrupt or insolvent shall take the benefit of any act in force for bankrupt or insolvent debtors, the then current   rent shall immediately become due and payable, and said term shall immediately become forfeited and void, but the next current   rent shall nevertheless be at once due and payable.

In witness whereof, &c.

Signed, sealed, &c.

SHORT HOUSE LEASE.

THIS INDENTURE, made the   day of   A.D. 18   , in pursuance of the act respecting short forms of leases,

BETWEEN   hereinafter called the Lessor   of the first part and   hereinafter called the Lessee   of the second part,

WITNESSETH, that in consideration of the· rents, covenants, and agreements hereinafter reserved and contained
on the part of the said Lessee   executors, administrators and assigns, to be paid, observed, and performed, he
the said Lessor ha   demised and leased, and by these
presents do   demise and lease unto the said Lessee
executors, administrators, and assigns, all th   certain
        . together with all the rights, members and ap-
purtenances whatsoever to the said premises belonging
or appertaining.

To HAVE AND TO HOLD, the said demised premises, with
their appurtenances, unto the said lessee   executors,
administrators and assigns for and during the term of
        to be computed from the   day of   one
thousand eight hundred and   and from thenceforth
next ensuing, and fully to be completed and ended, yielding and paying therefor yearly and every year, during
the said term hereby granted unto the said lessor
heirs, executors, administrators or assigns, the sum of
        dollars of lawful money of Canada, to be payable on
the following days and times, that is to say :   on the
        days of   and   in each year during the
said term, the first of such payments to become due and
be made on the   day of   next, and the last of
such payments to be made in advance, on the day of payment of rent, next preceding the expiration of the said
term.

And the said lessee covenant   with the said lessor to
pay rent: and to pay taxes : and to repair (reasonable
wear and tear, and accidents by fire or tempest excepted):
and to 'keep up fences, and not to cut down timber : and

that the said lessor may enter and view the state of repair, and that the said lessee will repair according to notice, and will not assign or sub-let without leave : and will not carry on any business that shall be deemed a nuisance on said premises : and that he will leave the premises in good repair :

And also that if the term hereby granted shall be at any time seized, or taken in execution, or in attachment, by any creditor of the said lessee, or if the said lessee shall make any assignment for the benefit of creditors, or becoming bankrupt or insolvent, shall take the benefit of any act that may be in force for bankrupt or insolvent debtors, the said term shall immediately become forfeited and void, and the full amount of the current rent shall be at once due and payable : and also, that if the said premises be destroyed, or so much injured as to become unfit for occupation by fire or other casuality not caused by the wilful default or neglect of the said lessee, executors, administrators or assigns, the said term hereby demised shall cease, and the current rent shall be duly apportioned and the due proportionate part thereof shall be at once due and payable.

Proviso for re-entry by the said lessor on non-payment of rent or non-performance of covenants, or seizure or forfeiture of the said term for any of the causes aforesaid, the said lessor covenant with the said lessee for quiet enjoyment.

In witness whereof, &c.

Signed, sealed, &c.

FARM LEASE.

THIS INDENTURE, made the   day of   A.D. 18   ,
BETWEEN   (hereinafter called the lessor   ) of
the first part; and   ·   (hereinafter called the lessee   )
of the second part ;

WITNESSETH, that for and in consideration of the yearly
rent, covenants, and conditions hereinafter reserved and
contained,   he   the said lessor   do   demise, lease, and
to farm let, unto the said lessee   executors, administrators and assigns, all that certain parcel or tract of land,
situate, lying and being in the   together with
all erections and buildings, barns, stables, and other out-
houses thereupon erected, standing and being, or hereafter
during the said term to be erected, standing and being,
and together also with all ways, paths, passages, waters,
watercourses, privileges, advantages and appurtenances
whatsoever to the same premises belonging, or in anywise
appertaining.

 To HAVE AND TO HOLD the same unto the said lessee
        executors, administrators and assigns, for the term
of   to be computed from the   day of   in the
year of our Lord one thousand eight hundred and
yielding and paying therefor yearly and every year during the said term unto the said lessor   the clear yearly
rent or sum of   of lawful money of Canada, on
the   day of the month of   in each and every
year during the said term, without any deduction, defalcation or abatement thereout on any account whatsoever, the first of such payments to become due and
to be made on the

And the said lessee   do   hereby for   heirs, executors, administrators and assigns, covenant promise
and agree to and with the said lessor,   heirs, and
assigns in manner following, that is to say: That
            the said lessee   executors, administrators,
or assigns, or some or one of them, shall and will well
and truly pay, or cause to be paid, unto the said lessor
   .   heirs, or assigns, the said yearly rent of
on the days and times, and in manner hereinbefore
mentioned and appointed for payment thereof, without
any deduction or abatement thereout on any account
whatsoever.   And also shall and will from time to time,
and at all times during the said term, well and truly
pay or cause to be paid, all taxes, rates, levies, duties,
charges, assessments, and impositions whatsoever, whether
parliamentary, municipal, or otherwise, which now are,
or which during the continuance of the said term hereby
demised, shall at any time be rated, charged, assessed or
imposed on said premises, or any part thereof.

And that the said lessee   will during the said term,
cultivate, till, manure and employ such part of the said
demised premises as is now, or shall hereafter be brought
under cultivation, in a good husband-like and proper
manner, so as not to impoverish or injure the soil, and
plough said land in each year during said term
inches deep, and at the end of said term will leave the
said land so manured as aforesaid.   And will crop the same
during the said term by a regular rotation of crops in a
proper farmer-like manner, so as not to impoverish or
injure the soil of the said land, and will use his best and
earnest endeavours to rid said land of all docks, wild

mustard, red roots, Canada thistles, and other noxious weeds. And will preserve all orchard and fruit-trees (if any) on the said premises, from waste, damage, or destruction ; And will spend, use, and employ, in a husband-like manner, upon the said premises, all the straw and dung which shall grow, arise, renew, or be made thereupon ; And will allow any incoming tenant to plough the said land after harvest in the last year of the said term, and to have stabling for two horses and bed room for one man. And will leave at least ten acres seeded down with timothy and clover seed.

And shall not nor will during the said term cut any standing timber upon the said lands, except for rails or for buildings upon the said demised premises, or for firewood upon the premises, and shall not allow any timber to be removed from off the said premises ; And also shall and will, at the costs and charges of the said lessee well and sufficiently repair and keep repaired the erections and buildings, fences and gates erected or to be erected upon the said premises.

And also shall and will at the expiration or other sooner determination of this lease, peaceably and quietly leave surrender and yield up unto the said lessor heirs or assigns the said premises hereby demised, in such good and sufficient repair as aforesaid (reasonable use and wear thereof, and damage by fire or tempest only excepted) ;

And also that it shall be lawful for the said lessor, heirs and assigns, twice or oftener in every year during the said term, to enter upon the said demised premises, to view the state and condition of the same, and that the said lessee   · executors, administrators or assigns, will repair the same according to notice ;

And also shall not nor will, at any time during the said term, assign transfer or sublet the said premises hereby demised without the license and consent of the said lessor   heirs or assigns, in writing, for that purpose first had and obtained ;

PROVIDED ALWAYS that if the said yearly rent hereby reserved, or any part thereof, shall be in arrear for twenty-one days after any one of the days appointed for payment thereof as aforesaid, whether the same shall be lawfully demanded or not : or if the said lessee,   . executors, administrators or assigns, shall assign or sublet the said premises without such license as aforesaid ; or in case of breach of any of the covenants herein contained, then, and in any of the said cases, it shall be lawful for the said lessor,   heirs, or assigns, into or upon the said premises, or any part thereof, in the name of the whole, to re-enter, and the same to have again, repossess and enjoy as in his and their first and former estate, and the said lessee,   executors, administrators and assigns, and all persons claiming under   thereout to expel, put out and remove, anything hereinbefore contained to the contrary notwithstanding ;

And the said lessor   do   hereby for   heirs and assigns, covenant, promise and agree to and with the said lessee,   executors, administrators and assigns, that he and they paying the said rent, and performing the covenants herein contained on   and their parts, shall and may peaceably and quietly enjoy the said premises during the said term, without any molestation, hindrance or disturbance of, from or by the said lessor   heirs and assigns, or any other person claiming under him or them

And also, that if the term hereby granted shall be at any time seized or taken in execution or in attachment by any creditor of the said lessee   or if the said lessee shall make any assignment for the benefit of creditors, or becoming bankrupt or insolvent shall take the benefit of any act that may be in force for bankrupt or insolvent debtors, the then current   rent shall immediately become due and payable, and the said term shall immediately become forfeited and void, but the next current   rent, shall, nevertheless, be at once due and payable.

In witness, &c.

Signed, sealed, &c,

LEASE OF LAND.

THIS INDENTURE made the   day of   A.D. 18 ,

BETWEEN   of the first part, and   of the second part,

WITNESSETH, that in consideration of the rent, covenants, and agreements hereinafter reserved, and contained, and to be paid, observed, and performed by the said part   of the second part,   executors, administrators, and assigns,   the said part   of the first part ha demised and leased, and by these presents do   demise and lease unto the said part   of the second part, executors, administrators, and assigns, all th   certain

Q

parcel   or tract of land and premises, situate, lying, and being

To HAVE AND TO HOLD the said parcel   or tract   of land, with the appurtenances, unto the said part   of the second part,   executors, administrators, and as- signs, from the   day of   one thousand eight hundred and   for the term of   from thence next ensuing, and fully to be complete and ended, yield- ing and paying therefor, unto the said part   of the first part,   executors, administrators, and assigns, the yearly rent or sum of   of lawful money of Canada, by equal   instalments on the   days of the months of   in each and every year during the said term, the first payment to be made on the   day of   next ensuing the date hereof.

And the said part   of the second part do   hereby for ·   heirs, executors, administrators and assigns, covenant, promise and agree with and to the said part of the first part,   heirs, executors, administrators and assigns, that   the said part of the second part,   executors, administrators and assigns, shall and will well and truly pay, or cause to be paid, to the said part   of the first part,   executors, administrators or assigns, the said yearly rent hereby reserved, at the times and in manner hereinbefore mentioned for payment thereof, without any deduction or abatement whatsoever thereout, for or in respect of any rates, taxes, assess- ments, or otherwise : and also shall and will, on or before the   day of   now next, at   own cost and charges, fence in the premises hereby demised, in such manner as will effectually protect the land adjoining thereto,

AND IT IS HEREBY AGREED, on the part of the said part
of the first part   heirs, executors, administrators,
and assigns, that if at any time within the said term of
      the said part   of the second part,   heirs,
executors, administrators, or assigns, shall desire to purchase the fee simple of the lands hereby demised,
shall be allowed to do so by paying the sum of   of
lawful money, aforesaid, provided the said rent shall
have been regularly paid up to the time when   may so desire
to purchase : and also, providing that the rent accruing
or to accrue, due for the remainder of the term above
created, then unexpired, shall also have been paid, but
the said part   of the first part shall not be bound to
give covenants or assurances for title other than for and
in respect to his own acts.

AND IT IS HEREBY AGREED, on the part of the said part
of the second part,   executors, administrators and
assigns, that if, at any time or times during the said term,
the said rent, or any part thereof, shall be in arrear and
unpaid for the space of thirty days after any of the days
or times whereon the same ought to be paid as aforesaid,
then it shall be lawful for the said part   of the first
part,   heirs, executors, administrators or assigns, to
enter into and take possession of the premises hereby demised, whether the same be lawfully demanded or not,
and the same to sell and dispose of either by public auction or private sale, as to   may seem best, and when
so sold to convey and assure the same unto the purchaser
or purchasers thereof his, her or their heirs or assigns, or
as he, she or they shall direct or appoint, without the
let, hindrance or denial of   the said part   of the

second part,   heirs, executors, administrators and
assigns : and further, that the non-fulfillment of the covenants hereinbefore mentioned, or any of them, on the part
of the lessee or lessees, shall operate as a forfeiture of
these presents, and the same shall be considered. null and
void to all intents and purposes whatsoever :, and also,
that the said part   of the second part,   executors,
administrators and assigns, shall not nor will, during the
said term, grant or demise or assign, transfer or set over
or otherwise, by any act or deed, procure or cause the
said premises hereby demised, or intended so to be, or
any part thereof, or any estate, term or interest therein,
to be granted, assigned, transferred or set over unto any
person or persons whatsoever, nor carry on any offensive
trade or business on the premises, without the consent in
writing of the said part of the first part,   heirs and
assigns, first had and obtained : and also that the said
part   of the second part will pay all taxes, rates, duties, and assessments whatsoever, whether municipal,
parliamentary, or otherwise, now charged or hereafter to
be charged upon the said demised premises, or upon the
the said part of the first part, on account thereof.

AND IT IS HEREBY DECLARED AND MUTUALLY AGREED,
by and between the parties hereto that time in the payment by the said part   of the second part,   heirs,
executors, or assigns, to the said part   of the first part,
          heirs, executors, or assigns, of the said sum of
          under the proviso or agreement above set forth in
that behalf, and within the period of   above limited
therefor, as the purchase money for the premises, shall be
strictly the essence of this contract, and that default in

payment by the said part   of the second part, of the said sum, within the said time or period of   from the date hereof above limited, over, above and in addition to all rents above reserved, shall render absolutely null and void so much of these presents as relates to the sale by the part   of the first part, or purchase by the part hereto of the second part, of the premises above mentioned, and the jurisdiction of equity, and of the several courts of this province, in reference thereto, shall be wholly barred, and the said part   of the first part shall be absolutely released and discharged from the performance or execution of the said agreement, and the said part   of the second part shall be deprived of all right to enforce the same, notwithstanding any rule (if such there be) that time cannot be made of the essence of a contract, or any other rule or maxim whatsoever.

In witness, &c.

Signed, sealed, &c.

(*Usual Affidavit of Execution.*)

___

STATUTORY LEASE.

THIS INDENTURE, made the   day of   in the year of our Lord one thousand eight hundred and   , in pursuance of the Act respecting Short Forms of Leases,

BETWEEN   hereinafter called the "Lessor   ," of the first part, and   hereinafter called the "Lessee   ," of the second part:

WITNESSETH, that in consideration of the rents, covenants and agreements hereinafter reserved and contained, on the part of the said Lessee   executors, adminis-

trators and assigns, to be paid, observed and performed,
the said Lessor   ha   demised and leased, and by these
presents do   demise and lease unto the said Lessee
        executors, administrators and assigns, all

To HAVE AND TO HOLD the said demised premises for
and during the term of   to be computed from the
        day of   in the year of our Lord one thousand
eight hundred and   and from thenceforth next
ensuing and fully to be complete and ended.

YIELDING AND PAYING therefor, yearly and every year
during the said term hereby granted unto the said Lessor
        heirs, executors, administrators or assigns, the sum
of   to be payable on the following days and times,
that is to say :—in equal portions, on the   · in each
and every year during the said term, without any deduction, defalcation or abatement whatsoever ; the first of
such payments to become due and to be made on the
day of

And the said Lessee   covenant   with the said Lessor
to pay rent ; and to pay taxes ; and to repair ; and to
keep up fences ; and not to cut down timber ; and that
the said Lessor   may enter and view state of repair ; and
that the said Lessee   will repair according to notice ; and
will not assign or sub-let without leave ; and · will not
carry on on said premises any business or occupation
which may be offensive or annoying to the said Lessor
or   assigns ; and that   will leave the premises in
good repair.

And also that if the term hereby granted shall be at
any time seized or taken in execution or in attachment
by any creditor of the said Lessee   or   assigns, or if

the said Lessee or   assigns shall make any assignment for the benefit of creditors, or, becoming bankrupt
or insolvent, shall take the benefit of any Act that may
be in force for bankrupt or insolvent debtors, the then
current   rent shall immediately become due and payable, and the said term shall immediately become forfeited
and void.

Proviso, for re-entry by the said Lessor   on nonpayment of rent, or on non-performance of covenants.

The said Lessor   covenant   with the said Lessee
for quiet enjoyment.

In witness, &c.

Signed, sealed, &c.

RENEWABLE LEASE.

THIS INDENTURE, made the   day of   A.D.
8   , in pursuance of the Act respecting Short Forms
d Leases,

BETWEEN   of the first part ; and   of
th second part :

WITNESSETH, that in consideration of the rents, cove-
nats, and agreements hereinafter reserved and contained,
on the part of the said party of the second part,
exeutors, administrators and assigns,   the said
pary of the first part, hath demised and leased, and by
thes presents doth demise and lease unto the said party
of th second part,   executors, administrators and
assigs, all that certain piece, parcel, or tract of land and
premes, situate, lying and being in   .   together
with he appurtenances :

To HAVE AND TO HOLD the said parcel or tract of land and premises hereby demised, with the appurtenances, unto the said party of the second part   executors, administrators and assigns, from the   day of   in the year of our Lord one thousand eight hundred and   for, and during, and until the   day of   which will be in the year of our Lord one thousand eight hundred and   renewable as hereinafter mentioned, yielding and paying therefor yearly, and every year during the said term of   years, unto the said party of the first part,   heirs, executors, administrators, and assigns, the clear yearly rent or sum of   of lawful money of Canada, in four equal quarterly payments o: in each payment, to be made on the first days of   in each and every year during the said term, without any deduction, defalcation, or abatement therefrom, for or in respect of any taxes, charges, rents assessments or impositions whatever, either now or here after to be taxed, charged, rated or assessed on the sai demised premises or any part thereof, or for or on account of the same, the first payment to become due n the   day of   one thousand eight hundred and And the said party of the second part, covenants wh the said party of the first part, to pay rent and to y taxes, and not to assign or sublet, without leave in wit- ing, executed in presence of two subscribing witness : Proviso for re-entry by the said party of the first rt, heirs, executors, administrators or assign on non-payment of rent, or non-performance of coventts. And the said party of the first part covenants wit the said party of the second part for quiet enjoyment ; And

also that immediately after the expiration of the said
term of   years, he, the said party of the first part,
his heirs and assigns, shall and will grant another lease
of the said hereby demised premises, with the appurtenances, containing the like covenants, conditions, provisoes
and agreements as are in this lease contained and expressed, and at and under a certain yearly rent, payable
in quarterly payments, the amount whereof to be ascertained in manner following, that is to say : To be fixed
on, and determined upon, and declared by two appraisers,
to be named and appointed, one of them by the said
party of the first part, his heirs and assigns, the other
by the said party of the second part,   executors,
administrators and assigns, with power to them the said
appraisers, to name and call in a third if they cannot
agree; and in such valuation and appraisement the'
amount of such rent shall be calculated altogether as
ground rent of a block or parcel of land situated as the
said premises are situated, and the value of any buildings,
tenements, houses or erections thereon, is not to be considered in any wise in making such appraisement : such
appraisement to be made within fourteen days after the
end of the term hereby granted : such rent to be payable
in quarterly payments as aforesaid, and to commence
from and immediately after the termination of the first
term : or, if the said party of the first part, his heirs and
assigns, decline making such renewal for a second term,
—which it shall be optional for him or them to do or
make (but of which intention to decline, the said party
of the first part,   heirs or assigns, shall give to the
said party of the second   executors, administrators

or assigns, or leave at his or their last known place of
abode, a notice, in writing, at least three calendar months
before the expiration of the said term of   years hereby granted, or any future term to be granted as hereby
provided),—then it is hereby expressly covenanted, declared and agreed upon, by and between the parties
hereto and their respective representatives, that all the
buildings, houses and erections, placed, erected and
being on said premises at the expiration of the first term
of   years, by the said party of the second part, executors, administrators or assigns, shall be duly valued
and appraised, by appraisers named and appointed on behalf of each party, as above particularly mentioned, with
power to them to name, refer to and call in a third person, should they not agree as above mentioned—such appraisement to be made within fourteen days from and
after the determination of the said first term hereby demised—who shall fix on the value under the conditions
aforesaid ; And the said party of the first part, hereby
for himself, his heirs, and assigns, covenants, promises
and agrees, to and with the said party of the second part,
        executors, administrators and assigns, that he or
they, or some one of them, will pay to the said party of
the second part,   executors, administrators and assigns, the full sum of money so to be fixed by the said
appraisers, or their referee, as the value of or compensation for said houses, buildings and erections, on the said
hereby demised premises then standing and being, within
one calendar month after such value is ascertained and
declared as aforesaid, a renewal for a second term having
been declined to be made by him or them as aforesaid ;

And also, that if any such renewal of a second term be
granted as aforesaid, under the terms and conditions
herein provided for granting the same, by the said party
of the first part, his heirs or assigns, to the said party of
the second part,   executors, administrators and assigns, that at the end of such renewed term, so to be
granted as aforesaid, the said party of the first part, his
heirs and assigns, shall and will grant a further renewed
lease to the said party of the second part,   executors,
administrators and assigns, of a further term of
years, precisely on the same terms and conditions as hereinbefore provided for the first renewal thereof, the amount
of rent payable quarterly to be ascertained by appraisers,
in the manner and form above provided and set forth, or
shall and will pay for all buildings and erections then
being on said premises (should such renewal be refused
or declined, and of which notice shall have been given as
aforesaid), at a rate to be ascertained by appraisement as
aforesaid, and within the time, and according to the
terms, conditions and agreements above mentioned and
expressed ; and so on at the end of every renewed term ;
it being the true intent and meaning of these presents,
and it is hereby expressly covenanted and agreed upon,
by and between the said parties hereto, their heirs, executors, administrators and assigns, that at the end of
the hereby granted term of   years, and also at the
end of every renewed term of   years, so to be
granted as aforesaid, the said party of the first part,
heirs and assigns, shall grant a renewed term or lease
of   years of the said hereby demised premises, and so on for ever, ascertaining the amount of

rent to be paid during such renewed term by appraisement, as hereinbefore provided, and always estimating
the amount of said rent as ground rent, and exclusive
and independent of all buildings and improvements thereon
erected, put, placed and being, until the said party
of the first part, his heirs or assigns, elect to determine
these presents, and all further renewal or renewals of the
hereby demised premises, and of which notice shall be
given as aforesaid, by paying within the term above
limited at the expiration of each term, for all such buildings, erections and improvements as may be put, placed,
erected and then being thereon, by the said party of the
second part,   executors, administrators or assigns,
at the appraised value, to be ascertained and estimated
by referees in manner hereinbefore provided.   And it is
hereby further covenanted and agreed upon, by 'and between the said parties of the first and second parts, for
themselves and their respective legal representatives,
that all dower and all charges and costs arising from the
demand of the same, either at law or in equity, that may
hereafter be made, and that may be chargeable on the
said premises, and legally and lawfully demanded therefor, shall be deducted from the rent reserved or to be
hereafter reserved, as aforesaid, for the said premises
such dower being limited to the ground (and not to apply to the improvements thereon), and the rents, issues
and profits thereof, it being hereby clearly admitted and
understood that the buildings and improvements to be
made and erected on said premises, will be made and
erected by the said party of the second part,   executors, administrators, and assigns, and that the said party

of the second part,   executors, administrators and assigns, shall be answerable only for the balance of such
rent, after deducting such dower and the charges accruing from demanding or enforcing the same, anything
herein contained to the contrary thereof in anywise notwithstanding. And also that if the said party of the
first part, his heirs, executors, administrators or assigns,
do and shall, at any time hereafter, neglect, decline or
refuse to pay to the said party of the second part,
executors, administrators or assigns, the full sum of
money so to be fixed and determined by the said appraisers, or their referee, as to the value or compensation for
the said houses, buildings and erections on the said hereby
demised premises then standing and being (upon being
lawfully demanded), for the space of one calendar month
after such value is ascertained, declared and demanded as
aforesaid (a renewal for a second, or for any subsequent
term, having been declined to be made by him or them, and
notice given as aforesaid), or if he or they refuse or neglect
to name and appoint an appraiser, for the purpose of ascertaining and determining such value, within the period
above fixed and prescribed, then, in either such case, the
said party of the second part,   executors, administrators and assigns, shall hold and enjoy the said premises for the further term of   years, reckoned from
the expiration of the preceding term, subject to the same
terms, conditions, rents and agreements contained and
provided for the term then last expired and ended ;
nevertheless, subject, after the termination of the term
so created, to all the conditions, provisoes and agreements contained in and by these presents for the renewal

of any term, or for the purchase of the buildings and improvements as aforesaid : It being clearly and fully understood and agreed upon, by and between the said parties to these presents, and their legal representatives, that the neglect or refusal to appoint an appraiser, on the part of the lessor, to estimate the value of the improvements as aforesaid, or the neglect or refusal of payment, after notice as aforesaid, for the value thereof, for the space of time above provided and mentioned (after due demand as aforesaid), shall, at all times hereafter, entitle and authorise the said lessee and   representatives to hold, own and enjoy the said premises for another term of   years, upon the terms and for the rents provided for in the preceding and then expired or expiring term, so ofter as payment of the purchase money for the buildings and improvements as aforesaid, shall be neglected or refused to be made, or the appointment of an appraiser, for the purposes of ascertaining such value, shall be neglected or refused to be made by the said lessor, or his legal representatives : and that, at the expiration of the term hereby created and provided for under the contingencies aforesaid, the original and first provisions and conditions contained in these presents shall then again operate and be in full force and effect. And the said party of the first part further covenants, that he, his heirs and assigns, will at any time within five years from the date hereof, upon payment by the said lessee, his executors, administrators or assigns, unto him or them, of the sum of   of lawful money of Canada, execute a deed, in fee simple, of the premises hereby demised,

unto the said party of the second part, his heirs and assigns, or as he or they may direct or appoint.

In witness, &c.

Signed, sealed, &c.

(Usual Affidavit of Execution.)

LEASE OF OIL AND MINING LANDS.

THIS INDENTURE, made the   day of   , A.D.
18   , in pursuance of the Act respecting Short Forms
of Leases, BETWEEN

WITNESSETH, that in consideration of the moneys, rents,
royalties, covenants, conditions and agreements hereinafter reserved and contained on the part of the said party
of the second part, his executors, administrators and assigns, to be paid, observed and performed, they the said
parties of the first part have demised and leased, and by
these presents do demise and lease unto the said party of
the second part,   executors, administrators and assigns, the lands following, namely : all and singular that
certain parcel or tract of land and premises situate, lying
and being in the township of   in the county of
and province of   being composed of   reserving thereout unto the said lessors, their executors,
administrators or assigns, a right of way in, over, out of,
upon and across the said demised premises, with their
servants, cattle, horses, waggons, carts and vehicles :

To HAVE AND TO HOLD the said demised premises for
and during the term of   years, to be computed from
the day of the date of this indenture and henceforth next

ensuing and fully to be complete and ended, for the following uses and purposes, that is to say : that the said
lessees, their heirs, assigns, employees or lessees are to
have at all times during the said term hereby granted
the exclusive right to enter upon and occupy the said
premises, and to take thereon all necessary teams, tools,
implements and machinery, and to work and use the
same for the purpose of putting down a shaft or shafts,
tubing or piping, or drilling, boring or digging a well or
wells for petroleum, oil, salt or any other mineral or vege-
table substance or deposit, which may be found or discovered to be upon, in or under the said premises hereby
demised ; with the right to erect a derrick or derricks,
building or buildings, which he or they may find necessary for drilling, boring, pumping or mining as aforesaid,
and for storing the products, and for all other purposes
connected therewith ; and are to have and to hold any
such petroleum, oil, salt or other substance so found and
obtained to himself, his heirs, executors, administrators
and assigns (except as hereinafter mentioned), with liberty at all times to remove the same ; yielding and paying
therefor unto the said lessors, their heirs, executors, administrators or assigns, the sum of   yearly
and every year during the continuance of the said
term ; and also the   part or share of all the petroleum,
oil, salt or other substance which may be obtained from
the said demised premises from time to time during the
continuance of this lease ; such part or share to be delivered by the said lessee, his executors, administrators or
assigns, unto the said lessors, their agents or assigns, at
the well or wells, in barrels or casks to be provided by

the said lessors at least   before, at the end of every
    and to be the   part of all the petroleum, oil, salt
or other substance, as had been obtained during the preceding   and the said lessee covenants with the said
lessors, that he the said lessee, his heirs, assigns, employees or lessees, will commence operations for obtaining such
oil or other substance on the premises hereby demised
within   days from the date hereof, and will commence
to put down at least one well on the said premises within
the said   days, and erect an engine house or houses,
derrick or derricks, and all things necessary for the same,
and will continue and prosecute the said well or wells,
with all earnest zeal, diligence and vigor   unto completion, and until the said well or wells shall have been
well and properly tested ; and that the said lessors, their
agents or assigns, may have access at any and all times
to the books and records of the said well or wells.
And the said lessors covenant with the said lessee, for
quiet enjoyment: and that the said lessee, his executors, administrators and assigns, may have the right at all times
during the term hereby created, of ingress and egress in,
upon, from and out of the said premises hereby demised,
with his or their servants, cattle, waggons, horses, carts
and vehicles,   the said lessee covenants with the
said lessors to pay rent and to pay taxes upon the said
demised premises

    Proviso for re-entry by the said lessors on non-payment
of rents and royalties or non-performance of covenants or
any of them.

    In witness, &c.
    Signed, sealed, &c.
    R

LEASE OF PART OF A HOUSE.

MEMORANDUM of an agreement made and entered into the   day of   18 , by and between A. B., of and C. D., of, &c.; whereby the said A. B. agrees to let, and the said C. D. agrees to take the rooms or apartments following, that is to say: being part of a house and premises in which the said A. B. now resides, situate and being No.   , in   street, in the city of   .

To HAVE AND TO HOLD the said rooms and apartments, for and during the term of half-a-year, to commence from the   day of   instant, at and for the yearly rent of   lawful money of Canada, payable monthly, by even and equal portions, the first payment to be made on the   day of   next ensuing the date hereof; and it is further agreed, that, at the expiration of the said term of half-a-year, the said C. D. may hold, occupy and enjoy the said rooms or apartments from month to month for so long a time as the said C. D. and A. B. shall agree, at the rent above specified; and that each party be at liberty to quit possession on giving the other a month's notice in writing.

AND IT IS ALSO FURTHER AGREED, that when the said C. D. shall quit the premises, he shall leave them in as good condition and repair as they shall be in on his taking possession thereof, reasonable wear excepted.

In witness, &c.

Signed, sealed, &c.

UNDERLEASE.

THIS INDENTURE, made the   day of   A.D. 18 ,
BETWEEN C. D., of   , of the one part, and E. F.,
of   , of the other part, witnesseth as follows :—

1. The said C. D. demises to the said E. F., his executors and administrators, the premises described in the first
schedule hereto, with their appurtenances from the date
hereof, for   years, except the last three days, at the
yearly rent of $, payable, etc. [*as in original lease*].

2. The said E. F., for himself, his heirs, executors and
administrators, covenants with the said C. D., his executors, administrators and assigns (hereinafter called "the
lessors"), that the said E. F., his executors and administrators (hereinafter called "the lessees"), will pay, etc.
[*follow the terms of the original lease to the end, substi-
tuting the assignor for the lessor, and the assignee for the
lessee.*]

In witness, &c.
Signed, sealed, &c.

LANDLORD'S INDEMNITY AGAINST RENT
AND TAXES.

To C. D.

In consideration of your becoming tenant of my premises, No.   , in   street, I agree to indemnify you
against the payment of any rent, taxes or rates chargeable upon the said premises, or upon any person in respect
of the occupation thereof, down to the commencement of
your tenancy.   Dated the   day of   A.D. 18 .

LETTER OF LICENSE.

(Extending time.)

—

To ALL TO WHOM THESE PRESENTS SHALL COME, we, who have hereunto subscribed our names and affixed our seals, creditors of I. B., of   send greeting:

WHEREAS the said I. B., on the day of the date hereof, is indebted unto us, the several creditors hereunder named, in divers sums of money, which at present he is not able to pay and satisfy, without respite and time to be given him for payment thereof : know ye, therefore, that we, the said several creditors, and each and every of us, at the particular request of the said I. B., have given and granted, and by these our present letters do give and grant, unto the said I. B., full and free liberty, license, power and authority to go about, attend, follow and negotiate any affairs, business matters or things whatsoever, or at any place or places whatsoever, without any let, suit, trouble, arrest, attachment, or any other impediment to be offered or done unto the said I. B., his wares, goods, moneys or other effects whatsoever, by us or any of us, or by the heirs, executors, administrators, partners or assigns of us or any of us, or by our or any of our means or procurement, to be sought, attempted or procured to be done, for and during   months next and immediately ensuing the day of the date hereof. And further, we the said creditors hereunder subscribed, do and each of us doth covenant and grant, for ourselves, our heirs, executors, administrators and assigns, respectively, and not jointly, or one for another, or for the heirs, executors, administrators or assigns of each other,

to and with the said I. B., that we or any of us, our
heirs, executors, administrators or assigns, or any of them
shall not nor will during the time aforesaid, sue, arrest,
attach or prosecute the said I. B., for or on account of
our respective debts, or any part thereof ; and that, if
any hurt, trouble, wrong, damage or hindrance be done
unto the said I. B., either in body, goods or chattels,
within the aforesaid term of   next ensuing the debt
hereof, by us or any of us the said creditors, or by any
person or persons, by or through the procurement or consent of us or any of us, contrary to the true intent
and meaning of these presents, then the said I. B., by
virtue hereof, shall be discharged and acquitted forever,
against such of us the said creditors, his and their heirs,
executors, administrators or assigns, by whom and by whose
will, means or procurement he shall be arrested, attached,
imprisoned or damaged, of all manner of actions, suits,
deeds, debts, charges, sum and sums of money, claims and
demands whatsoever, from the beginning of the world to
the day of the date hereof.

In witness, &c. this   day of   A.D. 18   .

Signed, sealed, &c.

MECHANICS' LIEN.

        of   under "The Mechanics' Lien Act of
18 ,"   claims a lien upon the estate or interest of
    of   in respect of the following   that is to
say : which   done for the said   on or before
the   day of

The amount claimed as due is the sum of

The description of the land to be charged is the following:

Dated at   this   day of   A.D. 18 .

County of   )
            To wit : }   make oath and say :

1.   name and residence   correctly set forth as above and   the owner of the property to be charged by the within declaration lives at

2. The   within mentioned has been   for the said   and upon his credit.

3. The   of the said   was completed on the day of

4. The   was as follows :

5. The sum claimed   is

Sworn before me at   )
in the County of   this }
    day of   A.D. 18 .)

        A Commissioner, &c.

MORTGAGE WITH DOWER.

THIS INDENTURE, made (in duplicate) the   day of   A.D. 18   , in pursuance of the Act respecting Short Forms of Mortgages,

BETWEEN   hereinafter called the Mortgagor   of the first part;   his wife of the second part; and   hereinafter called the Mortgagee, of the third part :

WITNESSETH, that in consideration of   of lawful money of Canada, now paid by the said Mortgagee   to the said Mortgagor (the receipt whereof is hereby acknowledged,) the said Mortgagor   do   grant and Mortgage unto the said Mortgagee heirs and assigns for ever :

All and singular th certain parcel or tract of land and premises situate, lying and being the said party of the second part hereby bars her dower in the said lands.

PROVIDED this Mortgage to be void on payment of of lawful money of Canada, with interest at per cent. per annum, as follows : and taxes and performance of statute labour.

The said Mortgagor covenant with the said Mortgagee that the Mortgagor will pay the Mortgage money and interest, and observe the above proviso.

That the Mortgagor ha a good title in fee simple to the said lands ; and that he ha the right to convey the said lands to the said Mortgagee ; and that on default the said Mortgagee shall have quiet possession of the said lands, free from all encumbrances.

And that the said Mortgagor will execute such further assurances of the said lands as may be requisite.

[TITLE DEEDS.]

And that the said Mortgagor ha done no act to encumber the said lands.

And that the said Mortgagor will insure the buildings on the said lands to the amount of not less than dollars currency.

And the said Mortgagor do release to the said Mortgagee all claims upon the said lands, subject to the said proviso :

Provided that the said Mortgagee in default of payment for months, may, upon giving notice in writing, enter upon and lease or sell the said lands ; provided that the Mortgagee may distrain for arrears of interest ; provided that in default of the payment of the interest hereby secured the principal hereby secured shall become payable ; provided that until default of payment the Mortgagor shall have quiet possession of the said lands.

In witness whereof, &c.

Signed, sealed, &c..

RECEIVED on the day of the date of this Indenture.

(*Usual Affidavit of Execution.*)

STATUTORY MORTGAGE.

THIS INDENTURE, made (in duplicate) the	day of	A.D. 18	, in pursuance of the Act respecting Short Forms of Mortgages, BETWEEN

WITNESSETH, that in consideration of	of lawful money of Canada, now paid by the said Mortgagee to the said Mortgagor (the receipt whereof is hereby acknowledged), the said Mortgagor	do	grant and Mortgage unto the said Mortgagee	heirs and assigns for ever :

All and singular, th	certain parcel or tract of land and premises

[DOWER.]

PROVIDED this Mortgage to be void on payment of	of lawful money of Canada, with interest	at	per cent. per annum, as follows ;	and taxes and performance of statute labour.

The said Mortgagor covenant with the said Mortgagee that the Mortgagor will pay the Mortgage money and interest and observe the above proviso ;

That the Mortgagor ha a good title in fee simple to the said lands; and that he ha the right to convey the said lands to the said Mortgagee and that on default the Mortgagee shall have quiet possession of the said lands, free from all encumbrances. And that the said Mortgagor will execute such further assurances of the said lands as may be requisite.

[TITLE DEEDS.]

And that the said Mortgagor ha done no act to incumber the said lands ; and that the said Mortgagor will insure the building on the said lands to the amount of not less than currency ; and the said Mortgagor do release to the said Mortgagee all claims upon the said lands, subject to the said proviso :

Provided that the said Mortgagee on default of payment for month may enter on and lease or sell the said lands :

Provided that the Mortgagee may distrain for arrears of interest ; provided that in default of the payment of the interest hereby secured, the principal hereby secured shall become payable; provided that until default of payment the Mortgagor shall have quiet possession of the said lands.

In witness whereof, &c.

Signed, sealed, &c.

RECEIVED on the day of the date of this Indenture, from

(*Usual Affidavit of Execution.*)

MORTGAGE (COMPOUND INTEREST).

THIS INDENTURE, made (in duplicate) the   day of
        18 , in pursuance of the Act respecting Short
Forms of Mortgages : BETWEEN

WITNESSETH, that in consideration of   of lawful
money of Canada, now paid by the said Mortgagee to
the said Mortgagor (the receipt whereof is hereby acknowledged) the said Mortgagor do grant and Mortgage unto the said Mortgagee   heirs and assigns, for
ever :

All and singular th certain parcel or tract of land
and premises situate lying and being

[DOWER.]

PROVIDED this Mortgage to be void on payment of   in
gold or its equivalent with interest thereon at   per
cent. per annum, as follows :   and taxes and performance of statute labour.

And it is hereby agreed that in case default shall be
made in payment of any sum to become due for interest
at any time appointed for payment thereof as aforesaid
compound interest shall be payable and the sum in arrear
for interest from time to time shall bear interest· at the
same rate as the principal money secured by these presents, and in case the interest and compound interest are
not paid in six months from the time of default a rest
shall be made and compound interest shall be payable on
the aggregate amount then due, and soon from time to time,
and all such interest and compound interest shall be a
charge on the lands, but the said Mortgagee shall, notwithstanding anything herein contained, be at liberty to

foreclose this Mortgage at any time on default of payment of principal or interest for ‑‑ months, on giving to the said Mortgagor executors, administrators or assigns, or leaving on said Mortgaged premises months notice in writing of intention so to do.

The said Mortgagor covenant with the said Mortgagee that the Mortgagor will pay the Mortgage money and interest, and observe the above proviso.

That the Mortgagor has a good title in fee simple to the said lands.

And that he has the right to convey the said lands to the said Mortgagee.

And that on default the Mortgagee shall have quiet possession of the said lands, free from all incumbrances.

And that the said Mortgagor will execute such further assurances of the said lands as may be requisite. And that the said Mortgagor ha done no act to encumber the said lands.

And the said Mortgagor will insure the buildings on the said lands to the amount of not less than currency.

And the said Mortgagor do release to the said Mortgagee all claims upon the said lands subject to the said proviso.

Provided that the said Mortgagee on default of payment for may notice enter on and lease or sell the said lands ; provided that the Mortgagee may distrain for arrears of interest ; provided that in default of payment of the interest hereby secured, the principal hereby secured shall become payable ; Provided that until default of payment the Mortgagor shall have quiet possession of the said lands.

In witness, &c.

Signed, sealed, &c.

RECEIVED on the day of the date of this Indenture, from

Witness :

(Usual Affidavit of Execution.)

LAND MORTGAGE (FUTURE ADVANCES).

THIS INDENTURE, made (in duplicate) the   day of A.D. 18   , in pursuance of the Act respecting Short Forms of Mortgages :

BETWEEN   hereinafter called the Mortgagor, of the first part;   his wife, of the second part; and   hereinafter called the Mortgagee, of the third part ;

WHEREAS the Mortgagee has advanced to the said Mortgagor, value to the amount of   dollars, and it has been agreed for further advances and the Mortgagor hath agreed to secure the Mortgagee (for the present debt of   and also for further debts to the said Mortgagee, whether the same be notes or book accounts owing by the Mortgagor) by the lands hereinafter mentioned:

WITNESSETH, that in consideration of   of lawful money of Canada, now paid by the Mortgagee to the Mortgagor (the receipt whereof is hereby acknowledged) and also in consideration of further advances by the Mortgagee to the Mortgagor, the Mortgagor doth grant and Mortgage unto the said Mortgagee, his heirs and assigns forever, all and singular th   certain parcel   or tract   of land and premises, situate, lying and being in the

PROVIDED this Mortgage to be void on payment of dollars, of lawful money of Canada, with interest at per cent. and all further advances by the Mortgagee to the Mortgagor as follows :   and taxes and performance of statute labour.

Provided that in default of the payment of the interest hereby secured, the principal hereby secured shall become payable.

The Mortgagor covenants with the Mortgagee, that the Mortgagor will pay the mortgage money and interest, and all further indebtedness of the Mortgagor to the Mortgagee, whether by note or account, and observe the above provisoes.

And that the Mortgagor has a good title in fee simple to the said lands.

And that he has the right to convey the said lands to the Mortgagee.

And that on default the Mortgagee shall have quiet possession of the said lands, free from all incumbrances.

The Mortgagor covenants with the Mortgagee that this Mortgage shall also form and be a security to the Mortgagee for future debts of the Mortgagor to the Mortgagee.

And that the Mortgagor will execute such further assurances of the said lands as may be requisite.

And that this Mortgage shall form a charge and claim against the aforesaid lands for all lawful indebtedness of the Mortgagor to the Mortgagee, whether due or becoming due.

And that the Mortgagor doth release to the Mortgagee all his claims upon the said lands subject to the said proviso.

Provided that the Mortgagee on default of payment for one month may, without notice, enter upon and lease or sell the said lands.

Provided that the Mortgagee may distrain for arrears of interest.

And the said party of the second part hereby bars her dower in the said lands.

Provided that until default of payment the Mortgagor shall have quiet possession of the said lands.

And that this Mortgage shall not be discharged until all lawful debts of the Mortgagor to the Mortgagee are fully paid and satisfied.

In witness, &c.

Signed, sealed, &c.

RECEIVED on the day of the date of this Indenture

(Usual Affidavit of Execution.)

MORTGAGE.

(Special form)

THIS INDENTURE, made (in duplicate) the   day of A.D. 18   , in pursuance of the Act respecting Short Forms of Mortgages : BETWEEN

WITNESSETH, that in consideration of   of lawful money of Canada, now paid by the said Mortgagee   to the said Mortgagor   , the receipt whereof is hereby ac-

knowledged, the said Mortgagor   do   grant and Mortgage unto the said Mortgagee   heirs and assigns for
ever, all and singular

To HAVE AND TO HOLD the same with the appurtenances
unto and to the use of the said Mortgagee   heirs and
assigns for ever, subject to the proviso for redemption
thereof hereinafter contained.

Provided this Mortgage be void on payment of
of lawful money of Canada, with interest at   per cent.
per annum, as follows :   and taxes, and performance of statute labour ; the said Mortgagor   covenant
with the said Mortgagee   that the Mortgagor   will pay
the Mortgage money, and interest, and observe the above
proviso ; that the Mortgagor   ha   a good title, in fee
simple, to the said lands ; and that   ha   the right to
convey the said lands to the said Mortgagee ; and that on
default, the Mortgagee   shall have quiet possession of
the said lands, free from all incumbrances ; and that the
said Mortgagor   will execute such further assurances of
the said lands as may be requisite ; and that the said
Mortgagor   ha   done no act to incumber the said lands ;
and that the said Mortgagor   will insure the buildings
on the said lands to the amount of not less than
currency ; and the said Mortgagor   do   release to the
said Mortgagee all   claims upon the said lands, subject to the said proviso.

And it is hereby declared and agreed by and between
the said parties hereto, that in case the said interest shall
not be paid on the days and times hereinbefore appointed
for payment thereof, then and so often as the same shall
be in arrear, interest shall become due and payable there-

on, at the rate aforesaid, from the time the same shall become due until payment thereof.

Provided that the Mortgagee on default of payment for   may enter on and lease or sell the said lands without notice.

And the Mortgagee covenant with the Mortgagor that no sale or lease of the said lands shall be made or granted by   until such time as   months' notice, in writing, shall have been given to the Mortgagor and the serving or giving of such notice shall be good and effectual, either by leaving the same with a grown up person on the said Mortgaged premises, if occupied, or by putting up the same on some portion thereof, if unoccupied, or, at the option of the Mortgagee   , by publishing the same for   successive times in some newspaper published in the

PROVISO: that the purchaser shall, in no case, be bound to ascertain that the default has happened under which the Mortgagee claim to lease or sell, and that the remedy of the Mortgagor for breach of the said covenant, shall be in damages only, and the sale under the said power shall not be affected.

Provided that the Mortgagee   may distrain for arrears of interest.

Provided that, in default of the payment of any instalment of the principal or interest hereby secured, the whole principal hereby secured remaining unpaid, shall become payable, but the Mortgagee   may waive   right to call in the principal, and shall not be therefore debarred from asserting and exercising   right to call in the principal upon the happening of any future default; provided that, until default of payment, the Mortgagor shall have quiet possession of the said lands.

In witness, &c.

Signed, sealed, &c.

RECEIVED on the day of the date of the foregoing Indenture

(Usual Affidavit of Execution.)

MORTGAGE BY WAY OF FURTHER CHARGE.
—

THIS INDENTURE, made the   day of   A.D. 18 ,

BETWEEN A. B., of   of the first part, and C. D., of   of the second part :

WHEREAS by an indenture of mortgage bearing date the   day of   A.D. 18 , and made between the said A. B. of the first part   his wife of the second part, and the said C. D. of the third part ; In consideration of the sum of   then advanced, lent and paid by the said C. D. to the said A. B., he the said A. B., did grant unto the said C. D., his heirs and assigns for ever, all and singular that certain parcel or tract of land and premises situate, lying and being in the   To hold unto the said C. D., his heirs and assigns, to and for his and their sole and only use for ever, subject to the proviso thereinafter contained for redemption of the said premises on payment by the said A. B., his heirs, executors, administrators or assigns, unto the said C. D., his executors, administrators or assigns, of the said sum of   with interest thereon, at six per cent. per annum, at the times and in

8

manner therein mentioned.   And whereas the. said
wife of the said A. B., has since departed this life. And
whereas the said principal sum of   still remains due
and owing to the said C. D., upon the security of the
said indenture of mortgage, but all interest thereon hath
been duly paid and satisfied up to the day of the date of
these presents.   And whereas the said A. B., having occasion for the further sum of   hath applied to and
requested the said C. D. to lend him the same, which he
hath consented and agreed to do on having the repayment
thereof, with interest, secured in manner hereinafter mentioned.

NOW THIS INDENTURE WITNESSETH, that in pursuance
of the said agreement and in consideration of the sum of
        of lawful money of Canada, this day lent, advanced
and paid by the said C. D., to the said A. B. (the receipt
whereof the'said A. B. doth hereby acknowledge and therefrom discharge the said C. D., his heirs, executors, administrators and assigns for ever, by these presents) ; He the said
A. B. doth hereby for himself, his heirs, executors and
administrators, covenant, promise and agree to and with
the said C. D., his executors, administrators and assigns,
that all and singular the said freehold messuages or tenements, land, hereditaments and premises comprised in and
conveyed by the hereinbefore recited indenture of mortgage with the appurtenances, shall from henceforth stand
and be charged and chargeable with, and be subject and
liable to, and shall continue and remain vested in, the
said C. D., his heirs and assigns, for securing the repayment as well of the said sum of   with interest from
the date hereof at the rate, upon the times and in manner

in the covenant of the said A. B., hereinafter contained, specified and set forth as of the said sum of   and interest by the said indenture of mortgage secured and made payable, and that the said premises or any part thereof shall not be redeemed or redeemable at law or in equity (or otherwise) until full payment to the said C. D., his executors, administrators or assigns not only of the said principal sum of   so lent and advanced and secured by the hereinbefore recited Indenture of Mortgage as aforesaid, and the interest to become due thereon respectively, but also of the said principal sum of   this day lent advanced and paid as aforesaid, and the interest thereof, according to the covenant hereinafter contained, anything in the hereinbefore recited Indenture of Mortgage to the contrary thereof notwithstanding. And the said A. B., doth hereby for himself, his heirs, executors and administrators, further covenant, promise and agree to and with said C. D., his executors, administrators and assigns that he, the said A. B., his heirs, executors, administrators or assigns, shall and will, on or before the day of   which will be A.D. 18 , well and truly pay or cause to be paid unto the said C.D., his executors, administrators or assigns, the said sum of   together with interest thereon from the date hereof in the meantime, at the rate of six per cent. per annum, half yearly on the days of   and   until the said principal sum is fully paid and satisfied, such interest to commence and be computed from the day of the date hereof ; and the first payment of interest to become due and be made on the day of   next, without any deduction, defalcation or abatement thereout, for or in respect of any taxes, charges or

assessments on the said land and premises, the said sum
of money, or the said party of the second part or otherwise howsoever. And it is hereby agreed and declared
between the said parties hereto, that all and singular the
trust, powers, remedies and provisions by the hereinbefore recited Indenture of Mortgage, given to or vested
in the said C. D., his heirs, executors, administrators or
assigns shall extend and be applicable to the securing and
paying to the said C. D., his executors, administrators
and assigns as well of the said sum of   and interest,
this day lent and advanced, as also of the said sum of
and interest thereon as aforesaid. And further, that if
default shall be made in payment of the said sum of
and interest or any part thereof, at the times hereinbefore appointed for payment thereof, he the said A. B.,
and his heirs and all persons claiming any interest in the
said premises in trust for him or them, shall and will at
the request of the said C. D., his executors, administrators or assigns, make, do, execute and perfect all such
further acts and deeds for the better securing the repayment of the said principal sum of   and interest, and
for more effectually charging the said premises, with the
repayment thereof, as by the said C. D., his executors,
administrators or assigns, or his or their counsel in the
law shall be reasonably devised, advised, or required.
And the said A. B., lastly, hereby covenants with the
said C. D., to insure the said premises in the sum of
and assign the policy of insurance in the manner upon
the terms and subject to the provisions, conditions and
stipulations in every respect in the said recited Indenture
of Mortgage, specified and set forth in lieu of the said

sum of   therein mentioned as to be insured upon the said premises.

In witness, &c.

Signed, sealed, &c.

RECEIVED on the day of the date hereof, &c.

MORTGAGE TO BUILDING SOCIETY.

THIS INDENTURE, made in duplicate the   day of A.D. 18 , in pursuance of the Act respecting Short Forms of Mortgages,

BETWEEN   of   hereinafter called "the Mortgagor," of the first part; The   Permanent Loan and Savings Company, hereinafter called "the Company," of the second part; and   wife of the said Mortgagor, of the third part,

WITNESSETH, that in consideration of   dollars now paid by the Company to the Mortgagor (the receipt whereof is hereby acknowledged), the Mortgagor doth grant and Mortgage unto the Company forever provided this Mortgage to be void on payment of   in equal   instalments of   on the first day of   the month of   in each year during the term of years. The first of said payments to become payable on the first day of   eighteen hundred and   together with all fines imposed by the Company on the Mortgagor on account of default in payment according to the Company's rules, and taxes and performance of statute labour.

Provided that on default of payment for   months of

any portion of the money hereby secured the whole of the instalments hereby secured shall become payable.

The Mortgagor covenants with the Company, that the Mortgagor will pay the Mortgage money and interest, and observe the above provisoes ; that the Mortgagor has a good title in fee simple to the said lands ; that he has the right to convey the said lands to the Company ; that on default the Company shall have quiet possession of the said lands, free from all incumbrances; that the Mortgagor will execute such further assurances of the said lands as may be requisite ; that the Mortgagor has done no act to encumber the said lands ; that the Mortgagor will insure the buildings on the said lands to the amount of not less than   dollars.

And the parties of the first and third parts do release to the Company all his, her or their claims upon the said . lands subject to the said proviso.

Provided that the Company, on default of payment for   months, may, without any notice, enter upon and lease or sell the said lands for cash or credit.

Provided that the Company may distrain for arrears of instalments.

And the said party of the third part, the wife of the Mortgagor, hereby bars her dower in the said lands.

The Mortgagor agrees, that neither the execution nor registration of this Mortgage shall bind the Company to advance the moneys.

And it is hereby declared, that in case the Company satisfies any charge on the lands, the amount paid shall be payable forthwith with interest, and, in default, the power of sale hereby given shall be exercisable, and in the event of the money hereby advanced or any part thereof being applied to the payment of any charge or incumbrance, the Company shall stand in the position and be entitled to all the equities of the person or persons so paid off.

In witness, &c.

Signed, sealed, &c.

RECEIVED on the day of the date of this Indenture

(*Usual Affidavit of Execution.*)

MORTGAGE TO BUILDING SOCIETY.

(Covenant not to sue upon.)

THIS INDENTURE, made the   day of   A.D. 18 ,

BETWEEN A. B. &c., trustees of the   Building Society, of the one part, and C. D., of   of the other part.

WHEREAS by Indenture bearing date the   day of   A.D. 18 , and made between   and the said C. D., of the   part; All and singular that certain parcel or tract of land and premises situate, lying and being   was granted, bargained, sold and conveyed to the said   heirs and assigns for ever.

AND WHEREAS by Indenture of Mortgage dated the   day of   A.D. 18 , and made between the said C. D. of the one part, and the said A. B. &c., trustees of the   Benefit Building and Investment Society of the other part, the ground messuages and premises comprised in and conveyed by the said hereinbefore recited Indenture, were conveyed to the said trustees, their successors and assigns for ever ; but upon the trust and subject to the provisoes therein contained, being trusts and provisions for securing the due and regular payment by the said C. D., his heirs, executors, administrators and assigns of all subscription moneys, fines, and other payments due and to become due and payable to the said Society on or in respect of the   shares of the said C. D. in the said Society (which in the now reciting Indenture of mortgage are stated to have been advanced to him immediately before the execution thereof), or otherwise as a member of the said Society by the said C. D., his heirs, executors, administrators and assigns.

And whereas the shares of the said C. D. in the said Society have been transferred to E. F. of   gentleman, and the messuages and premises comprised in and conveyed by the said firstly hereinbefore recited Indenture have been by Indenture bearing date the   day of   A.D. 18   , conveyed unto the said E. F., his heirs and assigns for ever   subject to the said hereinbefore recited Indenture of mortgage of the   day of   A.D. 18   , and the security thereby made and the payments of the moneys and observance of the rules of the said Society thereby secured.

And whereas the said E. F., in compliance with the rules of the said Society in that behalf, upon the transfer of the said shares to him, entered into a covenant with the said trustees for the payment of all subscriptions and other payments to become due to the said Society in respect of the said shares so transferred, and to observe the rules of the said Society and the covenants on the part of the said C. D., contained in the said hereinbefore re-

cited Indenture of mortgage of the   day of   A.D.
18 .   And whereas the said C. D. hath requested the
said A. B., &c., trustees of the   Building Society,
in compliance with the rules of the said Society, to release
him from all liability under the hereinbefore recited Indenture of mortgage of the   day of   A.D. 18   , and
they have accordingly agreed to enter into the covenant
heneinafter contained.

Now THIS INDENTURE WITNESSETH, that in pursuance
of the said agreement and in consideration of the premises, and in compliance with the rules of the said Society,
the said A. B., &c., as such trustees as aforesaid, do
hereby for themselves, their successors and assigns, covenant and declare, with and to the said C. D., his
heirs, executors and administrators, that they, the said
A. B., &c., trustees of the said   Building Society, their
successors or assigns, shall not nor will at any time or
times hereafter commence or prosecute against the said
C. D., or his heirs, executors or administrators, (in respect
of his estate) any action, suit, or other proceeding at law
or in equity for or in respect of the breach or non-performance of the covenants on the part of the said C. D.,
his heirs, executors, administrators or assigns, contained
in the said hereinbefore recited Indenture of mortgage
of the   day of   A.D. 18   , or any of them, but
nothing herein contained shall be construed as releasing
the said E. F. (as such purchaser as aforesaid), his heirs,
executors, administrators and assigns, from the performance of the said covenants, or as in any way prejudicing
or affecting the exercise of all the trusts, powers and
authorities contained in the said Indenture of Mortgage,

in like manner as if this Indenture had never been made
or executed.

In witness, &c.,

Signed, sealed, &c.

MORTGAGE OF REAL ESTATE TO SECURE
ENDORSEMENT.

—

THIS INDENTURE, made (in duplicate) the   day of
        A.D. 18   , in pursuance of the Act respecting
Short Forms of Mortgages, BETWEEN

WHEREAS the said Mortgagee   ha   endorsed the
several Promissory note   of the said Mortgagor   for the
sum of   of lawful money of Canada   cop   of which
        hereunto annexed and marked respectively
and whereas, the said Mortgagor   ha   agreed to execute
these presents for the purpose of indemnifying and saving harmless the Mortgagee   from the payment of the
promissory note   or any part thereof, or any note or
notes hereafter to be endorsed by the said Mortgagee
for the accommodation of the said Mortgagor   by way
of renewal of the said recited note   or any interest to
accrue thereunder, or otherwise howsoever.

WITNESSETH, that in consideration of the premises, and
of the sum of one dollar of lawful money of Canada, now
paid by the said Mortgagee   to the said Mortgagor   ,
(the receipt whereof is hereby acknowledged), the said
Mortgagor   do   grant and mortgage unto the said Mortgagee   heirs and assigns for ever, all and singular th

certain parcel   or tract   of land and premises situate, lying and being

[DOWER.]

PROVIDED this Mortgage to be void on payment by the said Mortgagor   of the said promissory note   or any renewals of the same, and saving harmless the said Mortgagee from all loss, costs, charges, damages or expenses, in respect to the said note   or renewals, and shall pay or cause to be paid the said promissory note so as aforesaid, endorsed by the said Mortgagee   cop   whereof hereunto annexed, and shall pay or cause to be paid all and every other note or notes which may hereafter be endorsed by the said Mortgagee for the accommodation of the said Mortgagor by way of renewal of the said note   and all interest in respect thereof, or otherwise then these presents shall cease and be utterly void, and taxes and performance of statute labour.

The said Mortgagor   covenant   with the said Mortgagee   that the Mortgagor   will observe the above proviso :

That the Mortgagor   ha   a good title in fee simple to ·the said lands ; and that   he   ha   the right to convey the said lands to the said Mortgagee.

And that on default the Mortgagee   shall have quiet possession of the said lands, free from all incumbrances ; and that the said Mortgagor   will execute such further assurances of the said lands as may be requisite :

And that the said Mortgagor   ha   done no act to incumber the said lands :

And that the said Mortgagor   will insure the build-

ing on the said lands to the amount of not less than
currency ;

And that the said Mortgagor do release to the said
Mortgagee all claims upon the said lands, subject ,
to the said proviso.

PROVIDED that the said Mortgagee on default of payment of any one of the said promissory note by the
said Mortgagor for months may, without notice,
enter on and lease or sell the said lands ; provided that
the Mortgagee may distrain for arrears of interest ;
provided that in default of the payment of the interest
hereby secured, the principal hereby secured shall become
payable ; provided that until default of payment the
Mortgagor shall have quiet possession of the said lands.

In witness whereof, &c.

Signed, sealed, &c.

RECEIVED on the day of the date of this Indenture,
    (Usual Affidavit of Execution.)

MORTGAGE OF LEASE.

THIS INDENTURE, made (in duplicate) the   day of
        A.D. 18   , in pursuance of the Act respecting
Short Forms of Mortgages.

BETWEEN   hereinafter called the mortgagor   of
the first part ;   hereinafter called the mortgagee   of
the   part.

WHEREAS, by a certain lease dated the   day of
one thousand eight hundred and   made between
        the said lessor   therein named did demise and

lease unto   all and singular th   certain parcel   or
tract of land and premises situate, lying and being

Now THIS INDENTURE WITNESSETH, that in consideration of the sum of   of lawful money of Canada,
now paid by the said mortgagee   to the said mortgagor
(the receipt whereof is hereby acknowledged), the said
mortgagor   do   grant and mortgage unto the said mortgagee   executors, administrators and assigns, all and
singular, the said above described parcel   of land, and
premises comprised in, and demised by the said hereinbefore in part recited lease together with the said   lease,
and all benefit and advantage to be derived therefrom :
To have and to hold the same, together with all houses
and other buildings, easements, privileges, and appurtenances thereunto belonging, or appertaining unto the said
mortgagee,   executors, administrators and assigns,
from henceforth for and during all the residue of the said
term of   years granted by the said lease, and for all
other the estate, term, right of renewal (if any), and other
the interest of the said mortgagor   therein or thereto,
subject to the payment of the rent and the observance and
performance of the Lessee's covenants and agreements in
the said Indenture of lease reserved and contained.

PROVIDED, this mortgage to be void on payment of the
full sum of   dollars of lawful money of Canada, with
interest thereon at   per centum per annum, on the
days and times following, that is to say :—   and
taxes and performance of statute labour :

The said mortgagor   covenant   with the said mortgagee   that the mortgagor will pay the mortgage money
and interest   and observe the above proviso.

And that the said in part recited lease is good, valid, and subsisting, and not surrendered, forfeited, or become void or voidable ; and that the rent and covenants therein reserved and contained, have been duly paid and performed up to the day of the date hereof.

And that the said mortgagor   ha   the right to convey the said lands to the said mortgagee ·

And that on default the mortgagee   shall have quiet possession of the said lands free from all incumbrances except as aforesaid

And that the said mortgagor will execute such further assurances of the said lands as may be requisite.

And that the said mortgagor   ha   done no act to encumber the said lands.

And that the said mortgagor will until default in payment of the said principal money or interest pay and perform the rent and covenants reserved and contained in said lease, and that the said mortgagor will insure the buildings upon said land to the amount of not less than
          currency :

And the said mortgagor   do   release to the said mortgagee   all   claims upon the said lands subject to the said proviso :

Provided that the said mortgagee   in default of payment for   month may   giving   notice enter on lease or sell the said lands.

Provided that the mortgagee   may distrain for arrears of interest : provided that in default of payment of the interest hereby secured, the principal hereby secured shall become payable: provided, that until default of payment the mortgagor   shall have quiet possession of the said lands :

In witness whereof, &c.

Signed, sealed, &c.

RECEIVED on the day of the date of this Indenture

(*Usual Affidavit of Execution.*)

MORTGAGE OF A LIFE POLICY.

THIS INDENTURE, made the   day of   A.D. 18 ,
BETWEEN   of   hereinafter called the Mortgagor, of the one part, and   of   hereinafter called the Mortgagee, of the other part. In consideration of   paid by the said Mortgagee to the said Mortgagor, WITNESSETH as follows :

1. the said Mortgagor covenants, that he, his heirs, executors or administrators, will, on the   day of pay to the said Mortgagee, his executors, administrators or assigns, the said sum of   with interest at the rate of   per cent. per annum.

2. For the consideration aforesaid, the said Mortgagor assigns to the said Mortgagee, his executors and administrators, a policy granted to the said Mortgagor, on the   day of   by the   Company, and numbered with all moneys ultimately payable thereon, and with power to the said Mortgagee, his executors administrators and assigns, and his and their substitute and substitutes, to recover and give receipts for the premises in the name or names of the said Mortgagor, his executors or administrators.

3. Provided, that if the foregoing covenant shall be

satisfied, the said Mortgagor, his heirs, executors administrators and assigns, shall be entitled, at his or their respective costs, to a re-assignment of the premises hereby assigned.

4. the said Mortgagor, for himself, his heirs, executors and administrators, covenants with the said Mortgagee, his executors, administrators and assigns, that he the said Mortgagor is entitled to execute this assignment of the premises, free from incumbrances, and that he and all necessary parties will, at the cost of his estate, do all acts required for perfecting such assignment, and effecting the recovery of the premises.

5. The holder or holders of this security may sell or surrender to the said Company the said policy or any policies effected in lieu thereof, as hereinafter mentioned, dealing with the same, as regards the purchaser's protection as absolute owners thereof.

6. The said Mortgagor, for himself, his heirs, executors and administrators, covenants with the said Mortgagee, his executors, administrators and assigns, that he the said Mortgagor, his heirs, executors and administrators, will pay interest after the rate aforesaid on all principal sums continuing secured hereon by two equal half-yearly payments, on the   day of   and the   day of   and will pay the premiums on the said policy when due, and will do or suffer nothing whereby the same may become void, voidable or lapsed ; and in any such event will, at his own cost, do all acts required to enable a policy in lieu thereof to be effected; and will repay to the said Mortgagee, his executors, administrators or assigns, on demand, with interest at the rate aforesaid, all

costs, charges and expenses incurred by him or them for
effecting and keeping up the said policy or any policy
ubstituted for the same as aforesaid.

7. Provided, that all the covenants herein contained
shall apply to any such substituted policy or policies in
the same manner as to the premises hereby assigned.

In witness, &c.

Signed, sealed, &c.

NOTICE TO THE INSURANCE COMPANY OF THE MORTGAGE.

To the   Company, their directors and secretary.
                                    [*Date and address.*]

Gentlemen,

Take notice, that, by indenture dated the   day of
      A.D. 18   , the policy granted by you upon the life
of   of   and numbered   , was assigned by him to
me to secure the sum of   and interest at the rate of
      per cent. per annum.

I am, Gentlemen,

Your obedient servant.

MORTGAGE BOND.

KNOW ALL MEN BY THESE PRESENTS, that I,   of the
      of   in the county of   and Province of   am
held and firmly bound to   both of the   of   in
the county of   and Province aforesaid, esquires, in the

T

sum of   of lawful money of Canada, to be paid to the
said   or to their certain attorney, executors, administrators or assigns ; for the payment of which sum, to be
well and truly made, I bind myself, my heirs, executors
and administrators, firmly by these presents, sealed with
my seal, dated this   day of   A.D. 18 ,

WHEREAS, by Indenture of Mortgage, dated on or
about the   day of   A.D. 18 , and made between
      of the one part, and the said   of the other
part, the said   for the consideration therein mentioned
did covenant with the said   their executors and administrators, that he the said   his heirs, executors or
administrators, would pay unto the said   or the survivor of them, or the executors or administrators of such
survivor, their or his assigns,   the sum of   on
the   day of   A.D. 18 , with interest for the same
after the rate of   per cent. per annum,   on the
first day of   and   in each year.

And whereas, before the execution of the said Mortgage,
the said   did require the said   and the said
did then agree to become personally bound for the due
payment of the said interest :

Now the condition of this obligation is such, that if
the said   his heirs, executors or administrators, should
from time to time and at all times hereafter, during the
continuance of the said mortgage, well and truly pay all
interest moneys by the said mortgage secured at the days
and times and in manner by the said mortgage appointed
for payment thereof, then this obligation to be void,
otherwise to remain in full force and virtue.

Signed, sealed, &c.

DISCHARGE OF MORTGAGE.

(Statutory.)

PROVINCE OF ONTARIO,   }   DOMINION OF CANADA,
          To WIT :

TO THE REGISTRAR of the   do certify that ha satisfied all money due on or to grow due on a certain mortgage made by   which mortgage bears date the   day of   A.D. 18   and was registered in the registry office for the   on the   day of A.D. 18 at   minutes past   o'clock   noon, in Liber   for   as No.   and that such mortgage has been assigned   [*Here state whether mortgage assigned or not.*] And that I am the person entitled by law to receive the money ; And that such mortgage is therefore discharged.

Witness my hand this   day of   A.D. 18 .

Witness :

ONTARIO :   }   I,
County of   of the   of
                     in the county of
          To WIT :   make oath and say :

1. That I was personally present and did see the within certificate of discharge of mortgage duly signed and executed by   the part   thereto.

2. That the said certificate of discharge of mortgage was executed at

3. That I know the said

4. That I am a subscribing witness to the said certificate of discharge of mortgage.

```
Sworn before me at          ⎞
in the county of             ⎟
this        day of           ⎬
A.D. 18                      ⎠
```
     A Commissioner for taking Affidavits, &c.

DISCHARGE OF PART OF MORTGAGED PREMISES.

(Statutory.)

PROVINCE OF ONTARIO,   ⎞
                ⎬ DOMINION OF CANADA.
     To WIT: ⎠

To THE REGISTRAR of the   I,   do certify that   ha   satisfied the sum of   dollars, part of the moneys mentioned in a certain mortgage made by   which mortgage bears date the   day of A.D. 18   and was registered in the registry office for the   on the   day of   A.D. 18 , at   minutes past   o'clock in the   noon, in Liber   for   as No.   and that such mortgage   and that   the person entitled by law to receive the money, and that such part of the lands as is herein more particularly described, that is to say :   is therefore discharged.

    Witness   hand this   day of   A.D. 18
    Witness :

    (Same Affidavit of Execution as on last Instrument.)

RELEASE PART OF MORTGAGED PREMISES.
(By deed.)
—

THIS INDENTURE, made (in duplicate) the   day of A.D. 18 ,

BETWEEN

WHEREAS by a certain mortgage, dated on the   day of   one thousand eight hundred and   and made between   for the consideration therein mentioned, the lands and premises hereinafter released were, together with other lands and premises, conveyed unto
for securing the sum of   and interest as therein mentioned :

AND WHEREAS the said part hereto of the first part ha agreed to release such part of the premises hereinafter described from the said mortgage security :

NOW THIS INDENTURE WITNESSETH, that in consideration of the sum of   of lawful money of Canada, now paid by the said part hereto of the   part, to the said part hereto of the first part (the receipt whereof do hereby acknowledge,) the said part hereto of the first part do by these presents grant, reconvey and release, unto the said part hereto of the   part,   heirs, executors, administrators and assigns, all and singular th certain parcel or tract of land and premises situate, lying and being

TO HAVE AND TO HOLD the same, with the appurtenances, unto the said part hereto of the   part heirs and assigns, to and for   their sole and only use for ever : Freed and absolutely acquitted, exonerated and discharged of and from the said Indenture of mortgage, and the principal money and interest thereby secured, and every proviso, covenant, matter and thing therein contained.

And the said part   hereto of the first part, do   hereby, for   heirs, executors, administrators and assigns, covenant, promise and agree, to and with the said part hereto of the   part,   heirs and assigns, that   the said part   hereto of the first part, heirs, executors, administrators and assigns, shall not nor will at any time hereafter proceed against the portions of the said lands hereby released by legal or equitable process, or otherwise nor look to the same, or any part thereof, for payment of the said principal moneys or interest, or any part thereof, nor disturb, molest or put to charge or damage. the part   hereto of the part,   heirs or assigns, or the present or future owners or occupiers of such hereby released portions of the said premises, for, or by reason, or on account of the said Indenture of mortgage, or anything therein contained

And that   ha   not done, permitted or executed any act, deed, matter or thing whereby the said hereditaments hereinbefore released have been or may be in any manner charged, affected or incumbered in title, estate or otherwise howsoever.

PROVIDED ALWAYS that nothing herein contained shall affect the said before in part recited mortgage, or its legal validity, so far as regards the unreleased portion of the said lands and premises, or any part thereof.

In witness, &c.

Signed, sealed, &c.

RECEIVED on the day of the date hereof
        (Usual Affidavit of Execution.)

NOTARIAL CERTIFICATE OF TRUE COPY.

PROVINCE OF ONTARIO, } To all to whom these presents may come, be seen or known.

To WIT : } I   a notary public by royal authority duly appointed residing at   do certify and attest that the paper writing hereto annexed is a true copy of a document produced to me by   and purporting to be   made by   dated the   the said copy having been compared by me with the said original. An act whereof being requested I have granted the same under my Notarial form and seal of office to serve and avail as occasion shall or may require.

NOTARIAL CERTIFICATES, &c.

TO ALL TO WHOM THESE PRESENTS SHALL COME :

I,   Mayor of the City of   in the   of do hereby certify, that on the day of the date hereof, personally came and appeared before me   the deponent named in the affidavit hereunto annexed, being a person well-known and worthy of credit, and by solemn oath, which he then took before me, in due form of law, did solemnly and sincerely depose to be true the several matters and things mentioned and contained in the said affidavit.

In faith and testimony whereof, I, the said Mayor, have hereunto signed my name, and caused the corporate seal of the said city of   to be put and affixed.

Dated at   aforesaid, the   day of   A.D. 18 .

(Signed)

Mayor of the said City of

} On this   day of   A.D. 18 ,
To wit :   } came and appeared before me   of
     within named who being duly sworn, maketh oath
and saith as follows :—

1. I was personally present and saw   of
within mentioned, duly execute, sign, seal and·deliver the
within paper writing or   as his act and deed.

2. I am a subscribing witness to the due execution of
the said paper writing, or   by the said.

3. The name "   " set and subscribed thereto as a
witness attesting such execution, is of the proper handwriting of me, this deponent.

Sworn before me at   in the City of   this
day of   A.D. 18 .

                    Mayor of the said City of

___

To all to whom these Presents shall come :

     I,   of the   of   in the county of
and Province of Ontario, Notary Public, by Royal authority duly appointed, do hereby certify that I was personally present on the   day of   A.D. 18   , at the
of   aforesaid, and did see   the person named in
the paper writing, or   hereunto annexed, duly execute,
sign, seal and deliver the same as his act and deed for
the purposes therein mentioned.   And that the name
thereto set and subscribed as the party executing the
same is of the proper handwriting of the said   the
grantor therein named.   And that the names   and
          thereto subscribed as the witnesses thereto, are of
the respective proper handwriting of   of   and
of me, this deponent.   And that the said   is personally known to me.

In testimony whereof, I have hereunto subscribed my
name, and affixed my seal of office at my Chambers in
the   of   aforesaid, this   day of   A.D. 18   .

Notary Public.

I,   of   in the county of   and Province
of Ontario, a Notary Public by Royal authority, duly
commissioned,   do hereby certify that on this   day
of   A.D. 18   , personally came and appeared   of
the said city of   the deponent named in the foregoing affidavit, and did then and there before   the
Mayor and Chief Magistrate of the said   state and
depose to be true, the several matters and things mentioned and contained in the said affidavit, and I do hereby
further certify that I am one of the witnesses to the execution of the foregoing   by the said   and that
the same was executed as it purports to have been.

In testimony whereof, I have hereunto set my hand
and seal of office this   day of   A.D. 18   .

NOTICE OF SALE UNDER MORTGAGE.
(42 Vic., Chapter 20, Ontario.)

To

In the matter of the sale of   lot   under "an
Act to give to mortgagees certain powers now commonly
inserted in mortgages."

I,   hereby require you on or before the
day of   18   , to pay off the principal money and in-

terest secured by a certain Indenture of mortgage dated
the   day of   18 , and expressed to be made between
          on all th   which said mortgage was re-
gistered in the registry office for the   on the
day of   18 , under the number   , and has since
become the property of the undersigned.

And I hereby give you notice that the amount due on
the said mortgage for principal, interest and costs respectively is as follows:

And unless the said principal money and interest and
costs are paid on or before the said   day of   18 ,
I shall sell the said property comprised in the said Indenture (and above described) under the authority of the Act
entitled "an Act to give to mortgagees certain powers
now commonly inserted in mortgages," at

Dated at   the   day of   18 .
Witness:

AFFIDAVIT OF SERVICE OF NOTICE OF SALE.

County of }   In the matter of the sale of
                                      lot
        To wit: }

I,   of   in the county of   make
oath and say:

1. That I did on   the   day of   one thousand
eight hundred and   at   in the county of
personally serve   with a copy of the within notice
of sale   by   delivering such copy to, and
leaving the same

2. That the within notice of sale is a true copy of the original notice so served by me as aforesaid.

Sworn before me at the
of   in the
county of   this
day of   18

A Commissioner for taking Affidavits in B. R., &c.

NOTICE OF PROTEST

—

day of   18 .

To

TAKE NOTICE, that a   dated on the   day of   18   for the sum of $ by   payable   after the date thereof, at the   and endorsed by   was this day presented by me for   at the said   and that   thereof was refused : And that   the holder   of the said   look   to you for payment thereof ; And also take notice that the same was this day protested by me for non-

Your obedient servant,

Notary Public.

—

NOTICE TO QUIT (BY LANDLORD).

—

To   OR WHOM ELSE IT MAY CONCERN :

I HEREBY GIVE YOU NOTICE to quit and deliver up, on or before the   day of   18   the peaceable and quiet possession of the premises you now hold of me, with the appurtenances, situate   in the   of in the Province of Ontario.

Dated this   day of   A.D. 18

Yours, &c.

Witness :

NOTICE TO QUIT BY TENANT.

To   Esq.

I HEREBY GIVE YOU NOTICE that it is my intention to quit and deliver up to you, on or before the •   day of   18 , the peaceable and quiet possession of the premises now held by me, with the appurtenances, situate at   in the township of   in the county of   in the Province of

Dated this   day of   A.D. 18 .

                                        Yours, &c.

Witness:

NOTICE CLAIMING DOUBLE RENT FOR HOLDING OVER.

To C. D.

I GIVE YOU NOTICE that if you do not deliver up possession of the house and premises situate No.   , in street, in the   of   on the   day of   according to my notice to quit, dated the   day of   I shall claim from you double the yearly value of the premises for so long as you shall keep possession of them after the expiration of the said notice, according to the Statute in that case provided.

Dated the   day of   A.D. 18 .

Witness:

NOTICE TO INCUMBRANCERS.

To

You and each and every one of you are hereby required

to take notice that and upwards is in arrear to
on a certain Indenture of Mortgage made by
to the said bearing date the day of
A.D. 18 , to secure the sum of $ and by which
said Indenture of Mortgage the following lands, tenements, hereditaments and premises are conveyed to the
said Mortgagee , that is to say :

And as payment thereof has not been made according
to the tenor and effect of the proviso for payment therein
contained, you and each one of you are required to take
notice that the said demand payment of the
arrears upon such Mortgage, and that unless payment of
the said arrears be made forthwith, will proceed to
sell the lands and tenements in the said Indenture of
Mortgage contained ; and that the same will be offered
for sale by Public Auction, at in the of
on the day of A.D. 18 , at
o'clock noon, and that when sold the land
and premises will be conveyed unto the purchaser or
purchasers thereof. And also take notice, that in case
the said lands and premises be not then sold, the said
will proceed, with or without any consent or con-
currence on your part, and without any further notice to
you, to enter into possession of the said premises, and to
receive and take the rents and profits thereof ; and
whether in or out of possession of the same, to make
any lease or leases of the same, as the said shall
see fit, and to sell and absolutely dispose of the said lands
and premises, either by auction or private sale, or partly
by auction and partly by private sale, as the said
may deem proper, and either for cash or upon such terms

of credit as they may think proper, and to convey and assure the same when so sold unto the purchaser or purchasers thereof, as he or they shall direct or appoint.

Dated at   this   day of   18 .

Yours, &c.,

Solicitor for the Mortgagee.

DEEDS OF PARTNERSHIP.

AGREEMENT CONSTITUTING A PARTNERSHIP AT WILL.

WE HEREBY AGREE to become partners as
Dated the   day of   A.D. 18 .
Witness:

A FULLER FORM WHERE ONE IS IN BUSINESS ALREADY.

AN AGREEMENT made this   day of   A.D. 18 ,
BETWEEN A. B. of   , and C. D. of   .

1. The said parties agree to become partners as from the date hereof.

2. The business is to be carried on at the house of the said A. B. where the books and other documents relating to the partnership shall be kept, but accessible at all times to the said C. D.

3. The partnership property shall consist of the stock in trade and implements of the said A. B. and of $, lodged in the   bank by the said C. D. in the joint names of the partners.

4. Each partner may draw out weekly a sum not exceeding   , on account of his share of the profits.

5. The profits of the business are to be divided on the

of   , and the   of   , between the partners in the following proportion, namely, three-fifths to
the said A. B., and two-fifths to the said C. D. and the
payments and liabilities are to be borne by them in the
like proportions.

In witness, &c.

Signed, sealed, &c.

DEED OF PARTNERSHIP.

AN AGREEMENT made this   day of   A.D. 18 ,
BETWEEN A. B. of   , and C. D. of   .

1. The said parties agree to enter into partnership as
        , under the firm of   for   years, from
the date hereof, or until the partnership is determined by
either party giving to the other a three months' notice in
writing, ending with a current year of the partnership.

2. The partnership business is to be carried on in convenient premises to be taken for the purpose in the
of   .

3. The partnership capital is to consist of the sum of
        to be contributed equally by the partners, and
lodged on or before the   day of   , to their joint
account at the bank of   , and of the property,
credits, and stock in trade of the firm for the time
being.

4. Each partner may draw   a week on account of
his profits, but if, at the periodical taking of accounts
hereinafter mentioned, either partner has drawn out during the past year a sum exceeding the profits to which he

shall be entitled, he shall repay the surplus to the partnership.

5. Neither partner shall sign any promissory note or bill other than a draft on a banker, in the name of the firm in the common course of business; nor shall give credit after warning from his co-partner ; nor shall, without his written consent, borrow money, or compound debts, or become surety or bail, or enter into any contract for more than   , or engage a servant to the firm, or take an apprentice, or engage in any other business.

6. Any engagement or liability entered into by either partner in contravention of the above clause is to be at his exclusive risk, and the firm is to be indemnified out of his separate property.

7. Accounts shall be kept in books of all partnership transactions, and such books, together with all other documents connected with partnership business, shall be kept at the principal place of business, and accessible to each partner.

8. On the first day of every year an account shall be taken of the partnership property, stock, credits and liabilities, and the sum found to be due to each partner shall be carried to his separate account.

9. On the taking of such accounts, they shall be entered, together with the valuation of the stock, in the partnership books, and each partner shall have a copy or abstract signed by both partners, and shall be bound thereby, unless within a year some manifest error be found therein, in which case it shall be rectified.

10. On the expiration or other determination of the

said partnership, a full written account shall be taken of all the partnership property, stock, credits and liabilities, and a written valuation shall be made of all that is capable of valuation, and such account and valuation shall be settled, and provision shall be made for the payment of the liabilities of the partnership, and the balance of such property, stock, and credits shall be divided equally between the partners, and each shall execute to the other proper releases and proper instruments for vesting in the other, and enabling him to get in such property, stock and credits.

11. If either partner shall die before the first day of January next, his executors and administrators shall be entitled to the share of the capital brought in by him, together with   per cent. interest in lieu of profits.

12. If either partner shall die after the said day, and during the continuance of the partnership, his executors and administrators shall be entitled to the value of the share of the partnership property, stock and credits, to which the deceased partner would have been entitled on the first day of January last preceding his death, together with   per cent. interest from that day in lieu of profits, and the surviving partner shall secure such sum by a bond in double the amount conditioned for the payment of such sum in twelve months by four quarterly instalments.

13. The surviving partner, his executors and administrators, shall execute a proper instrument indemnifying the executors and administrators of the deceased partner and his estate from all the liabilities of the partnership; and the executors or administrators of the deceased

v

partner shall release and assign to the surviving partner, his executors and administrators, all their interest in the property, stock and credits of the partnership, and shall empower him or them to get in and recover the same.

14. If either partner shall be guilty of a breach or non-observance of the fifth and seventh clauses above contained, the other, within three calendar months after such event shall have become known to him, may dissolve the partnership by notice in writing, declaring the same to be dissolved from the date of such notice, and the partnership shall thereupon cease and determine, and the partner to whom such notice shall be given shall be considered as quitting the business for the benefit of the partner giving such notice.

15. If, at any time during the subsistence of the partnership, or after its determination, any dispute shall arise between the partners, or between either of them, and the executors or administrators of the other, or between their respective executors or administrators, concerning any matter relating to the partnership, the same shall be referred to the award of such person as shall be appointed for that purpose by the parties within thirty days after such dispute shall arise, and in the event of no such appointment being made, then to a barrister-at-law to be appointed by   and such reference may be made a rule of Court.

In witness whereof, &c.

Signed, sealed, &c.

DEED OF PARTNERSHIP.

(Another form.)

ARTICLES OF AGREEMENT, made the   day of A.D. 18 , BETWEEN

WHEREAS the said parties hereto respectively are desirous of entering into a Co-partnership, in the business of   at   for the term and subject to the stipulations hereinafter expressed.

NOW, THEREFORE, THESE PRESENTS WITNESS, that each of them, the said parties hereto respectively, for himself, his heirs, executors and administrators, hereby covenants with the other of them, his executors and administrators, in manner following, that is to say :

First,—That the said parties hereto respectively shall henceforth be and continue partners together in the said business of   for the full term of   to be computed from the   day of   one thousand eight hundred and   if the said partners shall so long live, subject to the provisions hereinafter contained for determining the said partnership.

Second,—That the said business shall be carried on under the firm of

Third,—That the said partners shall be entitled to the profits of the said business in the proportions following, that is to say :

And that all losses in the said business shall be borne by them in the same proportions (unless the same shall be occasioned by the wilful neglect or default of either of the said partners, in which case the same shall be made good by the partner through whose neglect the same shall arise).

Fourth,—That the said partners shall each be at liberty, from time to time during the said Partnership, to draw out of the said business, weekly, any sum or sums not exceeding for each the sum of   per annum, such sums to be duly charged to each of them respectively, and no greater amount to be drawn by either of the said partners except by mutual consent.

Fifth,—That all rent, taxes, salaries, wages and other outgoings and expenses incurred in respect of the said business, shall be paid and borne out of the profits of the said business.

Sixth,—That the said partners shall keep, or cause to be kept, proper and correct books of account of all the partnership moneys received and paid, and all business transacted on partnership account, and of all other matters of which accounts ought to be kept, according to the usual and regular course of the said business, which said books shall be open to the inspection of both partners, or their legal representatives. A general balance or statement of the said accounts, stock in trade and business, and of accounts between the said partners, shall be made and taken on the   day of   in each year of the said term, and oftener if required.

Seventh,—That the said partners shall be true and just to each other in all matters of the said co-partnership, and shall at all times, during the continuance thereof, diligently and faithfully employ themselves respectively in the conduct and concerns of the said business, and devote their whole time exclusively thereto, and either of them shall not transact or be engaged in any other business or trade whatsoever : And the said partners, or either of them, during the continuance of the said co-partnership, shall not, either in the name of the said partnership, or individually in their own names, draw or accept any bill or bills, promissory note or notes, ✕ or become bail or surety for any person or persons, or knowingly or wilfully do commit or permit any act, matter or thing by which, or by means of which, the said partnership moneys or effects shall be seized, attached or taken in execution ; and in case either partner shall fail or make default in the performance of any of the agreements or articles of the said partnership, in so far as the same is or are to be observed by him, then the other partner shall represent in writing to such partner offending, in what he may be so in default ; and in case the same shall not be rectified by a time to be specified for that purpose by the partner so representing, the said partnership shall thereupon at once, or at any other time to be so specified as aforesaid by the partner offended against, be dissolved and determined accordingly.

Eighth,—That in case either of the said partners shall die before the expiration of the term of the said co-partnership, then the surviving partner shall, within six calendar months after such decease, settle and adjust with the representative or representatives of such deceased partner all accounts, matters and things relating to the said co-partnership, and that the said survivor shall continue to carry on henceforth, for his sole benefit the co-partnership business.

In witness whereof, &c.

Signed, sealed, &c.

AGREEMENT FOR LOAN TO PARTNERSHIP.

—

THIS AGREEMENT, made the   day of   A.D. 18 .
BETWEEN   of   and   of

1. The said   lends the sum of   to the said
   to be employed in his business of

2. The said   agrees to pay the said   his
executors or administrators, on or before every Mid-
summer and Christmas day, during the continuance of
this loan, by way of interest for the said sum, one-third
of the profits of the said business accruing during the
half year then last past, and in any event not less than

3. The said   is not to discharge the said loan,
except on the consent of the   his executors or
administrators, and the said   his executors or administrators, may at any time call in the principal on
days' notice in writing, and the principal shall *ipso facto*
become due if the interest or profits are ten days in arrear.

4. The said   for himself, his executors and administrators, covenants with the said   his executors
and administrators, that he the said   during the
continuance of the said loan, will faithfully render to the
said   his executors or administrators, on the occasion
of each payment, a full and true account of the outgoings and incomings of his said business during the
period for which such payment shall extend; And will
permit the said   his executors or administrators,
at all times, at the place of business of the said   to
inspect and take copies of the books of account, order-
books, bankers' pass-books, cheque-books, invoices, and
all agreements and contracts, and other books and writ-

ings whatsoever, connected with the said business of the
said   ; And the said   further covenants, as
aforesaid, that none of the said books or other writings
shall be removed from the said place of business at any
time during the continuance of this loan.

5. And the said   covenants, as aforesaid, that he,
his heirs, executors or administrators, at the expiration
of the said term, will pay to the said   his executors
or administrators, the said sum of   with interest for
the same, after the rate aforesaid.

In witness, &c.

Signed, sealed, &c.

CERTIFICATE OF PARTNERSHIP FOR REGIS-
TRATION (ONTARIO).

SCHEDULE.

PROVINCE OF ONTARIO,
County of
        To wit :

the undersigned   of the   of   in
the County of   and   hereby certify, that
have carried on and intend to carry on trade and business as   at   in partnership with   under
the firm of

And that the said partnership hath subsisted since the
        day of   one thousand eight hundred and
and that   the said   are and have been since the
said day the only members of the said partnership.

Witness   hand at   this   day of   one
thousand eight hundred and

Witness :

DEED OF DISSOLUTION OF PARTNERSHIP.

THIS INDENTURE, made the   day of   A.D. 18 ,
BETWEEN A. B., of   and C. D., of

WHEREAS it has been agreed to dissolve the partnership heretofore carried on by the said parties hereto,
under articles dated the   day of   . Now this
Indenture witnesseth as follows:

1. In consideration of one moiety of the profits of
such business up to the   day of   last, having been
received by the said A. B., and of   secured to him
by a bond bearing even date herewith of the said C. D.,
being the value of the share of the said A. B. in the
property, stock and credits of the partnership, and also in
consideration of an indemnity against the partnership
liabilities, by a bond, bearing even date herewith, of the
said C. D., indemnifying the said A. B. against the partnership liabilities, the said A. B. assigns and releases all
his interest in the property, lease, stock, credits and business of the partnership to the said C. D., his executors,
administrators and assigns, with power in the name of
the said A. B., his executors and administrators, to recover and give receipts for the same premises.

2. The said C. D., for himself, his heirs, executors and
administrators, covenants with the said A. B., that the
said C. D., his heirs, executors and administrators, will
discharge and keep indemnified the said A. B., his heirs,
executors and administrators, against all the liabilities
specified in the schedule hereto, but so that this covenant shall not be enforced so long as the said A. B., his
heirs, executors and administrators, are kept so indemnified as aforesaid.

3. Each of the parties hereto releases the other of them, his heirs, executors and administrators, from all claims in respect of the said partnership, and the articles constituting the same, preserving, nevertheless, in full force and effect the said bond of the said C. D.

In witness, &c.

Signed, sealed, &c.

DISSOLUTION OF PARTNERSHIP.
(*Another form.*)

WE, the undersigned, do hereby mutually agree that the partnership heretofore subsisting between us as

under the within articles of co-partnership, be and the same is hereby dissolved, except for the purpose of the final liquidation and settlement of the business thereof; and upon such settlement wholly to cease and determine.

In witness whereof, we have hereunto set our hands and seals, this   day of   A.D. 18 .

Signed, sealed, &c.

STATUTORY DISSOLUTION OF PARTNERSHIP (ONTARIO).

PROVINCE OF ONTARIO, }
County of   }   I,
formerly a member of the firm carrying on business as
      at   in the County of   under the style
of   do hereby certify that the said partnership was
on the   day of   dissolved.

Witness my hand at   the   day of   in the year of our Lord one thousand eight hundred and

NOTICE OF DISSOLUTION.

NOTICE is hereby given that the partnership heretofore subsisting between us, the undersigned, as   in the   of   has been this day dissolved by mutual consent. All debts owing to the said partnership are to be paid to   at   aforesaid, and all claims against the said partnership are to be presented to the said by whom the same will be settled.

Dated at   this   day of   A. D. 18 .

Witness :

NOTICE DISSOLVING A PARTNERSHIP IMMEDIATELY.

To   [*Date.*]

Sir,—I hereby dissolve the partnership between us from this day.

NOTICE OF DISSOLUTION UNDER A POWER IN THE DEED.

To   [*Date.*]

Sir,—I give you notice that I shall put an end to the partnership between us on the   day of   next, at which time I shall be ready to indemnify you, and shall expect you to indemnify me according to the articles.

Yours, &c.

BOND SECURING TO OUT-GOING PARTNER THE PAYMENT FOR HIS SHARE.

KNOW ALL MEN BY THESE PRESENTS, that I, C. D., of

my heirs, executors and administrators, am firmly bound to A. B., of   his executors, administrators and assigns, for the payment to him or them of the penal sum of   currency.

Dated this   day of   A.D. 18 .

The above-written obligation is conditioned to be void if the above-bounden C. D., his heirs, executors or administrators, shall pay to the said A. B., his executors, administrators or assigns, the sum of   on the   day of   and the sum of   on the   day of A.D. 18 .

Signed, sealed, &c.

BOND INDEMNIFYING OUT-GOING PARTNER AGAINST PARTNERSHIP LIABILITIES.

KNOW ALL MEN BY THESE PRESENTS, that I, C.D., of   my heirs, executors and administrators, am firmly bound unto A. B., of   his executors, administrators and assigns, for the payment to him or them of the penal sum of   currency.

Dated the   day of   A. D. 18 .

The above-written Obligation is conditioned to be void if the said C. D., his heirs, executors or administrators shall keep the said A. B., his executors and administrators, indemnified from all debts and liabilities of the said A.B. and C. D., which, up to the date of the said obligation, shall have arisen out of the partnership between the said A. B. and C. D., in the business of   heretofore carried on by them.

Signed, sealed, &c.

PARTY WALL: AGREEMENT RESPECTING A.

THIS AGREEMENT, made this   day of   A.D. 18 ,
BETWEEN D. L. of the City of Toronto, merchant, of
the first part, and P. S. of the said city, merchant, of the
second part.

WHEREAS the said D. L. is the owner in fee of the lot
and store known as number 90 in   street, in the
City of Toronto, and the said P. S. the owner in fee of
the lot known as number 92 in   street, aforesaid,
immediately adjoining to, and on the southerly side of
said lot and store number 90, on which lot of the said
P. S. he is about to erect a brick store.

AND WHEREAS it has been agreed by and between the
said parties, that the said P. S., in erecting his said store,
shall make use of the gable end wall of the said store of
the said D. L. immediately contiguous to and adjoining
the said lot of the said P. S., as a party wall, upon the
terms, conditions and considerations hereinafter mentioned, the said gable end wall, of the said D. L. so to be
used as a party wall, standing and being entirely on the
said lot of the said D. L.

NOW THEREFORE THIS AGREEMENT WITNESSETH, that
the said D. L., for and in consideration of the sum of
     dollars to him in hand paid by the said P. S., at or
before the ensealing and delivery of these presents, the
receipt whereof is hereby acknowledged, doth for himself, his heirs, executors, administrators and assigns, covenant, grant, promise and agree to and with the said
P. S., his heirs, executors, administrators and assigns, for
ever; That he, the said P. S., his heirs and assigns, shall

and may in erecting and building the said store upon the
said lot of the said P. S., freely and lawfully, but in a
workmanlike manner, and without any interruption, molestation, or hindrance of or from the said D. L., his
heirs, or assigns, make use of the said gable end wall of
the said store of the said D. L., immediately adjoining or
contiguous to the said lot of the said P. S., or such parts
and so much thereof, as he the said P. S. his heirs or assigns, may choose as a party wall.

And further, that should the said wall, hereby made a
a party wall, be at any future time or times injured or
destroyed, either by decay, lapse of time, fire, accident, or
other cause whatever, so as to require to be either repaired or rebuilt in whole or in part, then and in every
such case, the said D. L. and the said P. S. by these presents, for themselves respectively, and their respective
heirs and assigns for ever, mutually covenant and agree
to and with each other and their respective heirs and assigns for ever, that such reparation or rebuilding, as the
case may be, shall be at the mutual joint and equal expense of them the said D. L. and P. S., their respective heirs
and assigns forever; as to so much and such parts of the
said wall as shall be used by the said P. S. his heirs
and assigns, in erecting and building the said store,
which he is now about erecting on his said lot, and
as to all coping of the said gable end, whether such
coping be used by the said P. S., his heirs or assigns, in
erecting and building the said store or not, and as
to the residue of the said wall not used by the said
P. S., his heirs or assigns, in erecting or building the
said store, such reparation or rebuilding of such residue

of the said wall shall be at the sole and separate expense
of the said D. L., his heirs or assigns forever; and that
in every case of such reparation or rebuilding, should the
same be necessary and proper, and either party, his
heirs or assigns request the other to unite in the same,
and to contribute to the expense thereof, according to
the true intent and meaning of this agreement, then the
other party his heirs or assigns forever, may cause such
reparation or rebuilding to be made and done, and charge
the other party, his heirs and assigns forever, with the
proportion of the expenses, costs, and charges thereof,
according to the true intent and meaning of this agreement: and that in every case of such reparation or rebuilding, as the case may be, such repairs shall restore
the said wall to the state and condition in which it now
is, in all respects as nearly as may be; and that in every
case of rebuilding, such wall shall be rebuilt upon the
same spot on which it now stands, and be of the same
size and the same materials, as far as they may go, and
as to the deficiency with others of the same quality and
goodness, and in all respects shall be made of the same
quality and goodness as the present wall.   It being further in like manner mutually understood and agreed by
and between the said parties, that this agreement shall
be perpetual, and run with the land, and be obligatory
upon the heirs and assigns of the said parties respectively, forever, and in all cases and on all occasions, shall
be construed as a covenant running with the land: but
that this agreement shall not have the effect or operation of conveying to the said P. S., his heirs or assigns,
the fee simple of the one moiety or any other part of the

ground or land on which the said wall now stands, but only the right to the use and benefit of the said wall as a party wall forever.

In witness, &c.

Signed, sealed, &c.

PATENT RIGHTS.

PETITION.

To the Commissioner of Patents, Ottawa :

The petition of   , of the   of   , in the Province of Ontario,   sheweth,

That he hath invented new and useful improvements on   ,.not known or used by others before his invention thereof, and not being in public use or on sale for more than one year previous to his application in Canada, with his consent or allowance as such Inventor, the title or name whereof is

Your petitioner therefore prays that a patent may be granted to him for the said invention, and, for the purposes of the Patent Act of 18   your petitioner elects his domicile in the City of Ottawa, Province of Ontario.

Toronto, 1st September, 18   .

SURRENDER TO BE WRITTEN ON THE ORIGINAL PAPER.

To ALL TO WHOM THESE PRESENTS SHALL COME :

   , of the   of   , in the Province of Ontario,   , within named, sends greeting :

WHEREAS the within written patent for an improve-

ment on   is deemed defective or inoperative by
reason of insufficient description or specification, and the
error arose from inadvertance, accident or mistake, without any fraudulent or deceptive intention, and the Commissioner of Patents accordingly, in pursuance of the
statute in such respect hath agreed to accept a surrender
of the same.

Now know ye that the said   within named, doth
by these presents surrender and yield up the within
written patent, granted to him for improvements on   ,
and bearing date the   day of   18 .

In witness whereof the said   hath set his hand
and affixed his seal this   day of   A.D. 18 .

SPECIFICATION.

To ALL WHOM IT MAY CONCERN :

Be it known that I,   of   have invented a
new and useful   [*stating the use and title of the
          and if the application is for an improvement, it
should read thus :* "a new and useful improvement on a
(*or*, on the)   &c."]; and I do hereby declare that
the following is a full, clear and exact description of the
construction and operation of the same ; reference being
had to the annexed drawings, making a part of this
specification, in which figure 1 is, &c. [*describing* all the
sections of the drawings, and referring to the parts by
letters. Then should follow the *description of the construction and operation of the machine, &c., and the
principle upon which it is formed, and the several modes
in which the inventor has contemplated the application of
that principle or character by which it may be dis-*

tinguished from other inventions ; and, lastly, the *claim,* which should express the nature and character of the invention, and identify the parts claimed separately or in combination. If the specification is for an *improvement,* the original invention thereof should be disclaimed, and the claim confined to the improvement.]

Witness my hand, this   day of   A. D. 18 .

ASSIGNMENT OF LETTERS PATENT.

THIS INDENTURE, made (in duplicate) the   day of A. D. 18 .

BETWEEN   of the first part; and   of the second part.

WHEREAS the said part of the first part ha obtained letters patent of the Dominion of Canada   for the exclusive right and liberty to make, construct, use, and sell to others   which said letters patent bear date the   day of   one thousand eight hundred and

And whereas the said part of the second part ha agreed to purchase from the said part of the first part the right to manufacture, use, and sell the said   in and for the   limits hereinafter described, that is to say :   and in no other place or places

Now THIS INDENTURE WITNESSETH, that the said part of the first part for and in consideration of the said agreement; and of the sum of   paid by the said part of the second part to the said part of the first part, the receipt whereof is hereby acknowledged, doth hereby grant, assign, sell, transfer and set over unto the said part of the second part   executors, adminis-

W

trators, or assigns all that the full and exclusive right to   so secured by the said letters patent, as aforesaid, in and within   and in no other place or places for the term of   in entirety from the   day of   as fully and entirely in all respects within the limits aforesaid, as the same would have been held, used, and enjoyed by the said part of the first part, had this grant, assignment and sale not been made.   ·

And the said part of the second part hereby covenant with the said part of the first part that   will not import or cause to be imported into Canada the said invention after the expiration of one year from the granting of the said patent and that   shall and will before the expiration of   years from the date of the said patent commence and continuously carry on in Canada the construction or manufacture of the said invention or discovery so patented as aforesaid in default whereof the said part of the second part shall forfeit and pay to the said part of the first part the sum of   of lawful money of Canada, and also that the said part of the second part shall and will comply with all the present or future provisions and requirements of any act or acts of the Parliaments of Canada or Ontario regulating the Law of Patents in the Province of Ontario.

In witness whereof, &c.

Signed, sealed, &c.

ASSIGNMENT OF LETTERS PATENT.
(Another form.)

—

To all to whom these Presents shall come :
        of, &c., sends greeting :

WHEREAS the said   has invented a certain and has applied for and obtained letters patent under the great seal of   granting to him and to his assigns the exclusive right to make and vend the same, which letters patent are dated on the   day of   A.D. 18 .

And whereas   of, &c., has agreed to purchase from the said   all the right, title and interest which he the said   now hath in the said invention under the said letters patent, for the price or sum of

Now these presents witness, that for and in consideration of the said sum of   by the said   paid to the said   at or before the sealing and delivery of these presents, the receipt whereof is hereby acknowledged, he the said   hath assigned and transferred, and by these presents doth assign and transfer unto the said   his executors, administrators and assigns, the full and exclusive right to the invention made by him, and secured to him by the said letters patent, together with the said letters patent, and all his interest therein or right thereto.

In witness whereof the said   hath hereunto set his hand and seal, this   day of   A.D. 18 .

Signed, sealed, &c.

POWER OF ATTORNEY (BANK).

KNOW ALL MEN BY THESE PRESENTS THAT   do by these presents make, ordain, depute, constitute and appoint and in   place and stead put   to be true and lawful attorney for   and in   name to transact and manage all business with   ; to draw, accept, transfer and endorse all bills of exchange, drafts and promissory notes ; to pay and receive all moneys ; to give acquittances for the same ; to draw and sign all orders and drafts for payment of money on the said bank, or on their President, Manager, or other authorized officer or agent ; to settle, balance and arrange all books and accounts : and generally to do every act, matter and thing which the nature of   business with the said bank shall or may require as amply and effectually to all intents and purposes as   the said constituent   could do or have done in   own proper person, (save and except that nothing herein contained shall extend or be construed to extend to authorize the said attorney to accept any transfer of stock of or in the said bank ; nor to receive or give receipts for dividends that are now or that shall hereafter become due and payable for the same ; nor to sell, assign or transfer all or any part of   stock of or in the said bank ; nor to vote at any meeting of the stockholders of the said bank) hereby ratifying and confirming and promising to ratify and confirm all and whatsoever said attorney shall lawfully do or cause to be done in and about the premises aforesaid by virtue hereof this Letter of Attorney shall be and remain in full force and effect until due notice in writing of its revocation shall have been given to the said

In witness whereof   have hereunto set   hand and seal this   day of   A.D. 18 .

Signed, sealed, &c.

POWER OF ATTORNEY (BLANK).

KNOW ALL MEN BY THESE PRESENTS, that   do hereby make, nominate, constitute and appoint true and lawful attorney for   and in   name, place and stead, and for   sole use and benefit to

[*Here insert the particular objects for which the power is given*] and for all and every of the purposes aforesaid do   hereby give and grant unto   said attorney, full and absolute power and authority to do and execute all acts, deeds, matters, and things necessary to be done in and about the premises, and also to commence, institute and prosecute all actions suits and other proceedings which may be necessary or expedient in and about the premises as fully and effectually to all intents and purposes as   could do if personally present and acting therein, and also with full power and authority for said attorney to appoint a substitute or substitutes, and such substitution at pleasure to revoke   hereby ratifying and confirming, and agreeing to ratify, confirm and allow all and whatsoever   said attorney or such substitute or substitutes shall lawfully do or cause to be done in the premises by virtue hereof.

In witness whereof   have hereunto set   hand and seal this   day of   A.D. 18   .

Signed, sealed, &c.

NOTARIAL CERTIFICATE TO FOREGOING.

CANADA.
Province of
        To Wit :   }   I,   a Notary Public,

duly commissioned in and for said Province, residing

    do hereby certify and attest that the within Power of Attorney was duly signed, sealed and executed by the constituent   therein named in my presence and in presence of the other witness thereto subscribed ; that the signatures thereto subscribed of   as constituent and of   as witnesses, are the true and respective signatures of the said constituent   and witnesses, and that said Power of Attorney was so executed at   in Canada (where stamped paper is not used or required by law), on the date thereof.

    Act whereof being requested, I have granted these presents in Notarial form to serve and avail as occasion shall or may require.

    In testimony whereof I have hereto set my hand and affixed my Notarial seal at   this   day of A.D. 18 .

POWER OF ATTORNEY (GENERAL FORM).

KNOW ALL MEN BY THESE PRESENTS, that   for divers good causes and considerations,   thereunto moving, ha   nominated, constituted and appointed, and by these presents do   nominate, constitute and appoint   true and lawful attorney, for   and in name and on   behalf and for   sole and exclusive use and benefit to demand, recover and receive from all and every or any person or persons whomsoever all and every sum and sums of money, goods, chattels, effects and things whatsoever which now are or is, or which shall or may hereafter appear to be due, owing, payable

or belonging to   whether for rent or arrears of rent
or otherwise in respect of   estate, or for the principal money and interest now or hereafter to become
payable to   upon or in respect of any Mortgage or
other security, or for the interest or dividends to accrue
or become payable to   for or in respect of any shares,
stock or interest which   may now or hereafter hold in
any joint stock or incorporated company or companies,
or for any moneys or securities for money which are now
or hereafter may be due or owing or belonging to
upon any bond, note, bill or bills of exchange, balance
of account current, consignment, contract, decree, judgment, order or execution, or upon any other account.

Also to examine, state, settle, liquidate and adjust all
or any account or accounts depending between   and
any person or persons whomsoever. And to sign, draw,
make or endorse   name to any cheque or cheques or
orders for the payment of money, bill or bills of exchange, or note or notes of hand, in which   shall
be interested or concerned, which shall be requisite.
And also in   name to draw upon any bank or banks,
individual or individuals, for any sum or sums of money
that is or are or may be to   credit or which   or
may be entitled to receive, and the same to deposit in
any bank or other place, and again at pleasure to draw
for from time to time as   could do. And upon the
recovery or receipt of all and every or any sum or sums
of money, goods, chattels, effects or things due, owing,
payable or belonging to   for   and in   name and
as   act and deed to sign, execute and deliver such
good and sufficient receipts, releases and acquittances,

certificates, reconveyances, surrenders, assignments, me-
morials, or other good and effectual discharges, as may be
requisite.

Also in case of neglect, refusal or delay on the part of
any person or persons to make and render just, true and
full account, payment, delivery and satisfaction in the
premises him, them or any of them thereunto to compel,
and for that purpose for   in   name to make such
claims and demands, arrests, seizures, levies, attachments,
distraints, and sequestrations, or to commence, institute,
sue and prosecute to judgment and execution such
actions, ejectments and suits at law or in equity as
said attorney or attorneys shall think fit ; also to appear
before all or any Judges, Magistrates or other Officers of
the Courts of Law or Equity, and then and there to sue
plead, answer, defend and reply in all matters and
causes concerning the premises ; and also to exercise and
execute all powers of sale or foreclosure, and all other
power and authorities vested in   by any mortgage or
mortgages belonging to   as mortgagee.

And also, in case of any difference or dispute with any
person or persons concerning any of the matters aforesaid, to submit any such differences and disputes to arbitration or umpirage, in such manner as   said attorney
or attorneys shall see fit : and to compound, compromise
and to accept part in satisfaction for the payment of the
whole of any debt or sum of money payable to   or to
grant an extension of time for the payment of the same,
either with or without taking security, or otherwise to
act in respect of the same as to   said attorney or
attorneys shall appear most expedient.

And also, for   and in   name, or otherwise on
    behalf, to take possession of and to let, set, manage
and improve   real estate, lands, messuages and hereditaments whatsoever, and wheresoever, and from time
to time to appoint any agents or servants to assist him
or them in managing the same, and to displace or remove
such agents or servants, and appoint others, using therein the same power and discretion as   might do.

And also, as and when   said attorney or attorneys shall think fit to sell and absolutely dispose of
said real estates, lands and hereditaments, and also such
shares, stocks, bonds, mortgages and other securities for
money as hereinbefore mentioned, either together or in
parcels, for such price or prices, and by public auction or
private contract, as to   said attorney or attorneys
shall seem reasonable or expedient; and to convey,
assign, transfer and make over the same respectively to
the purchaser or purchasers thereof; with power to give
credit for the whole or any part of the purchase money
thereof; and to permit the same to remain unpaid for
whatever time and upon whatever security, real or personal, either comprehending the purchased property or
not, as   said attorney or attorneys shall think safe
and proper.

And further, for   and in   name as   act
and deed to execute and do all such assurances, deeds
covenants and things as shall be required, and   said
attorney and attorneys shall see fit, for all or any of the
purposes aforesaid; and to sign and give receipts and
discharges for all or any of the sum or sums of money
which shall come to his or their hands by virtue of the

powers herein contained, and which receipts, whether
given in   name or that of   said attorney or
attorneys, shall exempt the person or persons paying
such sum or sums of money from all responsibility of
seeing to the application thereof.

And also, for   and in   name, or otherwise,
and on   behalf, to enter into any agreement or arrangement with every or any person to whom   or
shall be indebted touching the payment or satisfaction of
his demand, or any part thereof ; and generally to act
in relation to   estate and effects, real and personal,
as fully and effectually, in all respects, as   could do
if personally present.

And   hereby grant full power to   said attorney to substitute and appoint one or more attorney or
attorneys under him, with the same or more limited
powers, and such substitute and substitutes at pleasure to
remove, and others to appoint,   the said   hereby
agreeing and covenanting for   heirs, executors and
administrators to allow, ratify and confirm whatsoever
          said attorney or his substitute or substitutes shall
do or cause to be done in the premises by virtue of these
presents, including in such confirmation whatsoever shall
be done between the time of   decease or of the revocation of these presents, and the time of such decease or
revocation becoming known to   said attorney or
attorneys, or such substitute or substitutes.

As witness   hand   and seal   this
day of   A.D. 18 .

Signed, sealed, &c

POWER OF ATTORNEY TO RECEIVE DEBTS.

KNOW ALL MEN BY THESE PRESENTS that   being about to leave this Province for distant parts, for divers good causes and considerations   thereunto specially moving, have made, ordained, nominated, constituted, and appointed, and by these presents do make, ordain, nominate, constitute, and appoint   true and lawful attorney for   and in   name, place, and stead, but for   sole and exclusive use and benefit, to ask, demand, sue for, recover and receive, all sum or sums of money, debts, and demands whatsoever, which now is, or are, or at any time hereafter during the continuance of these presents shall be due or owing to me by any person or persons, or on any account or accounts whatsoever within the Province aforesaid, and also to compound any such debt or debts, or sum or sums of money, or any other claim or demand whatsoever which I now, or at any time hereafter during the continuance of these presents, shall or may have, or be entitled to within the said Province, and make and receive all and every such composition or compositions, and upon the receipt thereof, or for any other purposes within these presents, for me, and in my name, to give, seal, and execute all and every such receipts, acquittances, releases, and discharges as my said attorney shall see fit in that behalf, and to endorse and sign my name to all drafts, bills, notes or cheques made payable to my order.

And for the purposes aforesaid   do hereby give and grant unto   said attorney full and absolute power and authority to do, perform, and execute all and every acts, deeds, matters, and things ; and also to commence, institute, and prosecute all actions, suits, and other proceedings, which may be requisite and necessary or expedient to be done, commenced, instituted, or prosecuted in and about the premises, as fully and effectually to all intents and purposes as   could do if personally present and acting in the premises with power to appoint a substitute or substitutes, for all or any of the purposes aforesaid, and such substitution at pleasure to revoke   the said   hereby ratifying and confirming and agreeing to ratify and confirm all and whatsoever   said attorney   or such substitute or substitutes shall lawfully do, or cause to be done, in or about the premises by virtue hereof.

In witness whereof   have hereunto set hand and seal ,this   day of   A.D. 18 .
Signed, sealed, &c.

POWER OF ATTORNEY.

(To receive Legacy.)

—

To all to whom these Presents shall come:

I,   of, &c., and .   my wife (late   ) one of the daughters and legatees, named in the last will and testament of   late of, &c. deceased, send greeting :

Whereas, the said   in and by his last will and testament, bearing date the   day of   A.D. 18 , did, amongst other things, give and bequeath unto his said daughter, the sum of   payable in six months after his decease (or did give and bequeath to her an equal share of his estate, as the case may be ;) And of his said

will appointed   executor, as in and by the said will
duly proved, and remaining in   in and for the
county of   relation being thereunto had, appears.

Now know ye, that I, the said   and   my
wife, have made, constituted, and appointed, and by
these presents do make, constitute, and appoint   of
         in the county of   our true and lawful
attorney, for us and in our names, and for our use, to
ask, demand, sue for, recover, and receive, of and from
the said   executor as aforesaid, or in whose hands
soever the same may be found, the said legacy or bequest
mentioned in the said will, and also all such other sum
or sums of money, debts, goods, wares, and demands
whatsoever, which are or shall be due, owing, payable,
and belonging to us by any means whatsoever, for or on
account of her full share, part, or dividend of the estate
aforesaid.

Giving and granting unto our said attorney, by these
presents, full power and authority in and about the
premises, to have, use and take, all lawful ways and
means, in our names for the purposes aforesaid, and upon
the receipt of any such debts, dues or sums of money (as
the case may be) acquittances, or other sufficient discharges, for us, and in our names to make, seal and
deliver.

And generally, all and every other act or acts, thing
or things, device and devices, in the law whatsoever,
needful and necessary to be done in and about the
premises, for us and in our names to do, execute, and
perform, as fully and amply, to all intents and purposes,
as we ourselves might or could do, if personally present ;

and attorneys one or more under him, for the purpose aforesaid, to make and constitute, and again at pleasure to revoke ;

Hereby ratifying, allowing, and holding for firm and effectual, all and whatsoever our said attorney shall lawfully do in and about the premises, by virtue hereof.

In witness, &c., this   day of   A.D. 18 .

Signed, sealed, &c.

POWER OF ATTORNEY.

(Custom House.)

—

KNOW ALL MEN BY THESE PRESENTS, that I,   of   in the county of   and Province of   merchant, have made, constituted and appointed, and by these presents do make, constitute and appoint, of   in the county of   of the said Province, gentleman, my true and lawful attorney, for me and in my name, place and stead [here set forth what the power is granted for], to receive and enter at the custom-house at   in the county of   any goods, wares or merchandize imported by me, or which may hereafter arrive, that are consigned to me ; to sign my name, and to seal and deliver for me, as my act and deed, any bond or bonds which may be required by the collector, of customs at   in the county aforesaid, for securing the duties on any such goods, wares or merchandize : Also to sign my name; to seal and deliver for me, and as my act and deed, any bond or bonds requisite for obtaining the debenture on any goods, wares or merchandize when exported ; and generally, to transact all business at the said custom-house, in which I am or may hereafter be interested or concerned, as fully as I could if personally present.   And I do hereby declare, that all bonds signed and executed by my said attorney shall be as binding on me as those signed by myself; and this power shall remain in full force and virtue until revoked by a written notice given to the said collector.

In witness, &c., this   day of   A.D. 18 .
Signed, sealed, &c.

POWER OF ATTORNEY.

(*To Manage and Sell Estates, &c.*)

—

KNOW ALL MEN BY THESE PRESENTS, that I,
of   for divers good causes and considerations me hereunto especially moving, have made constituted and appointed, and by these presents do make, constitute and appoint   of   my true and lawful attorney, for me and in my name to enter into and upon, and to take possession of all and singular my messuages, farms, lands, tenements and hereditaments whatsoever, and wheresoever situate in   .   And also, for me and in my name to make sale of and convey all or any of the said premises, and to sign receipts for the purchase moneys, and to sign, seal and execute, and as my act and deed, acts and deeds, deliver good, sufficient and valid deeds of conveyance and assurance, for conveying the said premises or any part thereof to any purchaser or purchasers of the same, his, her or their heirs and assigns ; and also, for me and in my name to contract with any person or persons for leasing any of the said premises,

and to make, seal, deliver and execute any lease or leases, demises or grants, for any term or terms of years not exceeding years, in possession, and not in reversion, and at such rent or rents as my said attorney shall think proper; and also, for me and in my name to ask, receive and recover of all tenants and occupiers whomsoever, of all and every the said premises, all rents and arrears of rent, issues and profits due and owing, or which at any time or times hereafter shall grow and become due and owing on account of same premises, and if need be to distrain for, sue or prosecute for the same; and also, for me and in my name to commence and prosecute any action or actions, suit or suits, as well real as personal and mixed, or otherwise, in any court of law or equity in the said Province, in relation to the said premises, and the same to prosecute and follow, or to discontinue or become nonsuit therein, as my said attorney shall see cause; and generally for me and in my name to do, perform and execute all and whatsoever shall be requisite and necessary to be done in and about the premises, as fully and effectually, to all intents and purposes as I might or could do if personally present; hereby promising to ratify and confirm all and whatsoever my said attorney shall lawfully do or cause to be done by virtue of these presents: And lastly, I do hereby revoke and make void all former powers of attorney, authorities and deputations, by me at any time heretofore made, given or executed, in any of the matters or things above mentioned, to any other person or persons whomsoever.

In witness, &c., this   day of   A.D. 18 .

Signed, sealed, &c.

POWER TO TRANSFER STOCK.

KNOW ALL MEN BY THESE PRESENTS, that I,
of   do make, constitute, and appoint   of
my true and lawful attorney, for me and in my name
and behalf, to transfer, assign, and set over unto
of   (or, *any other person or persons*),   shares
in the capital stock of the   bank, in   standing in my name on the books of said *corporation*, and to
do all necessary acts, and to make the necessary acquittances and discharges to effect the premises ; (add, if
desired, *and I do further empower him to substitute any
person or persons under him with like power*) ; hereby
ratifying and confirming all my said attorney (*or his substitute or substitutes*, to be added if desired,) shall lawfully do by virtue hereof.

In witness, &c., this   day of   A.D. 18 .
Signed, sealed, &c.

POWER TO RECEIVE DIVIDENDS.

KNOW ALL MEN BY THESE PRESENTS, that I,
of   do constitute and appoint   of   to receive from the cashier of the   bank (or the *treasurer of*) of the city of   the dividend or dividends now due to me, on all stock standing in my name
on the books of the said bank, and to receipt for the
same ; hereby ratifying and confirming all that by him
may lawfully be done by virtue hereof in the premises.

In witness, &c., this   day of   A.D. 18 .
Signed, sealed, &c.

x

POWER OF ATTORNEY (REVOCATION OF).

—

WHEREAS I,   of   did on the   day of
A.D 18   , by a certain instrument in writing,
or letter of attorney, make and appoint   of
to be my true and lawful attorney, in my name and for
my use, to (*here set forth what the attorney was authorised to do, precisely in the language of the original power,*)
as by the same writing, reference thereto being had,
will fully appear ; Now know all men by these presents,
that I, the said   for a good cause and valuable consideration, have revoked, recalled, and made void, and by
these presents do revoke, recall, and make void to all intents and purposes, the said recited letter of attorney, and
all powers or authorities therein granted, and all acts
and things which shall, or may be done or performed by
virtue thereof, in any manner whatsoever.

(*If another attorney is to be appointed, continue
thus :*—" And further know ye, that I, the said
do by these presents name, constitute, and appoint, and
in my place and stead put and depute   of   to
be my true and lawful attorney, etc.," or *as desired.*)

In witness whereof, &c., this   day of   A.D. 18   .
Signed, sealed, &c.

———

POWER OF ATTORNEY (REVOCATION OF).
(*Another form.*)
—

KNOW ALL MEN BY THESE PRESENTS, that I,
of   for divers good causes and considerations, me
hereunto especially moving, have revoked countermanded,
annulled and made void, and by these presents do revoke,

countermand, annul and make void, a certain deed poll or power of attorney, under my hand and seal, bearing date   to   of   given delivered and executed, and all powers and authorities whatsoever therein expressed and delivered.

As witness, &c, this   day of   A.D. 18 .

Signed, sealed, &c.

PROTEST (MARINE).

PROVINCE OF ONTARIO, ⎫
County of   ⎬
               To WIT : ⎭

BY PUBLIC INSTRUMENT OF PROTEST, be it known and made manifest to all whom it doth or shall or may concern, that on the   day of   in the year of our Lord one thousand eight hundred and   before me,   a Notary Public, by Royal authority duly appointed, in and for the Province of Ontario, formerly constituting Upper Canada, residing at   in the said county.

Personally appeared   master,   of the said   of   burthen, of the port of   and brought with him   mate on board of the said   each of whom, by me being duly sworn according to law, on their solemn oaths, did depose, declare, and say as follows : That

And further these deponents say not.

Subscribed and sworn before me at   in the County of   severally by the said   and   this day of   A.D. 18 .

Notary Public.

Wherefore I, the said Notary, at the request of the said   master,   of the said   as well on his own behalf, as on behalf of his   owners, freighters, officers and crew, have protested, and by these presents do most solemnly protest, against all and singular the cause and causes operating as aforesaid, to the serious detriment of the said   her cargo, sails, rigging, and other gearing, or any part or portion thereof, and more especially against the storm and heavy winds and gales, high and dangerous seas, experienced on her late voyage, bound as aforesaid ; and for all losses, costs, charges, damages, interest, and expenses whatsoever, suffered or sustained, for or by reason or means of the facts and circumstances set forth in the foregoing affidavit, to be claimed and recovered in time and place convenient. And these presents do serve and avail for that purpose.

In witness whereof, I have hereunto set my hand and official seal, the   day of   A.D. 18 · .

Notary Public.

I,   of the   of .   in the county of a Notary Public, by Royal Authority duly appointed, in and for the Province of Ontario, formerly constituting Upper Canada, do hereby certify that the within is a true copy of the deposition of   and   of the vessel   taken before me, this   day of   A.D. 18 , and now filed in my office.

Notary Public.

PROTEST (NOTARIAL).

On this   day of   in the year of our Lord one
thousand eight hundred and   at the request of
      the holder of the   hereunto annexed, I
a Notary Public for the Province of Ontario, by Royal
authority duly appointed, did exhibit the said
unto   at   being the place where the same is
payable, and there speaking to him did demand
of the said   to which demand he answered

Wherefore I, the said Notary, at the request aforesaid,
have protested and do hereby solemnly protest, as well
against all the parties to the said   as against all
other persons whom it may concern, for all interest, damages, costs, charges, expenses and other losses suffered
or to be suffered, for want of   of the said

And afterwards, on the day and year mentioned in the
margin, I, the said Notary Public did serve due notice
according to law, of the said presentation, non-
and protest, of the said   upon the several parties
thereto, by depositing in Her Majesty's post office at
      being the nearest post office to the place of the
said presentation, letters containing such notices, one of
which letters was addressed to each of the said parties
severally, the superscription and address of which letters
are respectively copied below, as follows, that is to say :

In testimony whereof, I have hereunto set my hand
and affixed my seal of office, the day and year first above
written.

Notary Public.

Notices mailed the   day of   A.D. 18   .
Protest, $0.50.   Postage   Notices $

QUIT CLAIM DEED.

—

• This Indenture, made (in duplicate) the   day of
    A.D. 18 ,

  Between   of the first part ;   wife of the said
party of the first part, of the second part ; and   of
the third part :

  Witnesseth, that the said part of the first part, for
and in consideration of   of lawful money of Canada,
to   in hand paid by the said part of the third
part, at or before the sealing and delivery of these
Presents (the receipt whereof is hereby acknowledged),
ha granted, released and quitted claim, and by these
Presents, do grant, release and quit claim unto the said
part of the third part   and assigns, all
estate, right, title, interest, claim and demand whatsoever,
both at law and in equity, or otherwise howsoever, and
whether in possession or expectancy, of, in, to or out of
all and singular th certain parcel or tract of land
and premises situate lying and being

  Together with the appurtenances thereto belonging or
appertaining ; to have and to hold the aforesaid land
and premises, with all and singular the appurtenances
thereto belonging or appertaining, unto and to the use of
the said part of the third part   heirs and assigns,
for ever; subject, nevertheless, to the reservations,
limitations, provisoes and conditions expressed in the
original grant thereof from the Crown.

  In witness whereof, &c.

  Signed, sealed, &c.

  Received on the day of the date of this Indenture, &c.
      (Usual Affidavit of Execution.)

RECEIPT FOR RENT.

LONDON, ONT., *1st September, 18* .

RECEIVED from   the sum of one hundred dollars, for half-year's rent of store on   street due this day.

$100.

RECEIPT IN FULL.

RECEIVED the   day of   A.D. 18 , from Mr.   the sum of fifty dollars, in full of all demands.

$50.

RECEIPT ON ACCOUNT.

TORONTO, ONT., *12th October, 18* .

RECEIVED from Mr.   the sum of one hundred dollars, on account of purchase-money of horse and buggy sold to him this day.

$100.

RECEIPT TO EXECUTOR.

RECEIVED the   day of   A.D. 18 , from and   Esquires, executors of the last will and testament of   deceased, the sum of one thousand dollars, in full of all demands against the estate of the said

$1,000.

RELEASE, GENERAL, OF ALL DEMANDS.

THIS INDENTURE, made the   day of   A.D. 18 ,

BETWEEN •   of the first part ; and   of the second part.

WHEREAS, there have been divers accounts, dealings and transactions between the said parties hereto respectively, all of which have now been finally adjusted, settled and disposed of, and the said parties hereto have respectively agreed to give to each other the mutual releases and discharges hereinafter contained in manner hereinafter expressed.

NOW THEREFORE THESE PRESENTS WITNESS, that in consideration of the premises and of the sum of one dollar, of lawful money of Canada to each of them, the said parties hereto respectively paid by the other of them at or before the sealing and delivery hereof (the receipt whereof is hereby acknowledged), each of them the said parties hereto respectively, doth hereby for himself and herself respectively, his and her respective heirs, executors, administrators, and assigns, remise, release and forever acquit and discharge the other of them, his and her heirs, executors, administrators and assigns, and all his, her and their lands and tenements, goods, chattels, estate and effects respectively whatsoever and wheresoever, of and from all debts, sum and sums of money, accounts, reckonings, actions, suits, cause and causes of action and suit, claims and demands whatsoever, either at law or in equity, or otherwise howsoever, which either of the said parties now have, or has, or ever had, or might or could have against the other of them, on any account whatsoever, of and concerning any matter, cause or thing whatsoever between them, the said parties hereto respectively, from the beginning of the world down to the day of the date of these presents.

\ In witness, &c.

Signed, sealed, &c.

GENERAL RELEASE (BY DEED POLL).

KNOW ALL MEN BY THESE PRESENTS, that   for and in consideration of the sum of   to   in hand paid by   have remised, released and forever discharged, and by these presents do for   heirs, executors, administrators and assigns, remise, release and forever discharge the said   heirs, executors and administrators, of and from all and all manner of action and actions, cause and causes of action, suits, debts, dues, sums of money, claims and demands whatsoever at law or in equity which ever had or now have or which   or   heirs, executors, administrators or assigns hereafter can, shall or may have by reason of any matter cause or thing whatsoever, from the beginning of the world to the date of these presents.

In witness whereof   have hereunto set   hand and seal this   day of   A.D. 18 .

Signed, sealed, &c.

RELEASE TO A GUARDIAN.

KNOW ALL MEN, &c., that A. B., &c., son and heir of B. B., deceased, hath remised, released and forever quit-

claimed, and by these presents doth remise, &c., unto
C. D., of   his guardian, all and all manner of action and actions, suits, reckonings, accounts, debts, dues
and demands whatsoever, which he the said A. B. ever
had, now hath, or which he, his executors and administrators, at any time hereafter can or may have, claim
or demand against the said C. D., his executors or administrators, for, touching and concerning the management and disposition of any of the lands, tenements
and hereditaments of the said A. B., situate, &c., or any
part thereof, or for or by reason of any moneys, rents or
profits by him received out of the same, or any payments
made thereout, during the minority of the said A. B., or
by reason of any matter cause or thing whatsoever relating thereto, from the beginning of the world to the day
of the date hereof.

In witness, &c., this   day of   A.D. 18 .
Signed, sealed, &c.

RELEASE TO EXECUTORS ON PAYMENT OF LEGACY.

KNOW ALL MEN BY THESE PRESENTS, that   of
        and   his wife, late   one of the daugh-
ters and legatees named in the will of   late of
deceased, do hereby acknowledge that they have this day
had and received of and from   and   executors of the last will and testament of the said .
deceased, the sum of   in full satisfaction and payment of all such sum or sums of money, legacies and be-
quests as are given and bequeathed to the said   by

the last will and testament aforesaid, and all interest accrued therefrom.

And therefore the said   and   his wife. do by these presents, remise, release, quit-claim and forever discharge the said   and   their heirs, executors and administrators, of the said legacy or legacies, and of and from all actions, suits, payments, accounts, reckonings, claims and demands whatsoever, for or by reason thereof, or of any other acts, matter, cause or thing whatsoever, from the beginning of the world to the day of the date of these presents.

In witness, &c., this   day of ·   A.D. 18 .

Signed, sealed, &c.

RELEASE FROM LEGATEE ON COMING OF AGE.

KNOW ALL MEN BY THESE PRESENTS, that whereas A. B., of   made his last will and testament in writing, bearing date   and among other legacies therein contained, did give and bequeath unto me, C. D., of   his son, the annual sum of   to be paid to me quarterly, until I should attain the age of twenty-one years ; and of his will constituted E. F. and G. H. joint executors, as in and by the said will may appear ; anp whereas the said E. F. and G. H. did jointly accept of the said executorship and trust, and I, the said C. D., have attained my said age of twenty-one years ; and whereas the said E. F. and G. H. have made up an account with me the said C. D., of all moneys received and paid by the said E. F. and G. H., and all transactions in

pursuance of the said executorship and trust ; and have
not only paid me the said C. D., the balance of such
accounts but also delivered unto me all the writings and
papers belonging to the estate of the said deceased A. B. :
Now know ye, that I the said C. D. being fully satisfied in the premises, have remised, released and forever
quit-claimed, and by these presents do remise, release and
forever quit-claim, unto the said E. F. and G. H., and
each of them, their and each of their executors and administrators, all reckonings and accounts, sum and sums
of money by them had and received in pursuance of the
said trust, or by means of their being executors to the
said A. B. as aforesaid ; and also of and from all other
reckonings accounts and demands whatsoever, from the
beginning of the world to the day of the date of these
presents.

In witness, &c., this   day of   A.D. 18 .
Signed, sealed, &c.

RELEASE OF A TRUST.

To ALL, &c., A. B., of, &c., sendeth greeting :

WHEREAS, by Indenture bearing date   made between, &c. [here recite the deed], in which said Indenture
the said A. B. doth hereby declare that his name was only
used in trust, for the benefit and behoof of C. D., of
      : Now, know ye, that I, the said A. B., in dis-
charge of the trust reposed in me, at the request of the
said C. D., have remised, released and surrendered, assigned and set over, and by these presents for me, my
executors and administrators, do freely and absolutely

remise, &c., unto the said C. D., his executors, &c., all the estate, right, title, interest, use, benefit, privilege and demand whatsoever, which I, the said A. B., have or may have, or claim, of or to the said premises, or of and in any sum of money, or other matter or thing whatsoever, in the said Indenture contained, mentioned and expressed ; so that neither I, the said A. B., my executors or administrators, or any of us, at any time hereafter, shall or will ask, claim challenge or demand, any interest, &c., or other thing, in any manner whatsoever, by reason or means of the said Indenture, or any covenant therein contained, but thereof and therefrom, and from all actions suits and demands, which I, my executors, administrators or assigns, may have concerning the same, shall be utterly excluded and forever debarred by these presents.

In witness, &c., this   day of   A.D. 18 .
Signed, sealed, &c.

RELEASE OF A PROVISO OR CONDITION.

KNOW ALL MEN, &c., that I, A. B., of   for divers good considerations, me hereunto moving, have remised, released and quit-claimed, and by these presents, for me, my executors, administrators and assigns, do, &c., unto   of   his heirs, executors, administrators and assigns, as well a certain proviso or condition, and all and every the sum and sums of money specified in the same proviso or condition, contained or comprised in an Indenture, of &c., bearing date, &c., made between me the said A. B., of the one part, and the said   of the

other part, and also all and all manner of actions and
suits, cause and causes of actions and suits, for or concerning the said proviso or condition.

In witness, &c., this   day of   A.D. 18 .

Signed, sealed, &c.

RELEASE OF EQUITY OF REDEMPTION.

THIS INDENTURE, made (in duplicate) the   day of
          A.D. 18 , in pursuance of the Act respecting
Short Forms of Conveyances: BETWEEN

WHEREAS, by an Indenture dated the   day of
one thousand eight hundred and   did grant and
mortgage unto   ·   the lands hereinafter described,
for securing payment of the sum of   and interest,
as therein mentioned:

NOW THIS INDENTURE WITNESSETH, that the said part
of the first part, in consideration of the sum of   of
lawful money of Canada, to   well and truly paid by
the said part   of the second part (the receipt whereof is
hereby acknowledged), do   grant, release and confirm
unto the said part   of the second part,   heirs and
assigns, all   And also all estate, right, title, interest
and equity of redemption of and in the said lands which
said part   of the first part now ha   or may hereafter
claim, either at law or in equity, of, in, to or out of the
said lands:

TO HAVE AND TO HOLD unto the said part of the second
part   heirs and assigns, to and for   and their
sole and only use for ever ; subject, nevertheless, to
the reservations, limitations, provisoes and conditions

expressed in the original grant thereof from the Crown :

The said part   of the first part covenant with the said part of the second part that he ha   the right to grant and release the equity of redemption of the lands before described : And that the said part   of the first part ha done no act to encumber the said lands : And that the said part   of the second part shall have quiet poesession of the said lands : And that the said part   of the first part will execute such further assurances of the said lands as may be requisite.

In witness whereof, &c.

Signed, sealed, &c.

RECEIVED on the day of the date of this Indenture, &c.

(Usual Affidavit of Execution.)

RELEASE OF DOWER (BY WIDOW).

THIS INDENTURE, made (in duplicate) the   day of A.D. 18   , BETWEEN

WHEREAS,   of the   of   in the county of   in the Province of   by an Indenture dated the   day of   one thousand eight hundred and   for the consideration therein mentioned did grant and convey to   therein described   heirs and assigns, all that certain piece or parcel of land, situate, lying and being   .

And whereas the said   departed this life on the   day of   one thousand eight hundred and leaving his wife the party of the first part him surviving.

And whereas the said party of the first part, the wife of the said   did not join in the execution of the said Indenture, and at the request of the said party of the second part she hath agreed to execute these presents for the purpose of releasing her dower in the said lands and premises hereinbefore described.

Now THIS INDENTURE WITNESSETH, that the said party of the first part, in consideration of the premises and of the sum of   dollars of lawful money of Canada to her in hand well and truly paid by the said party of the second part, the receipt whereof is hereby acknowledged, doth grant, release and quit claim unto the said party of the second part,   heirs and assigns, all dower and all right and title thereto which she the said party of the first part now hath in the said land before mentioned, or can or may or could or might hereafter in anywise have or claim whether at common law or otherwise howsoever in to or out of the lands and premises before mentioned and described.

To have and to hold the same unto the said party of the second part   heirs and assigns for ever.

In witness whereof, &c.

Signed, sealed, &c.

RECEIVED on the day of the date of this Indenture from, &c.

(Usual Affidavit of Execution.)

RELEASE OF DOWER (BY WIFE).

THIS INDENTURE, made (in duplicate) the   day of   A.D. 18   , BETWEEN

WHEREAS, the said party of the second part, the now present husband of the said party of the first part, by an

Indenture dated the   day of   one thousand
eight hundred and   for the consideration therein
fully set forth did grant and convey to   therein
described   heirs and assigns; that certain piece or
parcel of land, being

And whereas the said party of the first part, did not
join in the execution of the said Indenture for the purpose of barring her dower in the land thereby conveyed,
and she hath at the request of the said party of the
third part agreed to execute these presents by and with
the full consent of the said party of the second part
testified by his execution hereof.

Now THIS INDENTURE WITNESSETH, that the said party
of the first part, in consideration of the premises and of
the sum of   of lawful money of Canada, to her in
hand well and truly paid by the said party of the third
part, the receipt whereof is hereby acknowledged,
doth (with the approbation and consent of the said
party of the second part) grant and release unto the said
party of the third part   heirs and assigns, all dower
and all right and title thereto which she, the said party
of the first part, now hath or in the event of her surviving her said husband, the said party hereto of the second
part may have in the said land before mentioned, or can
or may or could or might hereafter in anywise have or
claim, whether at common law or otherwise howsoever, in
to or out of the lands before mentioned.

To have and to hold unto the said party of the third
part   heirs and assigns forever.

In witness whereof, &c.

Signed, sealed, &c.

Y

Received on the day of the date of this Indenture from, &c.

(Usual Affidavit of Execution.)

RELEASE FROM ONE JOINT TENANT TO ANOTHER.

—

THIS INDENTURE, made the　　day of　　A.D. 18　,
BETWEEN D. J., of　　widow of W. J., late of
　　and sister of S. C., of　　of the one part,
and the said S. C., of　　of the other part.

WHEREAS the said D. J. and S. C. are and stand jointly seized to them and their heirs, of and in all those messuages, &c., situate in the township of　　in the county of [*here insert an accurate description*].

Now THIS INDENTURE WITNESSETH, that for and in consideration of the sum of　　by the said S. C. to the said D. J. in hand paid at or before the sealing and delivery hereof (the receipt whereof is hereby acknowledged), she, the said D. J., hath granted, released and confirmed, and by these presents doth grant, release and confirm unto the said S. C. and his heirs, all and singular the above mentioned messuages, farms, lands, tenements, hereditaments and premises hereinbefore mentioned, to be the joint estate of them the said D. J. and S. C., with their and every of their appurtenances, and all ways, &c., and the reversion, &c., and all the estate, &c.: To have and to hold the said messuages, farms, lands and premises, with their appurtenances, to the said S. C. and his heirs, to the only proper use and behoof of the said S. C., his heirs and assigns forever. [Add cove-

nants by D. J. that she is lawfully seized of one moiety
of the premises, in joint tenancy with the said S. C.,
hath good right to grant,   for quiet enjoyment,
free from incumbrances,   and for further assurance.]

In witness, &c.

Signed, sealed, &c.

SETTLEMENT OF PERSONAL PROPERTY.

THIS INDENTURE, made the   day of   A.D. 18   ,
BETWEEN   of   , bachelor of the first
part,   of   , spinster, of the second part,
and .   of   and   of   of the
third part, in consideration of an intended marriage
between the said   and   *, witnesseth as
follows :—

1. The said   and   shall hold $
transferred into their names by the said   and the
lease of   at   , in the county of   ,
assigned to them by the said   , by an Indenture
of even date herewith, upon trust that they and the
survivor of them, his executors and administrators, or
their or his assigns, after the said marriage, and during
the joint lives of the said parties, shall pay the income
of the trust premises to the said   for her sole and
separate use (and so that no anticipation thereof shall
be valid), and after the death of either of them, to the
survivor, during his or her life.

2. Subject to the foregoing trusts, the premises shall
be held upon trust for such children or child of the marriage, and in such manner as the said parties shall by

deed appoint; and so far as there shall be no such appointment, then as the survivor shall by deed, will or codicil appoint; and so far as the same shall be unappointed in trust for the children of the marriage equally, or child, if but one, who shall attain twenty-one, or being a daughter, or daughters, shall marry, but so that no child shall take an unappointed share without bringing his or her appointed share into account.

3. And, on failure of the foregoing trusts, upon trust for the said　　　his executors and administrators.

In witness, &c.

Signed, sealed, &c.

SETTLEMENT OF WIFE'S PERSONAL ESTATE IN CONTEMPLATION OF MARRIAGE.

This Indenture of three parts, made this　　　day of　　　A.D. 18　　by and between A. B., of　　　spinster, of the first part, C. D., of　　　Esquire, of the second part, and E. F., of　　　gentleman, of the third part, witnesseth,

That, whereas a marriage is intended to be had and solemnized between the said parties of the first and third parts, and the said A. B. is possessed of certain personal estate, to wit, the sum of　　　＂　which is now deposited with the　　　Company in the City of Toronto, forty shares of the capital stock of the　　　bank in eleven shares in the capital stock of the　　　bank in　　　all which said A. B., with the consent of said party of the third part, is minded and disposed to transfer to the said party of the second part, in trust for her own proper use and benefit;

Now, therefore, in consideration of the premises, and of one dollar paid by the said C. D. to the said A. B. (the receipt whereof is hereby acknowledged), the said A. B. doth hereby assign, transfer and set over to the said C. D. and his executors and administrators, all the moneys, property and effects above mentioned (whereof separate transfers, according to the usages and rules of the aforesaid corporations, have been made, of even date herewith); To hold the same to him the said C. D. and his executors and administrators, upon the special trusts and for the use and purposes following, and none others, namely :

In the first place, that, until the solemnization of the said marriage, the said C. D. shall pay over to the said A. B., or shall empower her to receive for her own use, all the income, profits and dividends arising from the said moneys and effects, and from any other estate which may be substituted therefor, as is hereinafter provided.

Secondly.—That from and after the solemnization of the said marriage, and during the coverture of the said A.B., the said C. D. shall receive and collect the incomes, profits and dividends of the said trust moneys and effects, or of any other substituted estate, so often and whenever the same shall be payable, and, after deduction of all incidental expenses, shall pay over the same, or so much thereof as she shall not direct to be added to the principal for the purpose of accumulation, to the said A. B. upon her sole and separate receipt therefor, and free from the control or interference of her said husband or any other person whomsoever.

Thirdly.—That, in case of the decease of the said

A. B. after the solemnization of the said marriage, and during the life of her said husband, the said moneys and effects shall be transferred and paid over by the said trustee to such person or persons as she the said A. B. by any instrument or note in writing subscribed by her in presence of at least two competent witnesses, shall order and appoint to take and receive the same ; and in default of her making such appointment, the same shall be transferred and paid to the said E. F., being then her husband, and in case of his decease before the said property shall be actually transferred and paid over to him, then to such person or persons as would be the legal representatives of the said A. B. by the statute for the distribution of intestates' estates.

Fourthly.—That, in the event of the decease of the said E. F., leaving the said A. B. surviving, all the property then held in trust under this indenture shall be transferred and conveyed back to the said A. B. ; and, until so transferred, the trustee shall pay over to her, or empower her to receive, the income, profits and dividends of the same for her own use.

Fifthly.—That the said trustee shall have power, with the approbation or at the request of the said A. B., expressed in writing, to sell and dispose of the said trust estate, or any part of it, and the proceeds to invest in other personal or in real estate, according to the written direction of the said A. B.; and the estate so purchased shall be had and held by the trustee for the same uses and purposes, and upon the same trusts, as are declared in and by this indenture, of and concerning the property and estate first above mentioned, and may be sold and the proceeds reinvested from time to time in trust in manner aforesaid; and it is hereby declared, that the purchaser of any estate held in trust as aforesaid, shall not be bound to see to the application of the said purchase money.

Sixthly.—That, in case of the decease of the party of the second part, or of his resignation of the said trust, he or his executors or administrators shall convey, transfer and pay over the whole of the trust estate then held by him to such person or persons as may be appointed in writing by the said party of the first part to be the trustee or trustees under this indenture; and such new trustee or trustees shall have all the powers, and shall hold the trust estate subject to all the provisions herein set forth and expressed; and the receipt of such new trustee or trustees for the trust property shall be a complete acquittance and discharge to the said party of the second part, his executors and administrators; and in like manner other new trustees may be appointed from time to time, as occasion may require.

And the said party of the second party doth hereby signify his acceptance of the said moneys and effects, and doth engage to hold and manage the same upon the trusts and for the uses herein mentioned.

And the said party of the third part doth hereby signify his assent to the provisions of this indenture, and doth covenant to and with the said party of the second part and his successors in the said trust, to permit the said party of the first part, after the solemnization of the said intended marriage, to receive the aforesaid income and profits to her sole and separate use, and freely to dispose of the trust estate, by her will or by her testamentary appointment, to such person or persons as she may bequeath the same to, and not to interfere with the said trust estate otherwise than in conformity to the provisions of this indenture.

In witness, &c.

Signed, sealed, &c.

SETTLEMENT OF WIFE'S REAL AND PER-SONAL ESTATE IN CONTEMPLATION OF MARRIAGE.

THIS INDENTURE of three parts, made this   day of A.D. 18 , by and between A. M., of spinster, of the first part, W. M. and R. M., of   of the second part, and H. B., of   clerk, of the third part,

WITNESSETH, that whereas a marriage is intended to be had and solemnized between the said parties of the first and third parts, and the said A.M. is possessed of certain real and personal estate, to wit, one undivided seventh part of all the estate, real and personal, whereof her late father, W. M., Esquire, died, seized and possessed, all which the said A. M., with the consent of the said party of the third part, is minded and disposed to transfer and convey unto the said parties of the second part, in trust for her own proper use and benefit :

Now, therefore, in consideration of the premises, and of one dollar paid to the said A. M. by the parties of the second part (the receipt of which is hereby acknowledged), the said A. M. doth hereby give, grant, bargain, sell and

convey unto the said W. M. and R. M., and their heirs
and assigns, and to the survivor of them, and his heirs
and assigns, one undivided seventh part of all the estate
of which the said W. M., Esquire, died, seized and
possessed, consisting of real estate, bank, insurance, and
manufacturing stocks, furniture and other personal
property, wheresoever the same may be situated; To
have and to hold the same to the said W. M. and R. M.,
and their heirs and assigns, and to the survivor of them,
and his heirs and assigns forever, but upon the special
trusts and for the uses and purposes, and subject to the
powers and obligations following, and none other,
namely :

First.—That until the solemnization of the said
intended marriage, the said trustees shall hold the said
estate and property to and for the sole use of the said
A. M., and shall pay over to her, or empower her to
receive for her own use, all the rents, income and
dividends, arising from or out of the said trust funds or
estate.

Secondly.—That from and after the solemnization of
the said intended marriage, the said trustees shall collect
and receive the rents, income and dividends of the said
trust estates and moneys, or of any estates or property
which may be substituted therefor, as is hereinafter provided, so often and whenever the same may be due and
payable, and, after the deduction of all incidental expenses,
shall pay over the same to the said A. M., upon her sole
and separate receipt, and free from the control or interference of any person whomsoever, during her coverture
with the party of the third part.

Thirdly.—That in case of the decease of the said A.
M., after the solemnization of the said marriage, and
during the life of her said husband, the said trustees
shall hold the said estate to and for the use of such
person or persons as the said A. M., by any instrument
in writing subscribed by her in the presence of two
witnesses, shall name and appoint to take and enjoy the
same: And the said trustees shall forthwith execute and
deliver all such deeds and papers as they shall be advised
by counsel learned in the law to be proper and needful
to convey and set over the said trust estate and funds to
the person or persons so named and appointed; and in
default of such appointment, the said trustees shall hold
the said estate to and for the use of her said husband,
for and during his life, and shall collect and pay over to
him, from time to time, after deducting all incidental
expenses, all the rents, income, and the profits of the
trust estate, or may suffer him to collect and receive the
same, he keeping the real estate in good repair: And
from and after the decease of the said husband, the said
trustees shall hold the same to the use of such heirs, or
of the legal representatives of the said A. M. as would
be entitled to the same in and by the statutes of this
Province now in force, regulating the distribution of
intestates' estates, in case the said A. M, had died, seized
and possessed thereof intestate; And the trustees shall
execute and deliver all such deeds and instruments as
may be needful to transfer the said trust estate or funds
unto the persons hereby specified and named.

Fourthly.—That in the event of the decease of the said
party of the third part, leaving the said A. M. him

And it is hereby expressly agreed by and between all parties hereto that notwithstanding anything herein contained that if it should happen that a case of necessity of sufficient importance to require any part of the principal to be paid to the said party of 1st pt. and be so deemed by a Judge of the Court of Chy for Ontario to whom application for that purpose shall be made and such Judge shall grant his certificate or order for that purpose under the seal of the Court it shall and may be lawful for said parties of 2nd part to pay to said party of first part out of the principal of the said trust premises such sum or sums of money as such Judge shall certify as aforesaid in his opinion to be just and proper under the circumstances on the case made out before him — And it shall also be lawful for said parties of the 2nd part to retain the amount of costs of such application for any such order or orders certificate or certificates — All such sum or sums of money so to be paid to said party of the 1st part to be in all respects on the same terms as if such part or parts of the principal were a part of the ordinary income of said trust premises —

(
t
f
h
e
t
s
f
t
o
b
P
in
a
ex
m
u

pa

surviving all the estates and property then held in trust under this indenture, shall be conveyed and transferred back to the said A. M., and the trustees shall forthwith execute and deliver all such deeds and instruments as they shall be advised by counsel learned in the law to be needful and proper for that purpose.

[*Further provisions may be added respecting insurance, &c., and other duties of the trustees, as the case may require.*]

In witness, &c.

Signed, sealed, &c.

SETTLEMENT OF A POLICY ON HUSBAND'S LIFE EFFECTED IN THE NAME OF TRUSTEES.

—

THIS INDENTURE, made the   day of   A.D. 18   ,
BETWEEN A. B., of   bachelor, of the first part,
C. D., of   spinster, of the second part, and E. F., of   and G. H., of   of the third part, witnesseth as follows :

1. In consideration of an intended marriage between the said A. B. and C. D., it is agreed that, after the said marriage, the said E. F. and G. H., their executors, administrators and assigns, shall hold the moneys receivable on a policy for   on the life of the said A. B., granted on the   day of   by the   Insurance Company, in the names of the said E. F. and G. H., and numbered   and also the moneys receivable under every policy effected under the powers hereinafter given.

2. Upon trust that the said E. F. and G. H., or the

survivor of them, his executors or administrators or their or his assigns (with the written consent of the said A. B. and C. D., and after the death of either, with the written consent of the survivor if living), shall invest the said moneys and the moneys realized under this trust in or upon any public stocks, funds or securities.

3. The said trustees shall pay the income of the premises to the said C. D., if she shall survive the said A. B., during her life.

4. Subject to the foregoing trusts the premises shall be held in trust for such children or child of the marriage, as the said A. B. and C. D. shall by deed or will appoint, and so far as the same shall be unappointed in trust for such children equally, or child if but one, who, being sons or a son, shall attain twenty-one, or, being daughters or a daughter, shall marry; but so that no child shall take any unappointed share without bringing his or her appointed share into account.

5. On failure of the foregoing trusts the premises shall be held in trust for the said A. B., his executors, administrators and assigns.

6. Bonuses receivable under the said policy are to go in reduction or payment of premiums, either by virtue of any arrangement to be entered into for that purpose with the said company or otherwise.

7. The said A. B., for himself, his heirs, executors and administrators, covenants with the said E. F. and G. H., their executors and administrators, that he, the said A B., will pay the premiums on the said policy when due and will do or suffer nothing whereby the same may become void, voidable or lapsed, and, in the event of

such policy becoming void, voidable or lapsed, will at his own cost do all acts required to enable a policy in lieu thereof to be effected. And will repay to the said E. F. and G. H., their executors or administrators, on demand, with interest at per cent. per annum, all sums paid by them for effecting or keeping up the said policy or any policy substituted for the same as aforesaid.

8. Provided that all the covenants herein contained shall apply to any such substituted policy in the same manner as to the said policy already effected.

In witness, &c.

Signed, sealed, &c.

SETTLEMENT OF A POLICY ON THE HUS-BAND'S LIFE, AND ASSIGNED BY HIM TO THE TRUSTEES.

THIS INDENTURE, made the day of A.D. 18 ,

BETWEEN A. B. of &c. of the first part, C. D, of &c. of the second part, and E. F. of &c. and G. H. of &c. of the third part, witnesseth as follows :—

1. In consideration of an intended marriage between the said A. B. and C. D., the said A. B. assigns unto the said E. F. and G. H., their executors and administrators, a policy for on the life of the said A. B., granted to him on the day of 18 , by the Insurance Company, and numbered

2. Upon trust that after the said marriage the said E. F. and G. H., and the survivor of them, his executors or administrators, or their or his assigns (with the written consent of the said C. D. if living, and after the death of

either with the written consent of the survivor if living), shall invest the moneys receivable on the said policy, and on any other policy effected under the powers hereby given in or upon any public stocks, funds or securities.

(Insert Clauses 3, 4, 5, and 6, as in last Form.)

7. The said A. B., for himself, his heirs, executors and administrators, covenants with the said E. F. and G. H., their executors and administrators, that, notwithstanding anything by the said A. B. done or knowingly suffered, he is entitled to execute this assignment of the premises free from incumbrances, and that he and every person claiming under or in trust for him, shall, at his own costs, do all acts required for perfecting such assignment or recovering the moneys due under the same policy, or any other policy made pursuant to the trusts hereby created. And that the said A. B. will pay the premiums on the said policy when due, and will do or suffer nothing whereby the same may become void, voidable, or lapsed, and in the event of the said policy becoming void, voidable or lapsed, will at his own costs do all acts required to enable a policy in lieu thereof to be effected, and will repay to the said E. F. and G. H., their executors or administrators, on demand, with interest at   per cent. per annum, all sums paid by them for effecting or keeping up the said policy, or any policy substituted for the same as aforesaid.

8. Provided that all the covenants herein contained shall apply to any such substituted policy in the same manner as to the policy hereby assigned.

In witness, &c.

Signed, sealed, &c.

APPOINTMENT, BY WIFE, OF · PERSONAL ESTATE, TO TAKE EFFECT ON HER DECEASE.

—

To all to whom these Presents shall come,

I,   wife of   of, &c., send greeting :

Whereas, by Indenture triparite, bearing date, &c., made between the said   (by her then name and addition of   of, &c., spinster,) of the first part, the said   of the second part, and ·   and   of the third part, it was agreed by the said parties that the said   and   amongst other things, should stand possessed of certain capital stock in, &c., in the said indenture mentioned to have been transferred, on the day of the date thereof, to the said   and·   by the said   and any other estate which might thereafter be substituted therefor, in trust to receive and collect the incomes, profits and dividends of the said capital stock or substituted estate, so often and whenever the same should be payable, and to pay over the same, or so much thereof as the said   should not direct to be added to the principal for the purpose of accumulation to the said   during her coverture, upon her sole and separate receipt therefor, and free from the control or interference of her said husband or any other person whatsoever ; and in trust, upon the decease of the said   during the lifetime of her said husband, to transfer and pay over the said capital stock or substituted estate to such person or persons as she the said   by any instrument or note in writing subscribed by her in presence of at least two credible witnesses, should order and appoint to take and receive the same :

Now know ye, that I the said   by virtue and in pursuance of the said powers and limitations in the said Indenture contained, and in pursuance of every other power and authority in me now being, do direct and appoint the said   and   as soon after my decease as conveniently may be, to transfer and pay over to   of, &c., the whole of the said capital stock or substituted estate, and the incomes, profits and dividends thereon accrued, which shall not have been received by me, to her sole and separate use, according to the limitations, trust, and true intent of the said indenture.

In witness, &c., this   day of   A.D. 18   .

Signed, sealed, &c.   ℯ

APPOINTMENT TO CHANGE INVESTMENTS.

To ALL TO WHOM THESE PRESENTS SHALL COME, .

I,   wife of   of   &c., send greeting:

WHEREAS, by Indentures tripartite, bearing date, &c., made between, &c., it was agreed by the said parties that the said   and   trustees therein named, should stand possessed of   shares in the Bank of &c., and all dividends, incomes, and profits thereon, in trust for the sole and separate use of me the said during my coverture; and that the said   and should have power with the approbation, or at the request of me the said   expressed in writing, to sell and dispose of the said trust estate, or any part of it, and the proceeds to invest in other personal, or in real estate, according to the written direction of me the said and that the estate so purchased should be had and held by the trustees for the same uses and purposes, and upon the same trusts, as are declared in and by the said Indenture of and concerning the said bank shares; and that the same might be sold, and the proceeds re-invested from time to time in the like trust.

Now know ye, that I, the said   by virtue of the power of appointment limited to me in the before recited instrument, and of every other power and authority hereunto enabling me in this behalf, do hereby request, authorize, and appoint the said trustees to make sale of the whole of the said bank shares, and the proceeds thereof to invest by purchase in a certain tract or parcel of land, situate &c., *(describe the particular estate;)* and I do further declare, limit, and appoint the said *(trustees)* and their heirs, to stand seized of the said real estate to the same uses and purposes, and upon the same trusts, as in the said Indenture are declared of and concerning the said bank shares.

In witness, &c., this   day of   A.D. 18   .
Signed, sealed, &c.

SEPARATION, DEED OF.

THIS INDENTURE, made the   day of   A.D. 18   .
BETWEEN A. B., &c.; of the one part, and D. E., &c., and C., wife of the said A. B., of the other part.

WHEREAS some unhappy differences have lately arisen between the said A. B. and C., his wife, and they have mutually agreed to live separate and apart from each other; and previous to such separation he the said A. B. hath consented thereto, and also proposed and agreed

Z

that he, out of his own proper moneys would allow and pay the said C., his wife, during the term of her natural life, for her better support and maintenance, the annuity or yearly sum of   clear of all taxes, charges, and deductions whatsoever payable to her in such manner as hereinafter is mentioned (subject nevertheless to the proviso hereinafter contained, respecting the payment of the said annuity), and also that, in case the said C., his wife, should die before the said A. B., that then the said A. B. should pay to her executors or administrators the sum of   towards her funeral expenses.

Now this Indenture witnesseth, that the said A. B., in pursuance of his aforesaid proposal and agreement, doth hereby, for himself, his executors and administrators, and for every of them, covenant, promise and agree, to and with the said D. E., his &c., in manner and form following (that is to say), that it shall and may be lawful to and for the said C., his wife, and that he the said A. B. shall and will permit and suffer her the said C., from time to time, and at all times from henceforth during her natural life, to live separate and apart from him, and to reside and be in such place and places, and family and families, and with such relations, friends, and other persons, and to follow and carry on such trade and business, as she the said C., from time to time, at her will and pleasure, notwithstanding her present coverture, and as if she was a feme sole and unmarried, shall think fit.

And that the said A. B. shall not, nor will, at any time or times hereafter, compel her to cohabit with him, or molest, disturb or trouble her, for such living separate and apart from him, or any other person or persons whatsoever, for receiving, harboring, or entertaining her ; nor shall nor will, without the consent of the said C., visit her, or knowingly come into any house or place where she shall or may dwell, reside, or be : or send, or cause to be sent, any letter or message to her; nor shall or will, at any time hereafter, claim or demand any of the moneys, rings, jewels, plate, clothes, linen, woollen, household goods, or stock-in-trade, which the said C. hath now in her custody or possession, or which she shall or may hereafter buy and purchase, or which shall be devised and given to her, or she shall otherwise acquire, and that she shall and may enjoy, and absolutely dispose of the same as if she were a feme sole and unmarried.

And further, that the said A. B., his executors and administrators, or some or one of them, shall and will well and truly pay unto the said C., his wife, or her assigns, during the term of her natural life, for and towards her better support and maintenance, one annuity or yearly sum of   free and clear of all charges, taxes, and deductions whatsoever ; the said annuity or yearly sum of   to be paid and payable to her the said C. and her assigns, during her natural life, in four equal payments, each amounting to the sum of   on the first days of March, June, September and December in every year, or within ten days next following ; the first quarterly payment thereof to begin and be made on   or within ten days next following.

In consideration of which sum of   per annum, so hereby made payable to her the said C., in manner as aforesaid, she the said C. doth hereby agree to accept and

take the same, in full satisfaction for her support and
maintenance and all alimony whatsoever during her
coverture.

PROVIDED ALWAYS, and it is hereby expressly agreed
and declared, by and between all the parties hereto, and
the true intent and meaning of them and these presents
is and are, that in case he the said A. B., his executors
or administrators, shall at any time hereafter be obliged
to and shall actually pay any debt or debts which she the
said C., his wife, shall at any time hereafter during her
present coverture, contract with any person or persons
whatsoever, that then and in such case it shall and may
be lawful to and for the said A. B., his executors and
administrators, to deduct, retain to, and reimburse him
and themselves out of the said annuity or yearly sum of

so hereby made payable to her the said C. as aforesaid, all and every such sum and sums of money as he
and they shall be obliged to, and shall actually pay for or
on account of any such debt or debts, to be by her the
said C., at any time hereafter, so contracted as aforesaid,
together with all costs, charges and damages, which he
or they shall or may pay or sustain on account thereof,
anything herein contained to the contrary thereof in anywise notwithstanding.

In witness, &c.

Signed, sealed, &c.

SURRENDER OF LEASE.

KNOW ALL MEN BY THESE PRESENTS, that   in the
within written Indenture named and described, in con-

sideration of the sum of   lawful money of Canada, to
in hand well and truly paid by   at or immediately
before the sealing and delivery hereof, the receipt whereof
         do hereby acknowledge ; Do by these presents
assign, surrender and yield up unto the said   his
heirs, executors, administrators and assigns, all and
singular the lands, hereditaments and premises comprised
and described in the within Indenture of Lease, and
thereby demised, together with all the rights, members
and appurtenances to the same belonging or in anywise
appertaining ; and all the estate, right, title, interest,
benefit of renewal, claim and demand whatsoever, either
at law or in equity, of   the said   in, to, out of
or upon the same premises : To the intent that by virtue
of these presents, the residue now unexpired of the term
of   years of and in the said hereditaments and
premises created by the within Indenture of Lease, and
all other   estate, term and interest therein by virtue
of the said Indenture, may merge in the freehold reversion
and inheritance of the said premises, and be thereby
extinguished.

    And the said   for   heirs, executors and
administrators, do hereby covenant with the said
heirs, executors, administrators and assigns, that   the
said   now ha in   good right, full power and
lawful and absolute authority to assign, surrender and
yield up the said hereditaments and premises in manner
aforesaid, and according to the true intent and meaning
of these presents.

    In witness, &c.

    Signed, sealed, &c.

SURRENDER OF LEASE.
(Another form.)

To ALL, &c., A. B., of, &c., sendeth greeting:

Whereas, by Indenture, &c. [*recite the lease*]. Now know ye that I, the said A. B., in consideration of to me in hand paid by C. D., of &c., the receipt, &c., do hereby, for myself, my, &c., surrender and yield up, from the day of the date hereof, unto the said C. D., his, &c., the said Indenture of Lease, and all the messuages and premises aforesaid, and the term of years therein yet to come, with all my right, title and interest thereto, and which I have or claim, or hereafter can or may have or claim, either by virtue of said Indenture or otherwise howsoever; and that free and clear, and freely and clearly, &c. *(against incumbrances.)*

In witness, &c.

Signed, sealed, &c.

TRANSFER OF SHARES IN A COMPANY.

FOR VALUE RECEIVED, I   of   assign the whole of my right, title and interest, of, in and to shares in the   Company of   to   of and constitute him, his assigns and substitutes, my attorney and attorneys, with full power to receive in his or their name or names, certificates for the said shares, hereby obliging myself at his or their request to do all necessary matters and things for the more effectually transferring the said shares to him or them.

Witness, &c.

TRANSFER OF SHARES OF STOCK.

For value received, I   named in the certificates hereto annexed, which are numbered as follows, namely: No.   to No.   assign the shares of stock therein mentioned, to   of   and constitute him, his assigns and substitutes, my attorney and attorneys, with full power to receive, in his or their name or names, certificates for the said shares; hereby obliging myself, my heirs and executors, at the request of the said   or his assigns and substitutes, to do all necessary matters and things for the more effectually transferring the said shares to him or them.

Witness, &c.

TRUST DEED OF A CHURCH.

This Indenture, made (in duplicate) the   day of   A.D. 18 , in pursuance of the Act passed in the 35th year of the reign of Her Majesty Queen Victoria, and chaptered 107, and in pursuance of the Act respecting Short Forms of Conveyances; and in pursuance of the Act of the Legislature of Ontario, passed in the   year of Her Majesty's reign, chaptered   entitled "An Act respecting the   Church of Canada:"

Between   of the first part, and   the Trustees of the   Congregation of the   Church of Canada, of the   part.

Witnesseth, that in consideration of the sum of   of lawful money of Canada, now paid by the said Trustees to the said part of the first part (the receipt

whereof is hereby acknowledged)   he   the said
part of the first part do   grant and assign unto the
said Trustees and their successors in the said trusts

All and singular th

To HAVE AND TO HOLD the said parcel or tract of
land and premises unto and to the use of the said
Trustees and their successors in the said trusts, upon the
following trusts, namely:

UPON TRUST, &c.

The said part of the first part covenant with the
said parties of the   part, and their successors in the
said trust, that   ha the right to convey the said
lands to the said parties of the   part and their
successors in the said trust, notwithstanding any act of
the said part of the first part.

And that the said parties of the   part, and their
successors in the said trust, shall have quiet possession
of the said lands, free from all incumbrances.

And that the said part of the first part will execute
such further assurances of the said lands as may be
requisite.

And that   will produce the title deeds enumerated
hereon, and allow copies to be made of them at the
expense of the said parties of the   part, and their
successors in the said trust.

And that the said part of the first part ha   done no
act to encumber the said lands.

And the said part of the first part release to the said
parties of the   part, and their successors in the said
trust, all   claims upon the said lands.

And the said party of the   part hereby bars her dower in the said lands.

In witness, &c.

Signed, sealed, &c.

RECEIVED, &c.

(Usual Affidavit of Execution.)

INSTRUCTIONS FOR EXECUTING FOREGOING.

The *party of the first part* is to be the grantor, or person conveying the land.

The *party of the second part* is to be some member of the congregation, or other person, to whom the *legal* estate is to be conveyed, in order that, under the provisions of the deed, and by force of the *Statute of Uses*, it may vest, in the first place, in the trustees of the congregation ; and, in the event of the congregation ceasing to exist, as directed by the deed.

The *parties of the third part* will be the trustees of the congregation *by whatever name* that shall be chosen by the congregation. A convenient corporate name will be " *The Trustees of the*   *Church at*   ;" " *The Second*   *Church at*   ," or " *Zion Church at*   ," without using the word " *Trustees.*"

The *party of the fourth part* will be the wife of the grantor, and will be a party for the purpose of barring dower. Should there be no wife, the only alteration required is the erasure, by the pen, of the reference to the party of the fourth part, and of the clause containing the bar of dower.

The trustees should *adopt a corporate seal*, and may execute the deed by affixing their seal thereto; their chairman signing as chairman, but the others not signing. Execution by the trustees is not essential to the operation or validity of the conveyance.

It is recommended that, whenever practicable, congregations obtain the services of careful solicitors, to see that their deeds are properly filled up, executed, and proved for registering.

WILLS.

GENERAL DIRECTIONS FOR EXECUTING WILLS.

State as simply and concisely as possible, the manner in which you desire to dispose of your property. Attention must be paid to the formalities required in the execution of the will, as expressed in the attestation clause at the end.

All property may be disposed of by will. No person under the age of twenty-one years can make a will.

Every will should be signed at *the foot or end thereof* by the person making it, or by some other person, in his presence and by his direction, he making his mark thus X, and such signature must be in the presence of *two witnesses*, at least, who must sign their names under the attestation clause *before leaving the testator's presence*, in his presence, and in the presence of each other.

Against every *alteration and interlineation*, made before the will is executed, the testator and the witnesses must put their names, or initials, or which is better, enumerate them in the attestation clause. Nothing should be scratched out, or erased, or the will might be held incapable of proof.

No legatee under the will, should be a witness, al estate
the will would not be affected thereby, the gift admin-
person, or to the wife or husband of such person y such
, An executor is a good witness, but any legacy t sums
is thereby made void. It is better he should not be ees

A legacy to a friend is made void or "lapses" by y
death before the testator's.

A legacy to a testator's child, or other issue, does not
lapse by his death, if he has any issue living at the
testator's death; but the legacy takes effect as if he had
died immediately after the death of the testator.

A soldier in actual military service, and a mariner at
sea, may dispose of his personal property by any written
paper signed by him, though not attested.

A will is revoked by the marriage of the person making
it; except by marriage, it can only be revoked by another
will, or by destruction. After the will has been duly
executed, no addition or alteration may be made except
by a fresh will, or codicil, which must be attested in the
same manner as the original will.

After acquired property passes by the will.

WILL GIVING PROPERTY TO WIFE AND APPOINTING HER EXECUTRIX.

I, A. B., of, &c., declare this to be my last will and
testament. I do hereby give unto my dear wife
all my real and personal estate whatever and wheresoever, to hold unto her, her heirs, executors and administrators, according to the respective natures and quali-
ties of the said premises, absolutely and forever. And

I hereby appoint my said wife sole executrix of this my will, at the same time revoking all former and other wills, codicils, testamentary dispositions and appointments whatsoever by me at any time heretofore made.

In witness whereof I, the said A. B., the testator, have to this my last will and testament contained in this and the preceding   sheets of paper, set my hand and seal this   day of   A.D. 18   .

Signed by the said testator, as and for his last will and testament, in the presence of us, present at the same time, who, at his request, in his presence, and in the presence of each other, have subscribed our names as witnesses.

WILL, GIVING TO ONE PERSON ALL TESTA-TOR'S REAL AND PERSONAL ESTATE.

THIS IS THE LAST WILL AND TESTAMENT of me [*testator's name and description*]. I devise and bequeath all the real and personal estate to which I shall be entitled at the time of my decease, unto [*devisee's name, description and addition*], absolutely, and I appoint the said sole executor of this my will ; hereby revoking all former testamentary writings.

In witness, &c., (as before) this   day of   A.D. 18   .
Signed, &c., as before.

WILL, GIVING INCOME TO WIFE FOR LIFE, AND AFTERWARDS CAPITAL TO CHILDREN.

I, A. B., of, &c., hereby declare this to be my last will

and testament. I give all my real and personal estate unto C. D. and E. F., their heirs, executors and admin-istrators, upon trust, to sell and convert into money such real and personal estate, and to invest the sum or sums of money thus arising in the names of my said trustees in or upon the public stocks, funds or securities, or any real securities, and to vary the investment from time to time for any other of like nature. And to pay the annual income thereof to my dear wife   during her life, if she shall so long continue my widow; and after her decease or second marriage, then, as to the said trust fund and the yearly produce thereof, upon trust for all my children who, being sons, shall attain the age of twenty-one years, or, being daughters, shall attain that age or marry, in equal shares.

And I authorize my said trustees or trustee, at any time after the decease or second marriage of my said wife, to apply the whole or part of the income of the presumptive share or shares of any child or children of mine who, being a son or sons, shall be under the age of twenty-one years, or, being a daughter or daughters, shall be under that age and unmarried, towards his, her or their maintenance and education. And also to ad-vance any part of such presumptive shares (not exceeding one-half thereof) towards the advancement in life of any such children respectively.

And I hereby authorize my said trustees or trustee to release or compound any debts owing to me or to my estate, or to give time for payment, or to take such security for payment, and to adjust and pay all claims made upon my estate, whether the same shall be supported by legal evidence or not, and also to refer to arbitration any dispute respecting any debt claimed to be owing to or from me, and generally to act in the premises as my said trustees or trustee shall in their or his discretion think fit ; and all receipts given by my said trustees or trustee, acting in the execution of the trusts herein contained, shall exonerate the parties taking the same from all responsibility with respect to the application of the moneys therein expressed to be received.

And I hereby authorize the acting trustees or trustee of this my will, and the executors or administrators of the last acting trustee, by any instrument in writing, to substitute any person to be a trustee in the stead of any trustee who shall die, continue to reside abroad, disclaim, neglect, refuse, or become incapable to act in the trusts aforesaid, and all the said trust estates or premises shall forthwith be transferred, so as to vest the same in such new trustee or trustees, either jointly with the surviving or continuing trustee or trustees, or solely, as the case may be, and such new trustee, as well before as after such transfer, shall have the same powers as if originally appointed a trustee by this my will.

And I declare that the trustees for the time being of this my will shall respectively be chargeable only with such moneys as they respectively shall actually receive, and shall not be answerable for each other, nor for any banker, broker, or other person in whose hands any of the trust funds shall be placed, nor for the insufficiency or deficiency of any stocks, funds, shares or securities, nor otherwise, for involuntary losses.   And I appoint the said C. D. and E. F. to be executors of this my will.

In witness, &c. (as before) this   day of   A.D.
18 .

Signed, &c., as before.

WILL OF MARRIED WOMAN MAKING AN APPOINTMENT UNDER A POWER IN A WILL.

I,   wife of   of   in exercise of my power under the will of my father   appoint that the trust premises therein comprised shall, after my death, be held in trust for my children in the following proportions, namely, one-half for my child   and a quarter for each of my children   and

Signed by me this · day of   A.D. 18 .

Signed, &c., as before.

ANOTHER FORM GIVING EACH CHILD A SPECIFIC PORTION OF THE PROPERTY.

I,   wife of   of   in exercise of my power under the will of my father   appoint that the trust premises comprised in such power shall, after my death, be held in trust as follows, namely, that portion which is invested in   for my child   ; that portion which is invested in a mortgage on   for my child   ; and that portion which is invested in Railway Debentures for my son

Signed by me this   day of   A.D. 18 .

Signed, &c., as before.

WILL OF MARRIED WOMAN APPOINTING INCOME TO HER HUSBAND.

I,   wife of   of   in exercise of my power under the will of my father   appoint that the income of the trust premises comprised in such power shall be paid to my husband, if he shall survive me, for his life.

Signed by me this   day of   A.D. 18 .

Signed, &c., as before.

CODICIL TO A WILL.

This is a codicil to the last will and testament of me   of, &c., bearing date the   day of   A.D. 18 *(the date of the will).*

I do hereby revoke the bequest of all my household furniture to my son   and do give and bequeath the same to my daughter   to and for her own absolute use and benefit for ever.

I give and bequeath to my daughter   in addition to the legacy bequeathed to her by my said will, the further sum of

In all other respects I do confirm my said will.

In witness, &c. (as before) this   day of   A.D. 18 .

Signed, &c., as before,

CPSIA information can be obtained
at www.ICGtesting.com
Printed in the USA
LVHW080339230822
726640LV00009B/200

9 781376 415780